WIT

UTSA LIBRARIES

RENEWALS 691-4574

DATE DUE

WITHDRAWN
UTSA LIBRARIES

ELECTRONIC MEETINGS:

TECHNICAL ALTERNATIVES AND SOCIAL CHOICES

ADDISON-WESLEY SERIES ON DECISION SUPPORT

Consulting Editors
Peter G. W. Keen
Charles B. Stabell

Decision Support Systems: An Organizational Perspective
Peter G. W. Keen and Michael S. Scott Morton

Electronic Meetings: Technical Alternatives and Social Choices
Robert Johansen, Jacques Vallee, and Kathleen Spangler

ELECTRONIC MEETINGS:
TECHNICAL ALTERNATIVES AND SOCIAL CHOICES

Robert Johansen
Jacques Vallee
Kathleen Spangler
Institute for the Future
Menlo Park, California

ADDISON-WESLEY PUBLISHING COMPANY
Reading, Massachusetts • Menlo Park, California
London • Amsterdam • Don Mills, Ontario • Sydney

LIBRARY
The University of Texas
At San Antonio

Copyright © 1979 by Institute for the Future
Philippines copyright 1979 by Institute for the Future

All rights reserved. No part of this publication may be reproduced,
stored in a retrieval system, or transmitted, in any form or by any means,
electronic, mechanical, photocopying, recording, or otherwise, without
the prior written permission of the publisher. Printed in the United States
of America. Published simultaneously in Canada. Library of Congress
Catalog Card No. 78-66749.

ISBN 0-201-03478-6
ABCDEFGHIJ-MA-798

SERIES FOREWORD

Changes in transportation and communication—the infrastructures of society—have led to the eclipse of distance and the foreshortening of time. Our concept of space has enlarged to include the entire globe, now connected in something approaching "real-time." *Electronic Meetings* explores one apect of this development: the use of audio, video, and computer technologies to facilitate information exchange, negotiation, problem solving and decision making within groups whose members may be separated by both space and time.

Electronic Meetings is the second book in the Decision Support Series. The series focuses on decision making in ill-structured and complex managerial tasks, and on the use of technology to improve decision making performance. The idea of "decision support" stems from a perspective which emphasizes *effectiveness* rather than efficiency; the *use* of information rather than "information flows" and "data"; and the *needs, skills and habits* of the individual decision maker, rather than the standard operating procedures of the organization. From the decision support perspective, computer technology is a tool to assist managers—not an end in itself.

Electonic Meetings contributes to this series by examining an aspect of decision making omitted in most discussions of computer use: making meetings more effective. The authors deal mainly with the uses of telecommunications in the complex and relatively unstructured context of group problem solving and cooperative information exchange among peers. This is in contrast to more structured functions such as message switching and data transfer. In many ways, electronic meetings are to the broader issue of communication within organizations what decision support is to information systems. Both electronic meetings and decision support systems require an approach that stresses support and extension rather than automation and efficiency of communication.

Identifying a particular system as "good" requires a very clear idea of what it means to make meetings "effective." Therefore, we need to understand how each system can be used and how it can affect group processes. *Electronic Meetings* does this. It not only provides a clear and comprehensive introduction to the technologies of communication, but emphasizes the context and criteria for effective use.

This book provides an important model for thinking about technological alternatives. Researchers and practitioners find it difficult to visualize and evaluate the effects of technological changes in complex social contexts. *Electronic Meetings* meets this need by using imaginative scenarios to integrate and operationalize a vast amount of research and experience in the relevant technologies. This is an instructive and stimulating approach, which avoids predictions in an area where forecasting is virtually impossible, but clarifies the implications of potential futures. It should become an important method of evaluation for anyone concerned with the development and implementation of systems for support of decision making and communication in complex organizational contexts.

Organizing for effective communication is often something we take for granted. We also tend to view the ability to perform effectively in a group as an art. We have not seen this as a situation in which we can make choices. New technologies create options, however, and *Electonic Meetings* provides a starting point for thinking about these options both at the macro level—technologies to select—and at the micro level—how to use a technology effectively once it is in place. The book enables us to recognize and use the opportunities being created by technological developments to rethink and improve how we meet.

PGWK

CBS

ACKNOWLEDGMENTS

This book grew directly from the Intermedia Project at the Institute for the Future, an independent nonprofit research group. The Intermedia Project was supported by the Charles F. Kettering Foundation of Dayton, Ohio; Robert Johansen and Jacques Vallee were co-leaders and shared equally in the responsibilities. Kathleen Spangler was an active member of the Intermedia Project team and was a full partner in expanding the project results into this book. Thus, the three authors should be considered equal contributors to the end product.

R. Garry Shirts of Simile II in LaJolla, California, was a consultant to the Intermedia Project during its various phases. Though not an author of this book, he made invaluable contributions to the scenarios of Chapter Four and to the "teleconferencing tutorial" in Appendix B.

Kent Collins, our project monitor at the Kettering Foundation, played a major role in both the initial vision of this reseach and the final results. We are deeply grateful for his support and that of the Kettering Foundation.

Background and organizational work were crucial to this project, and several Institute staff members made significant contributions. In particular, Jeanne Muzzicato helped in organizing the summaries of social evaluations in Appendix A as well as the bibliography. Carreen Jensen also assisted in organizing the summaries in Appendix A. Their work was meticulous and crucial to the overall effort. Roberta Edwards, the Institute's graphic artist, was responsible for the design of the tutorial materials in Appendix B. Dr. Roy Amara, as president of the Institute, provided the guidance and administrative structure which made this effort possible.

Outside the Institute, we received assistance from several sources. Suzanne Harris carefully edited the final manuscript of the book. Toni Vian, a freelance artist, prepared the illustrations.

Our colleagues doing research related to teleconferencing systems were very helpful to the project and deserve much of the credit for our final product. This is still a small research community, but it is one in which we are proud to be involved. In particular, a critics board provided many useful comments on a draft of the scenarios in Chapter Four. Included on this board were:

Paul Bohannon
Department of Anthropology
University of California at Santa
    Barbara

Bruce Christie
PACTEL
London, England

Larry Day
Bell Canada
Montreal, Canada

Martin Elton
Communications Studies
    and Planning Ltd.
London, England
and
Alternate Media Center
New York University

Douglas Fuchs
Cablecommunications Resource
    Center/West
Palo Alto, California

E. C. Frohloff
Bell Canada
Montreal, Canada

Donald George
Carleton Unviersity
Ottawa, Canada

Arthur Hastings
Mountain View, California

Nicole Mendenhall
Public Service Commission
Ottawa, Canada

Roger Pye
Communications Studies
    and Planning, Ltd.
London, England

Michael Tyler
Communications Studies
    and Planning, Ltd.
London, England

Nozomu Takasaki
The Research Institute of
    Telecommunications and
    Economics
Tokyo, Japan

Ederyn Williams
British Post Office
London, England

We would also like to thank Andrew Hardy of Stanford University for his help in verifying the many citations and the wording of the findings presented in Appendix A. Bruce Christie was very helpful in reviewing each of the "strengths" and "weaknesses" of the media for accuracy. Roger Pye assisted greatly in checking the accuracy of the bibliography. Any errors which still remain are, of course, the responsibility of the authors.

In addition to these formal reviews, discussions with other researchers and users of teleconferencing systems undoubtedly contributed greatly to whatever insight is contained in this book. While such discussions are impossible to acknowledge precisely, the NATO Science Symposium on the Planning and Evaluation of Telecommunication Systems (Bergamo, Italy, September 1977) was particularly useful to us as we wrote the final chapter of the book. Informal meetings, both at the Institute for the Future and during our visits to other groups, have helped us refine our own thinking about teleconferencing systems and their social effects.

Finally, Peter Keen and Charles Stabell, editors of the series of which this book is a part, provided initial encouragement and sustained guidance as the book neared completion. Their reactions were of great help to us as we revised the various drafts of the book. William Gruener at Addison-Wesley provided both freedom and support, in satisfying balance.

CONTENTS

1   ELECTRONIC MEETINGS:
    A SYNTHESIS AND A PROBE   1

2   THE TECHNOLOGY:
    ALTERNATIVES TO FACE-TO-FACE MEETINGS   5

    Video Teleconferencing   5
    Computer Teleconferencing   8
    Audio Teleconferencing   12
    Teleconferencing Now and in the Future   15

3   THE CULTURE:
    MEDIUM CHARACTERISTICS AND GROUP COMMUNICATION   17

    Physical Separation   18
    Access to Remote Resources   20
    Limited Communication Channels   21
    Control of Group Interaction   23
    Dependence on Technology   24
    The Sensitive Zones   25

4   THE CAMELIA SCENARIOS:
    USES AND MISUSES OF TELECONFERENCING   27

    Effective Use of Video Teleconferencing   41
    Ineffective Use of Video Teleconferencing   47
    Effective Use of Computer Teleconferencing   59
    Ineffective Use of Computer Teleconferencing   75
    Effective Use of Audio Teleconferencing   85
    Ineffective Use of Audio Teleconferencing   93
    Effective Use of Face-to-Face Conferencing   102
    Ineffective Use of Face-to-Face Conferencing   107
    Unanswered Questions   116

5   *THE POTENTIAL:*
    ORGANIZATIONAL AND SOCIETAL IMPACTS   *117*

    The Utopian Temptation   117
    The Promises—and Pitfalls—of Utopia   120
    The Problems with Utopia   127

6   *DECISIONS:*
    ORGANIZING ELECTRONIC MEETINGS   *131*

    Benefits and Cautions: A Summary   131
    New Communication Choices   132
    Developing a Critical Perspective   134
    The Improvement of Communication   138

    APPENDIX A:
    A SUMMARY OF SOCIAL EVALUATIONS
        OF TELECONFERENCING   *141*

    APPENDIX B:
    SPINOFF: A TELECONFERENCING TUTORIAL   *193*

    Bibliography   *225*

ONE

Electronic meetings are alternatives to face-to-face meetings. They are meetings in which visual images, the spoken word, or typewritten messages are exchanged electronically by people who may be far apart. They offer a promise of meetings-at-a-distance, a promise of more effective communication to replace, enhance, or extend that which currently occurs.

The technology for electronic meetings already exists. Perhaps the most glamorous is the television-like technology of video teleconferencing.[1] Video systems are designed to duplicate as closely as possible the feeling of a face-to-face meeting without imposing the burden of travel. In a video teleconference, participants can see the reactions of their colleagues—whether they are smiling or frowning, bored or interested. They can also show one another pictures, graphs, and three-dimensional objects much as they would in a face-to-face meeting.

Computer-based teleconferences are *least* like face-to-face meetings. There is no conference room at all: participants use portable typewriter terminals which are linked by normal telephone lines to a central computer. The computer then serves as a "meeting place" for a print-based discussion. The computer also performs a number of services in the course of the meeting. For example, it keeps a complete record of the discussion and will retrieve comments on request. Also, it can be instructed to poll participants on some question, with automatic analysis and feedback of results. And since there is no need for everyone to be present simultaneously in a computer conference, participants can drop in whenever it is most convenient.

More familiar than either video or computer-based conferencing is audio teleconferencing. Audio meetings are a natural extension of the person-to-person telephone call. In place of the telephone handset, there is a conference room carefully designed to provide high-quality voice transmission as well as equipment for send-

---

[1] In this book, we use the terms "electronic meeting" and "teleconferencing" interchangeably. We define both of these terms as small group communication through an electronic medium. Unfortunately, this broad definition has not been adopted in all the literature of this field. "Teleconferencing" in particular is often used as a shorthand term for a specific medium under study by a group, such as audio, video, or computer-based teleconferencing. Only the broad definition will be used in this book; specific media will be designated as such.

ing photocopies or even "electronic blackboard" drawings over normal—and inexpensive—telephone lines. And if not-so-high quality is acceptable, more portable facilities also can be arranged easily.

All of these media offer the opportunity to improve communication. They mean that people who are separated by the time and expense of travel can get together more quickly and less expensively. And since electronic meetings are easier to arrange than face-to-face meetings, more people can participate in important decisions. They can share more resources and consider more perspectives. They can try out new forms of organization which are not constrained by time and space.

However, the technical feasibility of electronic meetings does not guarantee that any of these possible benefits will become actual benefits. It is not enough to find a way to send a picture, a voice, or a word from "here" to "there." There must also be judgments about such factors as why the information is sent, when, how often, at what level within an organization, and with what cultural backdrop. Any mistake in this analysis will mean a mismatch between the technology and the people it should be serving. Any mismatch could mean miscommunication or no communication at all.

An appraisal of the potential of electronic meetings should thus be more than a technological appraisal. As interested researchers in Europe told us: "We are certain that those things [teleconferencing media] can be developed. What we want to know is what they will do to the way we think and the things we think about."

In recent years, over 100 studies have explored the social and psychological effects of electronic media on group communication. Users of teleconferencing have answered questionnaires and sat through interviews. They have reported their impressions of the media—for example, that video is more effective than audio for forming an impression of others. Or that it is possible to develop a sense of personal contact in a computer conference. Laboratory experiments have quantified information exchange rates and accuracy of perceptions in audio compared to video or audio and video compared to face-to-face. Field tests have attempted to clarify the kinds of communication tasks—bargaining or getting to know someone or exchanging technical information—which are best suited to each of the new media.

The findings of these studies provide a starting point for assessing both the benefits and pitfalls of electronic meetings. But isolated findings, out of context, offer only partial insights and fragmented guidelines for potential users of teleconferencing. Thus, this book is both a synthesis and a probe. It synthesizes a broad spectrum of social evaluations of audio, video, and computer-based teleconferencing. At the same time, it probes the meanings of current evaluations of teleconferencing in a future setting in which such technologies are readily available.

The core of this probe is a series of scenarios, and the setting for the scenarios is an imaginary country we call Camelia. Camelia is a small developing nation which depends on a few agricultural products for its economic well-being. In the future time of the scenarios, however, Camelia is facing a drought. Many people are concerned about the country's future, and a few organizations are in a position to help. The U.S. State Department and the church-supported Council of African Missions both might provide direct aid. An international activist group, Lutte Contre la Famine, is mobilizing support for Camelia. A multinational agricultural corporation has invested heavily in Camelia and could be a key to a more stable Camelian economy. But there is a communication problem here: no one knows exactly how much relief is needed or available. And those who could answer these questions haven't been talking to one another.

The Camelia problem is the kind of situation which might be featured on the evening news any night of the week. It is easy to imagine a commentator asking: "So why doesn't someone bring these people together face to face and let them work out a solution before the Camelians starve?" In the near future, however, that same commentator might suggest a teleconference: "Why not just hook all these people up in an electronic meeting and let them work out a solution before the Camelians starve?"

In this book, we try to respond to this question. Chapter Two surveys the technology of teleconferencing, describing systems which are currently in operation and offering some preliminary assessments of their likely effects on group communication. Chapter Three then takes a look at the nature of small group communication and performs a kind of sensitivity analysis, examining those dimensions of small group communication which might be most sensitive to the introduction of an electronic medium. In Chapter Four, we give life to this analysis as we let the characters from the Camelia conferences describe both effective and ineffective uses of each medium in the near-crisis situation of the Camelian drought. The skeleton for these scenarios is constructed from the findings of the various social evaluations of the media. Integrated into the context of an international meeting and dramatized by could-be characters, these findings begin to suggest how intelligent choices can be made among media—including face-to-face—and how, once chosen, an electronic medium can be used most effectively.

Next, Chapter Five steps beyond the limits of current findings and, indeed, beyond small group communication, to explore organizational and societal issues which could arise as electronic media become more widely used. It is the most speculative chapter in the book as it looks critically at the utopian possibilities of electronic meetings.

Finally, Chapter Six speaks directly to potential users of electronic meetings. It summarizes the benefits and problems of teleconferencing, and it offers four propositions to guide users in their own evaluations of the new media.

Appendix A contains a systematic summary of many of the social evaluations performed so far. Findings are paraphrased and organized around "strengths" and "weaknesses" of each medium. A table classifies the studies according to the basic characteristics of their approach to evaluation. Appendix B is a "teleconferencing tutorial." Suitable for classroom or more general use, this tutorial is similar to a simulation game. It provides participants with first-hand exposure to the major issues in using teleconferencing effectively.

This book, then, is about electronic meetings: small group meetings which occur over electronic media such as audio, video, or computer-based systems. But the book is more about meetings than electronics. The technology of teleconferencing merely creates the context for group communication. The nature of that communication is the true subject of this book.

TWO

Electronic meetings may have their roots in comic strips. Certainly comic strip and fantasy images of electronic meetings can be traced at least to the early 1900's, when Buck Rogers thought nothing of communicating with projected images or calling instant meetings through invisible circuits.

In the practical world of electronics, these visions have been brought to life in three basic alternatives to meeting in person. Video teleconferencing uses a television-like image, as well as sound; computer teleconferencing is print-based communication through keyboard terminals, and audio teleconferencing relies only on the spoken word, with occasional extra capacity for telecopying or telewriting. Each of the three alternatives also has its own history, which is reflected in the type of systems available. An examination of a few of these systems will illustrate the distinctive character of each medium and, at the same time, begin to suggest the possible impact of the media on group communication.

VIDEO TELECONFERENCING

In the 1971 novel *Diabolus*, David Saint John has an intelligence agent discussing a point in the office of the CIA station chief in Paris:

> Peter finished his coffee and looked around. Evans was sitting quietly next to the drape-hung wall. There was no sound in the insulated room, but Peter knew they were shielded by an electronic barrier, impenetrable to any form of bugging. In one corner stood the TV screen and camera that permitted conferences with the Director via satellite.

While such technology is more casually available in spy novels than in the real world, video teleconferencing is certainly a technical reality. The assumption behind video teleconferencing, usually unquestioned, has been that the closer a medium can come to face-to-face communication the better. Engineers have thus struggled to make video images lifelike in size and quality. As a result, video teleconferencing offers glamor, but also a technical complexity that, so far, has limited the number of operational conference rooms.

5

Some Promising Systems

A system in use at the Department of Energy typifies advanced video conferencing equipment.[1] It connects Germantown, Maryland, with Washington, D.C., spanning a distance of 20 miles. The system transmits black-and-white images of conference groups, with up to six participants in a group. In each room, there are several cameras for self-view, overview, and close-ups. A tripod camera permits blackboard views, and an overhead projector displays written documents. The cameras are voice-switched with buttons for manual override in front of the center chair. The cost of the system is about $5,000 a month, under a special regulatory arrangement which does not include all of the actual costs. At this cost, seven or eight conferences a month, with five people at each end, are necessary to produce a savings over the cost of travel. Its use to date seems to meet this requirement.

Ohio Bell uses a video conferencing system which is simpler than most video systems but still adequate for its users' needs.[2] These users are Ohio Bell personnel in Cleveland and Columbus, where the conference rooms are located. An efficiently designed table at each location seats three people, and a single camera focuses on all three at the same time. A camera directly above the table accommodates written documents. All of this equipment is off-the-shelf and inexpensive. (In fact, much of it was salvaged from unused equipment in Ohio Bell's television studios.) However, transmission is by means of standard television circuits, which are expensive.

The Ohio Bell system is used heavily, especially during the winter when travel in Ohio is often difficult. Video meetings are not limited to just a few of Ohio Bell's staff, either. They are held by a broad range of groups on a broad range of topics. This high usage developed without sophisticated technology or organized promotion of the system. It is perhaps the best current example of a simple video system which seems well matched to its users' needs. The simplicity of this system also contrasts sharply with the technological elegance of many large corporate video rooms.

The facilities at Arthur Andersen, Inc., are an example of such a corporate system.[3] Connecting four cities across the United States, these rooms were designed for top-level management meetings. The San Francisco facility is a dramatic executive board room for face-to-face meetings, with thick carpets, a large table, wood paneling, and a view of the San Francisco Bay. For video conferencing, however, the drapes are drawn and a control panel tilts up from the table. The paneling slides away to reveal discrete cameras and monitors, as participants all move to one side of the table, facing the cameras. These facilities are perhaps the most luxurious video conference rooms in the world and would match the fantasies from Tomorrowland or James Bond movies.

While there are many video systems that link several conference rooms, it is difficult to link more than two sites at any one time. Probably the most successful multi-site system is operated by the Metropolitan Regional Council in New York

---

[1]Division of Computer and Communications Operations, Department of Energy, Washington, D.C. 20545.

[2]Ohio Bell, 100 Erieview Plaza, Cleveland, Ohio 44114.

[3]Arthur Andersen and Co., Inc., 69 West Washington Street, Chicago, Illinois 60602.

City.[4] Headquartered in the World Trade Center in Manhattan, this system has nine studios in county seats surrounding the city. All are equipped with television cameras which require an on-site operator. A case study evaluation performed by RAND in 1974 concluded that the system had been well received and was serving its purpose of facilitating interaction among county governments. There were some technical problems, such as transmission failures and the inability of more than one person to speak at a time, but these were later corrected. The system is actually a hybrid of teleconferencing and broadcast television. It is used primarily for continuing education, personnel management, and purchasing. Each site paid about $16,000 in 1977 for operating costs of its participation in the system.

While all of these video systems are for private use, public visual conferencing services are also currently available in Australia, Canada, Great Britain, Japan, and the United States.[5] Each of these services is provided by the country's communications carrier, and users come to centrally located public conference rooms connecting major cities. To introduce and test these services, the carriers occasionally have offered free usage on a limited basis. In such tests, evaluations have been generally positive, but use of the systems has not matched expectations. Travel to the public conference room is frequently cited as a major barrier to expanded use. Accordingly, AT&T is now marketing corporate video conference rooms which can be installed on each company's premises. And Japan's NT&T has introduced its public facilities in hotels, hoping to improve access for potential users.

Still, the question persists: why has video teleconferencing not been used more— even when it is easily accessible? The low usage figures are a frequent embarrassment to system promoters and a puzzlement to evaluators. A variety of explanations have been offered. For example, some say that low usage can often be traced to the awkwardness or impossibility of connecting more than two video teleconference rooms simultaneously. Thus communication is often limited to two locations, while many groups have members at several sites. Another explanation is that video requires new communications skills which have not yet been developed. Others raise more basic questions about the utility of video: they question whether video teleconferencing, as currently conceived, is anything more than conspicuous consumption.

An Expensive Way to Meet

A television-quality video image is very expensive. It requires the transmission of a large amount of information, and this information must be updated continually as people move. Video is thus referred to as a "wide band" communications medium:

---

[4]New York Metropolitan Regional Council, One World Trade Center. New York 10023.

[5]Telecom Australia, 59 Lt. Collins Street, Melbourne, Victoria 3000, Australia; Bell Canada, Special Services, 620 Belmont, Montreal, Quebec, Canada; Post Office, Telecommunications Headquarters, 207 Old Street, London EC1V 9PS, England; Nippon Telephone and Telegraph, 1-6 Uchisaiwai-cho 1-Chome, Chiyoda-ku, Tokyo 100, Japan; American Telephone and Telegraph, Visual Communications Services, 295 North Maple Avenue, Basking Ridge, New Jersey 07920.

the bandwidth (size of the signal carrier) must be very large in order to send all this visual information continuously. In contrast, a facsimile system which sends photocopies is a "narrow band" medium because information can be sent more slowly—usually a few minutes per page.

The costs associated with the bandwidth required for video are formidable. The figures are difficult to estimate, but at current rates in the United States, video teleconferencing is at least five times as expensive as audio teleconferencing over comparable distances (Panko, Hough, and Pye, 1976). The video teleconferencing system between Sydney and Melbourne, Australia, has a full cost of about $400 per hour of usage. A comparable figure is estimated for the Japanese NTT system, connecting Tokyo with Osaka. The Picturephone® Meeting Service is currently available at experimental rates of $6.50 per minute from San Francisco to New York or Washington, $4.50 from Chicago to New York, $3.50 from Chicago to Washington, and $2.50 from New York to Washington. Even these rates, which are high enough to inhibit many potential users, do not cover the full costs of the service. Nevertheless, video conferencing rates are still likely to compare favorably with travel costs.[6] Also, it is possible that technological developments will produce major cost reductions. The key sources of hope here are video compression techniques, optical fibre signal transmission, efficient use of satellites, and other transmission innovations. While none of these possibilities promises cheap video conferencing, lower costs do seem probable in the future.

The Video Profile

Video teleconferencing is a group-to-group medium, typically with only two groups meeting at any time. Video conference rooms are usually permanent and often elegant. However, while video systems try to mimic face-to-face meetings, even clever system design cannot eliminate basic differences between an electronic meeting and meeting in person. Many people still feel uncomfortable "on camera." Associations with television and movies probably create this discomfort, which is fueled by the studio atmosphere of some systems. It may help to see distant participants as they speak, but an image on a television monitor is *different* than face to face, and participants must adjust to this difference.

Video conferencing appears to work for many meetings. But a gnawing question remains: Is the full visual information always *necessary* for those meetings?

COMPUTER TELECONFERENCING

It is ironic that some of the simplest ideas can be put into practice only when a very complex level of development has been reached in a related field. The availability of

---

[6]It should be noted here that even such high costs may not be impediments to use of video. Interviews with Australian users, for instance, indicated that the costs were considered reasonable. Business clients saw cost as no problem, while government users saw cost as a bureaucratic problem—video teleconferencing didn't fit their budget categories. See Susan Ellis, Vince McKay, and Michael Robinson, *Follow-Up Study of Users of the Melbourne-Sydney Confravision Facility*, Swinburne Institute of Technology, Australia, 1976. The user costs for the Australian system, however, are below the actual cost for a self-supporting system.

electronic memories could have permitted the establishment of networks of tele-types many years ago. Yet, such print-based group conferencing developed only when casual access to terminals, powerful time-sharing systems, and text editors was made possible by the advances of computer science in the late 1960's.

A Hybrid Medium

Computer conferencing is a hybrid medium, which borrows its terminology from computer science even though its purpose, culture, and evaluation strategies all come from the field of communications. This dual quality has created some identity crises for the designers and users of the medium; it has also generated a dilemma for those who are concerned with regulating communications media. The designers of computer conferencing systems find it difficult to win supporters among computer scientists, who view their work as simplistic: after all, the use of a processing machine to send messages is not particularly impressive. Similarly, communications experts, who lack a feeling for the genuine power of the computer, ask: "Why can't we do the same thing with a telephone or with TELEX?"

The answer is rather simple. Computer conferencing offers group commu-nication irrespective of time or space, and it is generally less expensive than the telephone and TELEX once the terminal itself (an increasingly common device) is amortized. For example, the PLANET system, offered by Infomedia[7] on a time-sharing computer, typically costs less than a quarter per 15 words for any distance. Use of systems on special-purpose machines will cost even less in just a few years. Terminals rent from $100 to $150 a month, with costs going down. Murray Turoff (1975b) has suggested that the cost of computer conferencing will be about $1 per hour for computing costs by 1980. While such a forecast appears to be optimistic, it seems safe to assume that the medium will not be expensive to operate by the mid-1980's—perhaps even less expensive than audio teleconferencing.

From Forecasting to Communicating

Computer conferencing developed in a community with specific needs: forecasting and policy formulation through "expert" interaction. Experts are typically dispersed across the country or even in several countries; assembling them for face-to-face meetings is often a difficult task. Furthermore, such meetings can isolate them from their usual sources of information. With computer conferencing, experts could con-fer through computer terminals in their offices or homes. Response-elicitation pro-grams could systematically query the experts or test for consensus among them.

Today, computer conferencing is not restricted to experts and can involve a wide range of print-based communication activities. Users type their messages to other conference participants on standard computer terminals, usually linked by telephone to a computer network. They receive printed messages at their terminals each time they join a computer "activity." Such activities typically involve 3 to 25 people, although everyone need not be present simultaneously. In fact, one of the most attractive features of computer conferencing is that participants can come in at

---

[7]Infomedia, 430 Sherman Avenue, Palo Alto, California 94306.

their own convenience, see what has happened since they were last present, respond, and leave. Between conferencing sessions, they can check their libraries, draft responses, reflect on solutions to current problems, or talk to others without disrupting the "meeting" or appearing rude. Computer conferencing can also facilitate use of other computer resources such as data analysis packages, data bases, or models. In short, computer conferencing is a medium that each participant uses only when he or she chooses.

A Range of Applications

Some of the most enthusiastic users of this medium have been government agencies. Their uses of computer conferencing have ranged from routine administrative tasks to crisis situations. For example, at the Federal Preparedness Agency, the Resource Interruption and Monitoring System (RIMS) allows regional centers across the United States to monitor crisis situations.[8] Connected continuously via the computer link, these centers are called into full operation as crises occur. Data bases and other information sources are available to support conference-like discussions among the centers.

In the Canadian government, a computer conferencing and messaging system connects regional offices of the Nonmedical Use of Drugs Directorate.[9] The conferencing capability is part of a management information system called MINT, which also includes a capability for simple message sending.

The PLANET system mentioned above was first used by several government agencies in field tests conducted by the Institute for the Future. The National Aeronautics and Space Administration, for example, used PLANET to coordinate the use of the Communications Technology Satellite test centers around the United States. The Department of Energy and the U.S. Geological Survey have both used PLANET to support joint research among their various branches.

Computer conferencing has also found non-governmental applications. Users of the CONFER system at the University of Michigan have developed several educational applications for the medium, including committee meetings, seminars, and inter-university communication.[10] And a number of seminar-style conferences sponsored by a variety of foundations and private organizations have focused on topics ranging from psychic research to world climate changes. Perhaps the most impressive example of such conferences was an international meeting sponsored by the European Management Forum, using the PLANET system. The subject of the two-month conference was technology transfer, and a dozen experts from five countries contributed to the discussion.

---

[8]Crisis Management Division, Federal Office of Preparedness, GSA Building, 18th and F Streets NW, Washington, D.C. 20405. This system is an extension of systems such as EMISARI, PARTYLINE, and DISCUSSION, developed by Murray Turoff and his colleagues at the former Office of Emergency Preparedness.

[9]Nonmedical Use of Drugs Directorate, Department of Health and Welfare, 365 Lausier Street West, Ottawa, Ontario, Canada K1A 1B6.

[10]CONFER, Center for Research on Learning and Teaching, 109 East Madison, Ann Arbor, Michigan 48104.

The Need to Type

A common first question about computer-based conferencing is: "Will people really use a medium which requires them to type all of their thoughts?" The answer is that some will and some won't. Computer conferencing does not require skilled typing. Many of the users of the PLANET system have been one-finger typists. They report that typing is not an insurmountable barrier to the use of the medium. Furthermore, their participation patterns—the number of messages they send and the length of those messages—do not appear to differ significantly from those of more practiced typists. Almost every new user of computer conferencing will apologize once or twice for typing errors, but these errors seem to become irrelevant rather quickly.

There are people, however, who never get over the discomfort of typing. Some simply don't attend the conference. Another option is to have someone else do the typing, in much the way a secretary types an executive's letters. Some users have chosen this option, and ordinarily, this seems to be a workable solution. However, it can occasionally create some interpersonal problems. For example, if two people happen to be online simultaneously, it is common to exchange a few friendly words. But a paid typist may not know how to respond to such an exchange and may simply ignore it, typing only the prepared messages. Since there is no way of knowing that the typist is not the real author of the messages, the other participant may feel ignored. Such feelings could eventually impede cooperation in the group.

Power or Simplicity?

Because the computer has the power to do much more than simply route messages from one point to another, one of the most important design questions is: just how many services should a computer conferencing system provide? It is possible to differentiate the basic elements of computer-based group communication from other computer services such as text editors, data bases, and journal systems. At present, some systems, such as the Electronic Information Exchange System at the New Jersey Institute of Technology, combine computer-based communications with these other computer services to form a complex and powerful package.[11] In contrast, other systems (such as the PLANET system) provide only a nucleus of functions for group communication. The issue here is power versus simplicity, and there are arguments on both sides. These two approaches may both prove fruitful over the long term; they may simply be aimed at different user populations and task environments.

The Profile of Computer Conferencing

Computer conferencing is the strangest of the new teleconferencing media. With no images of the participants nor voices nor even a shared moment in time, a computer conference hardly seems like a "meeting" at all. Yet people are using the medium to do many of the things they might normally do in face-to-face groups. And they are doing them by sitting down at a typewriter computer terminal, often in the privacy of their own offices or even their own homes. Such a communications medium ob-

---

[11]New Jersey Institute of Technology, 323 High Street, Newark, New Jersey 07102.

viously provides new opportunities for people to work together while geographically separated, but its unique characteristics potentially could produce an altered state of communication.

AUDIO TELECONFERENCING

The apparent simplicity of audio conferencing is deceptive. It is easy to view this medium as a simple extension of the telephone: if two people can talk to each other so easily, why not three, four, or even 12? For many years, the telephone company has provided a "conference call" service that is, in effect, a basic form of audio teleconferencing. However, the telephone traditionally has been viewed as a two-party communications medium. It's for "calling somebody up," not holding a meeting. People simply do not think of the telephone as a group communications medium. Furthermore, the design of the telephone handset does little to encourage its use for long periods, and speakerphones usually do not offer adequate quality to provide a genuine alternative. Nevertheless, telephone technology seems to be quite adaptable to group conferencing needs, as demonstrated by systems developed specifically for this purpose.[12]

Permanent and Portable Systems

The technology for audio conferencing can be either permanent or portable. Typical of the permanent audio conferencing installations is the system at the Union Trust Company in Connecticut.[13] The conference rooms in Stamford and New Haven look much as they did before the audio equipment was installed; the only obvious signs of their new function are six movable table microphones and the speaker cabinets in two corners of each room.

Another permanent facility is the Remote Meeting Table in England.[14] This system includes 11 conference rooms—seven in London and the rest in other UK cities. The conference tables have built-in speakers for six remote participants; each person's voice is heard through only one speaker, labeled with his or her name. Thus, the voices of the participants are "seated" around the table much as in a face-to-face conference.

The NASA audio system is perhaps the most extensive network of permanent audio conferencing rooms currently in operation.[15] At NASA, the need for audio conferencing grew out of the early U.S. space program, as geographically dispersed contractors and NASA sites worked together on the Apollo Project. In addition to

---

[12]While most audio teleconferencing systems to date have been designed specially for a small number of users, there are plans to offer "dial-up" conferencing for regular telephone subscribers in many U.S. cities over the next few years.

[13]Union Trust Company, 300 Main Street, Stamford, Connecticut 06904.

[14]Telecommunications Division, Civil Service Department, Riverwalk House, Millbank, London S.W.1 England.

[15]NASA Headquarters, 600 Independence Avenue, SE, Washington, D.C. 20003.

voice transmission, the conference sites were also equipped for high-quality tele-copying capabilities to allow immediate exchange of diagrams and technical information. Today, rooms have both audio and telecopy equipment. A facility in Huntsville, Alabama, provides the "audio bridges" for rooms engaged in a conference.

The NASA System is used for regular committee meetings and exchanges among NASA sites, as well as for coordination among members of specific projects. The project-oriented uses, in which geographically separated work groups have a high need to communicate with each other and a common task to be performed, seem to be the most effective.

A variety of portable audio conferencing equipment, available from a number of manufacturers, can transform an ordinary conference room into an electronic meeting center. The University of Wisconsin–Extension relies on such equipment to conduct continuing education courses on a regular basis.[16] Portable units are available at 200 sites around the state, many in public buildings. Professors remain on campus in Madison or Milwaukee or hold class from some more convenient location. Students simply attend class at the nearest court house or public library.

The costs of both permanent and portable systems are low. Audio teleconferencing uses inexpensive telephone lines. For systems which use the existing telephone network, the cost is especially low, although it increases as more people join the conference. Permanently installed audio conferencing systems which use dedicated lines are more expensive to use, but they provide greater reliability and generally higher voice quality. Also, the higher cost can be justified by higher use. The University of Wisconsin-Extension, for example, estimates that its system costs only 25 cents per student contact hour, not including the instructor's time (Parker and Riccomini, 1976).

A Quality Problem

One problem which has plagued audio teleconferencing is that of acoustical conditions in conference rooms. Hough (1976) describes the Bank of America audio system in San Francisco, which is generally acknowledged as one of the highest quality systems:

> "Achieving this system required unusual measures. Most surprising of all are the structural aspects. The room is completely isolated mechanically from the rest of the building, despite its being in the middle of the building, on one of the top floors. Moreover, no wall is parallel to any other wall."

Such elaborate designs may be possible for large organizations that can afford to establish permanent conference rooms, but they are certainly impractical for those who need the flexibility and economy of portable systems.

---

[16]Educational Telephone Network, Division of Educational Communications University of Wisconsin-Extension, Madison, Wisconsin 53706. Nearly 50 other such systems are in existence on a smaller scale. A report containing a survey and analysis of these systems is available from the Institute for the Future.

The problems of acoustics arise primarily in conference room-to-conference room situations in which more than four people share each location. For smaller groups, acoustical arrangements are much easier. Interestingly, some of the simplest systems are also the most effective—in spite of the room acoustics problems. The Western Electric 50-A system, for instance, is a simple portable speakerphone, yet it is basic equipment for the very successful University of Quebec audio teleconferencing program. Thus, while acoustical problems are annoying in the design of teleconferencing rooms, they are manageable if groups are kept small and some care is taken in room design.

Order of Speaking: A Frequent Communication Problem

Perhaps the toughest problem in audio teleconferencing is the issue of *order of speaking.* In face-to-face, visual signals usually aid in determining who speaks when; gestures and motions indicate when someone is almost finished speaking and even help to identify others who are waiting to speak next. In audio teleconferencing, however, there are no such visual cues, and the establishment of speaking order—and sometimes even identifying *who* is speaking—are basic problems.

The engineers' response to this problem is voice-switched microphones: a speaker's voice captures the sound channel and forces others to wait until he or she is finished. Small group interaction is more complicated than that, however, and a voice-switched system can be very annoying. A cough or sneeze, for example, grabs the microphone as easily as a spoken word. (The engineers' response here is a "cough button" which a participant can press when necessary.) Beyond the cough problem, voice-switching can also limit group spontaneity. Speakers keep the floor as long as they continue to talk; interruption of the speaker is technically impossible. So, when one speaker is finished, the other eager participants jump in with vigor—only to find the microphone lured away by another's voice.

The alternative to voice-switched microphones is an "open system" which allows everyone to speak at once. Such a system is more flexible but still leaves unsolved the problem of speaking order. The result is often a staccato of simultaneous speaking patched with periods of awkward silence.

While interpersonal logistics within an audio teleconference remain problematic, emerging systems show definite improvements. Speaker identification is one remedy for the social problems of audio, and several systems are experimenting with alternative ways of identifying speakers. Also, Telecom Australia is testing a multilevel, open microphone system. Here, the speaker is given a higher volume level than the other participants, but it is still possible for others to interrupt by activating buttons on their own microphones. The system is also tied to a microcomputer which permits queueing of speakers waiting their turns. The queueing order is displayed on a lighted panel with the names of all participants. This system, still in the testing stage, even features lights which pulse to the rhythm of the speaker's voice. Such advances illustrate some potential variants of audio teleconferencing, but raise questions about the degree to which any mechanical system can insure smooth interpersonal exchanges. Even with the best technologies, some problems seem likely. And *too* many gimmicks could certainly impede group communication.

The Audio Profile

Compared to video, audio teleconferencing might be viewed as an "intermediate" technology. The equipment is simpler than video equipment, and it costs less to use. At the same time, audio appears to be adequate for many meeting tasks. And it may also be accessible to more groups. Audio conferencing may, of course, require a little more discipline of its users: they must pay closer attention to who is speaking and what is being said. For the future, the most important question is whether users, who take one-to-one telephone calls for granted, can develop the same confidence in the technology for group conferencing by voice only.

TELECONFERENCING NOW AND IN THE FUTURE

The essential differences among the three media for teleconferencing are the differences among visual, voice, and typewritten communication. These fundamental characteristics are not likely to change in the near future. But new capabilities will almost certainly be added, and the media probably will become more accessible.

The introduction of new capabilities will be closely linked to the cost of transmission. Much in demand will be clever systems which use inexpensive narrow band transmission. Slow-scan video, which sends a still image every few seconds, is an example. Such systems will, in effect, create hybrid media between the categories we identify as audio and video. At the same time, if the cost of transmitting wideband signals decreases, the range of meeting options will be even broader.

Even within the current range of systems, electronic meetings are really options for only a few people. Most of the systems are private, and the public services are restricted. AT&T's public Picturephone® Meeting Service currently services only five cities. Computer conferencing, which is probably accessible from more locations than either video or any dedicated audio system, is still limited by the need for each participant to have a computer terminal. Furthermore, none of the teleconferencing facilities currently extends far beyond the advanced industrial countries. It is not now possible (without a great deal of effort) for a group of Canadians to meet electronically with a group in South America or for a group in the United States to arrange a teleconference with people in Africa.

For the purposes of this book, we assume that all three media will become more widely accessible and more familiar to the public. We also assume that the distinctions between audio, video, and computer-based teleconferencing will continue to be meaningful. While future media are likely to combine characteristics from each of the media, these distinctions help to focus the issues involved in selecting and using electronic media for group communication.

THREE

Why not just hook all these people up electronically and let them work out a solution before the Camelians starve?

There is a sense of urgency in this question which, however well intentioned, obscures the complexity of group communication. The plea rests on a too-simple assumption: that getting people together is the primary problem of communication. Establishing contact, either electronically or face-to-face, *is* a prerequisite to communication. But it is only a beginning. Furthermore, it may be the beginning of new problems as well as new communication. Electronic meetings ease the task of making contact; they do not, however, erase the complexity of group communication.

E. T. Hall offers a valuable insight when he says that "culture is communication and communication is culture."[1] When defined as culture—a labyrinthian concept—communication emerges as the complex phenomenon it really is. As culture, communication goes well beyond the exchange of words when people meet in a group. It includes the use of physical space and of time. It also includes other traditional components of culture—play and learning, defense and allocation of resources, assignment and recognition of social roles.

Choices about each of these components of communication are influenced by a variety of rules, assumptions, and perceptions. Many of these guiding assumptions are less than conscious, and most of them are guidelines for meeting *in person.* So when someone chooses to hold an electronic meeting, the old unconscious rules for meetings need revision. And choices about whom to invite, how to establish the agenda, how long and how often to meet all become more prominent. So do choices of leadership styles, protocols for speaking, and procedures for making group decisions.

"Just hooking all these people up electronically" overlooks the importance of these choices. It assumes that "things can't get any worse." But they probably can. And electronic meetings probably can increase the number of ways in which communication can get worse. The potential for easier communication may also be the potential for easier *mis*communication.

Teleconferencing, then, does not eliminate the possibility of ineffective meetings. Instead, it changes the nature of meetings in ways which increase the possibilities for both good and bad outcomes. These changes are linked to the fundamental characteristics of electronic meetings via all three media: physical separation of the

---

[1]Edward T. Hall, *The Silent Language*, New York: Anchor Books, 1973, p. 191.

17

participants, access to remote resources, narrow communication channels, potential for control of group interaction, and dependence on technology. Any of the choices about communication in a small group—about leadership and protocols and agenda—should thus be preceded by an examination of the positive and negative implications of these characteristics.

PHYSICAL SEPARATION

The most obvious difference between an electronic meeting and face-to-face encounters is the physical separation of participants. An ethereal electronic pulse is the only common "space" for the group. If the participants are far apart, physical separation may also mean a separation in time, as the exchange crosses time zones. This separation redefines communication possibilities in some rather obvious ways: objects cannot be exchanged; the sense of touch disappears. While some participants have their early morning coffee, their cross-country colleagues may be hungry enough to break for lunch. There can be no coffee break chit-chat and no hallway meetings.

But the lack of a shared space also influences communication in more subtle ways. For example, it eliminates the possibilities of using interpersonal distance to communicate.[2] The distance between any two members of a group expresses their feelings toward each other and toward what is being said. It can be supportive or insulting. Communication can proceed without it, but an important cue is lost. Could the miniaturized image of a person on a video screen across the room be interpreted as a detachment from the meeting agenda?

The use of conventional distances to communicate attitudes may be one factor in the *sense of social presence* in a meeting—a sense often found lacking in electronic meetings. Short, Williams, and Christie (1976) suggest, in fact, that the sense of social presence varies from medium to medium:

> Although we would expect it to affect the way individuals perceive their discussions, and their relationships to the persons with whom they are communicating, it is important to emphasize that we are defining Social Presence as a quality of the medium itself. We hypothesize that communications media vary in their degree of Social Presence, and that these variations are important in determining the way individuals interact. We also hypothesize that the users of any given communications medium are in some sense aware of the degree of Social Presence of the medium and tend to avoid using the medium for certain types of interactions; specifically, interactions requiring a higher degree of Social Presence than they perceive the medium to have. Thus, we believe that social presence is an important key to understanding person-to-person telecommunications.[3]

---

[2]Hall comments on the importance of social distance in group communication by saying that, "Spatial changes give a tone to communication, accent it, and at times even override the spoken word. The flow and shift of distance between people as they interact with each other is part and parcel of the communication process." E. T. Hall, *op. cit.*, p. 180.

[3]John Short, Ederyn Williams, and Bruce Christie, *The Social Psychology of Telecommunications*, London, England: John Wiley and Sons, Ltd., 1976.

This view of social presence may link the concept too rigidly to the characteristics of each teleconferencing medium. It is easy to imagine how different people could perceive varying degrees of social presence in the *same* medium. Field tests of computer-based teleconferencing, for instance, have shown that some people see this print-based medium as low in social presence while others have the opposite impression.[4] These varied reactions are clearly linked to the nature of the user groups and their communication needs, as well as the specific characteristics of the medium they are using.

It seems doubtful that social presence is a static variable, attached in simple ways to each teleconference medium. Rather, a sense of social presence can perhaps be cultured by teleconference leaders or encouraged by initial learning sessions. Furthermore, it is not clear that a strong sense of social presence is always best. The use of interpersonal distance, for example, varies from culture to culture. Everyone has probably witnessed a scene in which people from North and South American cultures negotiated the distance between themselves, with the North American feeling that the Latino was too pushy while the South American tried to understand why the North American was being so "cold" and remote. The different meanings associated with interpersonal distance might just as easily interfere with communication as facilitate it. Also, the separation of participants eliminates the fear of physical violence which, however subtle, is at least possible in any face-to-face encounter. Could safety from violence encourage "good fights" in electronic meetings?

A related impact of physical separation is that an electronic meeting is, in a sense, out of context. That is, it doesn't take place in a single cultural context or place. Such a displacement may save participants from uncomfortable meetings in unfamiliar surroundings. But it may also disguise important information about both goals and interpersonal needs of the conference participants. In particular, the abstract, electronically created context of a teleconference may obscure differences in perspectives of participants; participants could end up focusing too much attention on words which make little sense without an understanding of the organizational or cultural context of the speaker.

While physical separation is an unmistakable feature of electronic meetings, not everyone in every teleconference will be isolated. In fact, as we have noted, video teleconferences and some audio conferences will be group-to-group meetings. Such meetings combine the dynamics of face-to-face interaction with remote exchanges. Not surprisingly, differences between groups can become exaggerated in these conferences, and personal alliances within each group may be reinforced.

It is tempting to view physical separation as a necessary evil of teleconferencing—as something groups tolerate to gain savings in time and travel. However, this substitution mentality probably discourages creative uses of the unique communications environment of meetings-at-a-distance. Also, the view of electronic meetings as second-best does not acknowledge one very attractive complement to physical separation—namely, access to remote resources.

---

[4]See Jacques Vallee, Robert Johansen, Hubert Lipinski, Kathleen Spangler, and Thaddeus Wilson, *Group Communication through Computers, Volumes 3 and 4*, Institute for the Future, 1976, 1978.

ACCESS TO REMOTE RESOURCES

Many people, and hence many viewpoints, are routinely excluded from face-to-face meetings for logistical reasons of convenience, cost, and accessibility. Geographic distances remain a major barrier to dialogue on important organizational and societal issues. They limit access to both human and data resources that would otherwise be considered vital to the work of a group. They frequently foster duplication of effort and, in the extreme, parochialism.[5]

Teleconferencing provides an opportunity to organize groups in a non-parochial fashion, to tap resources that may be far away. Decisions about whom to consult or what information to use do not have to be constrained by what is closest. Distant experts can consult with a group more effectively: they can avoid tiring travel which may leave them less "expert"; and they can remain close to their own resources. Similarly, with computer conferencing, a data base on the other side of the world can be searched instantly and the results entered and evaluated immediately in the conference proceedings.

As suggested in Chapter Two, electronic meetings can facilitate cooperation among geographically separated branches of the same organization—the use of audio conferencing by NASA is an example—or between separate organizations. The U.S. Department of Energy uses computer-based teleconferencing to assist in coordinating the activities of regional laboratories in various parts of the country. This application has also spawned serendipitous interorganizational communication between scientists doing similar work at the Department of Energy and the U.S. Geological Survey. In this case, scientists who happened to be using computer conferencing for other purposes found they had research interests in common with each other and then established a joint conference. Teleconferencing thus seems to expand the opportunities to contact distant colleagues and sometimes even to discover new colleagues.

In spite of these apparent benefits, increased access to resources could actually overwhelm a group. Simple increases in the number of inputs to a group do not always lead to increased effectiveness. Without a social structure to integrate the various views and new sources of information, a group can easily drift into what Doyle and Straus call "The Multi-Headed Animal Syndrome."[6] Many people will be pulling in different directions, all of them feeling that they are acting in the common good but that others are not cooperating. Too much information too fast would only add to this problem, no matter how high the quality of the information.

An overemphasis on the opportunities of *access* could also encourage a too-narrow view of experts and expert information. The expert could become someone "out there" who is available to solve all of the problems if only he or she could be

---

[5]In describing alternative modes of organizing an institution, Wilensky points out that "intelligence failures are greatest if location is emphasized" as the basis for organization. He explains that "good intelligence cuts across arbitrary political boundaries" and that specialization by territory "overelaborates administrative apparatus" that makes the transfer of information from one area to another more difficult. See Harold L. Wilensky, *Organizational Intelligence*, New York: Basic Books, 1967, p. 55.

[6]Michael Doyle and David Straus, *How to Make Meetings Work*, New York: Wyden Books, 1976, p. 20.

reached. The expert's facts and figures might be viewed as the "truth" when they are only limited truths at best; at worst, they might not even be accurate information.

Teleconferencing probably has the potential to isolate the so-called expert from interaction with the group. Experts play many roles other than that of a data bank. They learn about the important political battles in a group, encouraging objectivity here and taking sides there. They cajole people into new perspectives on their problems. They may even lay groundwork for communicating with other important resources outside the group. But all of these supportive functions require a cultivation of relationships. If experts are simply plugged into a conference to answer questions without knowing their context, is the group likely to lose some of this support? Will experts lose some of their expertise?

Access will not mean the same thing in an electronic meeting as it does face-to-face. The kind of information which is exchanged and the way it is used will necessarily change. Just as a student having a beer with his professor might learn things he wouldn't learn in the lecture hall, electronic media will set new standards for accomplishing various meeting tasks. At least some of these standards will reflect a third fundamental characteristic of teleconferencing—limited channels for communication.

LIMITED COMMUNICATION CHANNELS

Compared to face-to-face, all teleconferencing media offer more restricted channels for the many types of communication which normally occur in small group interaction. These restrictions vary from medium to medium. Audio and computer conferencing, for example, filter out the body language which is preserved (although altered) in a video conference. Computer conferencing further filters voice intonations out of the discussion, but adds a dimension of literacy which is not so apparent in audio, video, or even face-to-face meetings.

In all three media, though, many of the nonverbal messages will be invisible or at least difficult to discern. Communication will be more focused. Differences in cultural background, organizational commitment, and goals and objectives will be less perceptible. These limitations could inhibit group effectiveness in several ways.

First, the narrowness of electronic media might foster a false sense of consensus, encouraging what Irving Janis calls "groupthink."[7] Groupthink is the reverse of the Multi-Headed Animal Syndrome noted above; it is the product of *too much* cohesiveness in a group—cohesiveness which screens out divergent ideas and tends to produce low-quality group decisions. While restricted communication channels may not build cohesiveness *per se*, they may easily limit the perspectives considered in a group by establishing an illusion of consensus. Once established, such an illusion might be aggravated by the isolation of participants from each other. In addition, the type of outside information accepted into the decision-making process could become limited to that which "fits" the available communication channels.

The supression of diverse perspectives does not necessarily produce consensus, however. Stereotyping of participants and polarization of issues are equally probable—and troublesome. Without enough breadth of communication, efforts to

---

[7]Irving Janis, *Victims of Groupthink*, Boston, Massachusetts: Houghton Mifflin Company, 1972.

explore the underlying sources of differences will probably be frustrated. It is easy to imagine that different organizational perspectives might bring charges of elitism; differences in cultural perspectives might elicit charges of racism. Such charges may eradicate the trust which is vital for any group communication.

Trust is always tentative. But it is particularly so in the initial stages of a meeting before expectations of others are tested in interaction. Much of the communication early in a meeting is, in fact, testing of trust. Laing captures the complexity of this testing process in his description of husband-wife interactions:

> Husband acts on wife so that wife will experience husband's actions in a particular way. But wife has to *act* in such a way before husband can realize that she experiences his act conjunctively or disjunctively to his intention; thus, husband's behavior towards wife affects her experience of him, which, mediated back to him by her behavior towards him, in turn influences his experience of her.[8]

Laing is describing interaction of only two people; as the group grows, the dynamics become even knottier.[9] When such complex dynamics are funneled through the narrow channel of an electronic medium, intentions may not be perceived accurately. The result is likely to be what Laing calls "spirals of misperception"—and mistrust.

These are some of the negatives—false consensus, failure to recognize and reconcile differences in perspectives, and a brittleness of group trust. In favor of limited channels, we need to point out that restricted communication can also help focus a discussion on critical group tasks. In some situations, trust is not really an issue. The group task is well-defined, and the need for divergent perspectives is low. In such situations, a lot of nonverbal messages are extraneous. Electronic meetings might then increase effectiveness by filtering unnecessary and distracting signals.

Electronic meetings could even allow some groups to bypass typical social protocols and become intimate more quickly. In a computer conference, Richard Bach made this observation:

> We are convention bound to comment on the weather, current events, where do you live, what do you do for a living, et cetera. In computer conferencing I can say, and delight in it, "M. Baudot, what for you is real?" In this capacity the system is sort of an intellectual ComputerMate. You can draw preliminary conclusions about a person in minutes that take long times to draft face to face, occluded as face-to-face is with appearance, manner, speech patterns, *und so wieder.*

Though perhaps not typical, Mr. Bach's reaction suggests that the "restrictions" of electronic communication channels need not always be limitations.

The size of communication channels in electronic meetings will undoubtedly elicit varied responses from participants. Some will see these media as terribly limiting, forcing complex communication through simple channels. Others may ac-

---

[8]R. D. Laing, N. Phillipson, and A. R. Lee, *Interpersonal Perception*, New York: Perrenial Library, 1966, pp. 34–5.

[9]In fact, Laing's metaphor for the entanglement of selves which occurs in groups is simply "knots." R. D. Laing, *Knots*, New York: Pantheon, 1971.

tually experience a new sense of freedom within the limitations so clearly set by teleconferencing media. Whatever the emotional reaction of participants, however, the narrowness of communication channels will introduce a *potential* for control of group communication in ways which simply could not occur face-to-face.

CONTROL OF GROUP INTERACTION

While channels of communication in an electronic meeting are more limited than in face-to-face, they are also more easily controlled. Teleconferencing systems often have control panels or consoles. Leaders of video conferences can decide who should be seen on the screen or can switch the view away from the group altogether. In both audio and video conferences, participants in the same room can disconnect their microphones or press "cough buttons" when they want to speak to each other without being heard at the remote site. Volume controls can reduce shouts to whispers. In a computer conference, the organizer of the meeting often has special controls which other participants do not, such as the ability to erase messages, to block all private messages, or to close one conference and open another.

The design of a teleconferencing system will also shape the kind of communication which can occur. A computer conferencing system can be structured to ask direct questions of participants, to specify the form of their response, and to tally the results according to predetermined formulas. A voice-switched audio system technologically prohibits two people from speaking at once. These built-in controls are attempts to eliminate the need for certain social choices, to make communication more orderly and rational, maybe even conflict-free.

On the surface, the orderly nature of electronic meetings suggests that they might promote the carefully deliberated sequential exchanges which typify many formal negotiations. Ironically, this well-ordered, rational consideration of the demands of all parties is often the *least* effective way to reach a solution in which everyone's needs are met. First, the sequential exchange of one demand for another can oversimplify the problem so that many complex differences become collapsed into just a few, highly polarized issues. Furthermore, rigidly controlled interaction inhibits informal interpersonal communication which might focus on areas of consensus and foster some feeling of group trust.

After a detailed review of laboratory experiments in the use of audio and video teleconferencing in conflict situations, Short, Williams, and Christie conclude:

> In contrast to problem-solving discussions, conflict is clearly a major area of sensitivity to medium of communication. Medium can affect the likelihood of reaching agreement, the side which is more successful, the nature of the settlement reached, the evaluation of the other side and the individual opinions after the discussion.[10]

On the positive side, the potential to control group interaction via teleconference, like the limits of electronic channels, can certainly aid in focusing the efforts of a group on the task at hand. More control might also mean more effective pro-

---

[10]John Short, Ederyn Williams, and Bruce Christie, *op. cit.*, p. 109.

cedures for promoting equality of participation, for reducing the importance of personal likes and dislikes in solving a problem, or for ensuring that all important topics are covered within a limited time period. But we suggested at the beginning of this chapter that communication is much more than verbal exchanges on a topic—that it includes more subtle dynamics such as play and developing and defining relationships. If the procedures for group communication are too rigid, if interaction is controlled too much, there could be little room for interpersonal relationships.

DEPENDENCE ON TECHNOLOGY

A final defining characteristic of teleconferences is their basic dependence on some form of electronic equipment. Whether it uses telephone lines, microwave circuits, computers, or satellites, each form of teleconferencing introduces *some* sort of machine dependence into group communication. This dependence is perhaps the corollary to increased control: if electronic media provide the technology for more orderly meetings, they also render meetings more vulnerable to failures in the technology—and the possibility of complete loss of control.

Machines have been accused of choosing awkward moments at which to fail. And in electronic meetings, there are likely to be many potentially awkward moments. A broken connection during an emotional exchange might be devastating. At best, it would probably slow the whole communication process as group members restart and try to recover their momentum. At worst, a system failure might be interpreted as an intentional act—the slamming of an electronic door. Group trust would likely deteriorate.

Less obvious system failures might produce equally damaging results. For example, spurious numbers or letters in a computer transcript might go undetected, but they could distort an important presentation of data or signal the wrong instructions to some participant. Such occurrences may prove rare; however, it will be difficult to predict when they might occur and what their impact will be.

Most users of electronic media will trust the technology without question—until something goes wrong. Then they will make contingency plans against future malfunctions. These will be useful but probably not infallible. And even if the technology performs flawlessly, users of teleconferencing media may still experience a loss of control in the meeting situation. In a conventional conference room, meeting participants can move chairs around, sit on the floor, or open the window; they can change the meeting environment to make it more hospitable to the task at hand. But the environment in an electronic meeting probably will not be so adaptable. In a video conference room, cameras are set for predetermined chair positions; microphones will place limits on how many people participate in an audio conference. Since electronic technology will be too complex for most people to tamper with, users are likely to accept these constraints as unalterable. In fact, they may be only partially aware of the constraints which teleconferencing imposes upon them.

There is a contradiction in electronic meetings between the apparent increase in control and the possibility of greater loss of control. This contradiction, even if it remains unconscious, will change the dynamics of group communication; group behavior in the meeting will likely reflect some loss of initiative, perhaps even a reduced sense of responsibility for the communication which is taking place.

THE SENSITIVE ZONES

The decision to use a teleconferencing system to improve communication sets a dynamic process in motion. It not only introduces new organizational choices for the meeting organizer; it can also change the way people feel about what they are doing. It changes their relationships with other members of the group and the way they perceive themselves as a group. And in the long term, it may change long-standing conventions for communicating in small groups as well as in organizations and even whole societies.

Some areas of small group communication will be particularly sensitive to this change process. The recurring themes in this chapter begin to map these areas: the building and maintenance of group trust is one. The recognition and reconciliation of diverse perspectives, particularly cultural differences, is another sensitive zone. So are group conflict and the use of outside resources, especially outside experts.

To explore these sensitive zones in more detail, we will return to the question which opened this chapter—the suggestion to hook up a group of people and let them work out a solution to a near-crisis. We propose to organize several electronic meetings. Each will consider the ways in which one of the media can be used either very effectively or very ineffectively. Each will build on the existing social evaluations of electronic media. Since these meetings will be imaginary, we will call them scenarios—the Camelia Scenarios.

FOUR

The characteristics of electronic media—physical separation, access to remote resources, narrow communication channels, increased control, and dependence on technology—increase the potential for both improvements and disappointments in meetings. Similarly, each medium has its own set of strengths and weaknesses for group communication. Effective uses of a medium are those which capitalize on its strengths; ineffective uses are those in which the weaknesses prevail. However, certain strengths will be more important in some contexts than in others; so will certain weaknesses. Accordingly, guidelines for effective meetings are really context- sensitive, and descriptions of effective uses of the media might best be described for a well-defined communication situation rather than in the abstract.

In this chapter, we have chosen to dramatize the strengths and weaknesses of teleconferencing by taking an imaginary leap to a future world where the media are being used for an international meeting. The meeting has been arranged by a foundation official in response to an impending crisis—a drought in the fictitious African country of Camelia. It is a bilingual communication situation (French and English), involving a blend of data interpretation, information exchange, negotiation, and decision-making.[1] Eleven people, representing local, regional, and international points of view, participate in the meetings. Although there is no immediate crisis, the threatening drought is serious enough and the time frame short enough to provoke a definite need to communicate and a recognizable outcome from the proceedings.

Since the purpose of the scenarios is to illustrate both *effective* and *ineffective* uses of audio, video, and computer teleconferencing as well as face-to-face communication in this situation, there are two scenarios for each of the media. These scenarios were developed from the "strengths" and "weaknesses" of each medium, included in the Summary of Social Evaluations of Teleconferencing in Appendix A. The focus is on small group communication—the issues of choice among media, of leadership, and of self-presentation. The reader should keep in mind that we are *not* attempting to forecast political or social realities of the future. We have purposely refrained from any major variance from the current world situation. Certainly, the

---

[1]This situation was inspired, in part, by the novel *L'Imprecateur* by R. V. Pilkes (Paris: Le Seuil, 1976). This book was awarded the Femina Prize in 1976; it describes the collapse (both physical and cultural) of a large business organization in which multilevel communication problems become overwhelming.

sociopolitical variables we have ignored will have profound effects on the ways in which teleconferencing media are used in the future. Such effects, however, could only have been considered here at the expense of our concentration on the important communication choices in a meeting.

While the scenarios are dramatizations of the strengths and weaknesses of the four media as revealed by evaluations to date, they are necessarily more. The current evaluations do not tell us how an African economic minister will get to know an American diplomat in a computer conference. Or how a voice-only medium will convey three distinctly different cultural perceptions of a problem like a drought. To answer questions like these, we have had to *interpret* the research findings, to relate them to such basics of communication as trust and the need to communicate or the availability of feedback channels. And occasionally, we have had to guess.

This chapter, then, begins with two memos from Bill Owens, our imaginary foundation official, who describes the situation in Camelia and proposes a conference. The memos are followed by two scenarios for each medium; in these scenarios, the same general variables combine, as a result of different uses of the media, to produce the success or failure of the conference. After each pair of scenarios, an analysis traces the links between events in the scenarios and the medium "strengths" and "weaknesses" which inspired them. These analyses identify some of the contradictions in the findings to date and explain the position that we took in these cases. They note the points at which we feel we are on the *terra firma* of the research data and those points at which we are speculating. In so doing, they also identify some of the major leadership issues embodied in the scenarios.

MEMO TO: Planning Committee, The Foundation

FROM: Bill Owens, Program Director, Task Force on Food
           Supply

DATE: 3 January 1985

SUBJECT: CAMELIA DROUGHT PROJECT

I have returned from Camelia and Paris with a feeling of
urgency regarding the threat of drought in Camelia. The
country had an extremely dry and poor growing season last
year, and a seriously under average rainfall over the past
three months. As you are aware, an extended drought would
compound the already severe problems of malnutrition in that
area. My meetings on this trip confirmed our earlier belief
that there is no comprehensive international activity underway to assess the extent, seriousness, impacts, and likely
duration of the possible drought; nor is there any concerted
effort to mobilize those organizations essential to short- or
long-term remedial action.

I see several possible goals for the Foundation, should
we decide to become involved in this situation. The most
important from our standpoint is to establish communication
among the major actors. Possible tasks would be to:

- evaluate the validity of the existing data;

- place the current weather conditions in the context
  of regional climate trends;

- assess the possible impact of a continuing drought;
  and

- develop alternative responses for an effective relief
  program.

During my trip, I identified several likely participants for such a study. In Lagos, I met with officials of the African Agricultural Board, notably Eduardo Ribera, who was extremely concerned by the discrepancies in the data and is anxious to hear the American experts on this question. In Timbalwe, Camelia, I had little opportunity to verify the reports about the impending drought. Certainly, everyone I met there was concerned, and some emergency measures were already in evidence in the city. I did meet with economic minister Abu Arume and his staff, who stated they would be willing to discuss the problem in meetings, provided the discussions weren't held in the United States. They would probably send three representatives. In Paris, I met with Helene Dubarieux of the Lutte Contre la Famine (LCF). She is an attractive, talented French woman who has an attitude of suspicion toward technology and appears to harbor an emotional skepticism—sometimes hostility—toward the involvement of the advanced nations in the Camelian situation. The LCF itself is a respected activist group with a strong involvement in countries such as Camelia.

I wasn't able to get an appointment with Jack Morris, who is the Euro-African representative of the Consolidated Produce Organization, but I spoke to him on the phone, and he advised me to extend an invitation to George Clemmons, Jr., the chairman of Consolidated Produce, based in Nebraska. I think he reflected their general attitude of doubt regarding the predictions of drought in Camelia, which he said may be grossly exaggerated. I could feel a good deal of potential antagonism toward Consolidated Produce during my trip abroad, and I think it would be politically advisable for a member of our board to contact Mr. Clemmons directly and find out how he would feel about being involved in the meetings.

In addition to the Camelians, the LCF, and Consolidated
Produce, I think we should identify one or two American
climatologists, a representative of the Council of African
Missions, and someone from Project Progress. That makes
about a dozen people who probably have never met as a group,
although some of them have known one another individually.

In organizing this conference, we should think carefully about the various modes of conferencing open to us.
We could, of course, hold the meetings face to face. I
would prefer to have them in Camelia, but Clemmons may not
agree to this. Paris also might be a logical place.
Facilities would be placed at our disposal by the French
government, which would also provide translations. (The
Camelians speak French, but I don't believe Clemmons does.
My French is pretty bad, and I don't think Morris fares
much better. Ribera and Dubarieux strongly recommended
conducting the meetings in two languages.)

If we decide not to rely solely on face-to-face meetings, then we have three other options, which can be used
alone or in combination: video, audio, and computer-based
teleconferencing. Computer conferencing would not be a
problem in terms of equipment. Even Timbalwe has a World
Net connection, and I have seen their terminals. They have
the high-speed type with a graphic display capability, so we
could discuss models and trends. I can arrange to have a
couple of interpreters standing by on the network. Similarly, audio conferencing would be no problem: there are
facilities at all sites through the local phone companies or
government agencies. In Camelia, they would even make the
emergency lines available to us if we ran into noise problems with the normal circuits.

If we decide to go the video route, I think we should use one of the commercial video conferencing services which are worldwide and can supply interpreters and camera technicians at all sites with very little advance notice. Their equipment will send a color image through a satellite to as many as 10 sites simultaneously. We need to think about the number of sites necessary for such a conference.

A word about costs: all of the electronic media are potentially less expensive than face-to-face meetings. Video is at the high end of the cost scale while audio and computer conferencing are comparable. However, it is important to note that the type of communication developed will vary considerably from medium to medium, making real cost comparisons difficult. Thus, our choice should not be determined as much by cost considerations (since all of the media are within our grasp) as by our communication needs.

This situation presents us with a fine opportunity to facilitate a collaborative network; but at the same time, if such an attempt backfires, the consequences in terms of economic and social conditions in Camelia, to say nothing of our reputation, could be severe.

MEMO TO: Planning Committee, The Foundation

FROM: Bill Owens, Program Director, Task Force on Food
           Supply

DATE: 5 January 1985

SUBJECT: PARTICIPANTS IN THE CAMELIAN DROUGHT MEETINGS
           (Please keep confidential)

     Since several of you have asked about suggested par-
ticipants in the proposed Camelian Drought Conference, I
decided to circulate this memo with my own (candid) perceptions of them. I have selected the participants carefully in order to represent all of the important points of
view on the Camelian drought. However, I want to limit the
core group to 10 in order to enable full interchange of
viewpoints. Naturally, these descriptions should be kept
confidential, since they are only my own views.

     Let me begin at the center of the potential crisis,
which is Camelia. This large country in what used to be
French Africa is a quasi-democracy with a history not unlike
the rocky road traveled by most developing countries.
Abu Arume, the economic minister, is a key to power in the
country's agricultural and rural development policies. He
is politically astute, with an innate instinct for the
political arena. To Americans, he has often appeared
domineering and may even be perceived as bizarre. He
appears to have great leverage within Camelia, however, and
his role is vital to the success of the conference. To give
you a sense of his style, Arume is said to have changed
the course of a national council meeting through a single
15-minute speech. During the speech, he flung his coat on

the parliamentary floor and threw his military medal across
the room. When he finished, some council members were
actually in tears. Obviously flabbergasted, they left in
awe--and probably in some fear--of Arume. I share this
anecdote with you even though it may have become something
of a legend by now. Arume is explosive, but he is crucial
to the success of the conference.

Camelia will also be represented by two other government officials, Francoise Mwanga and Cyprian N'dolo.
Ms. Mwanga has a Ph.D. from the School of Public Policy at
Berkeley and is the first female head of the Camelian Office
of Planning. (Actually, the office was only established 10
years ago.) I don't know a lot about her, except that her
training is good and she may be able to serve in a supporting role. I don't expect her to be dominant, though.
Similarly, I don't expect too much initiative from Cyprian
N'dolo, but as a top Camelian Weather Bureau official, he
has access to important information about current conditions
there and is well respected by the local farmers.

Bishop Ampleby, a 40-year-old veteran of such meetings,
works with the Council of African Missions. He has the air
of a rugged explorer even on those rare occasions when he
wears his holy collar. He is easy to talk with and relaxing
to be around; he is also knowledgeable and tough. He
currently manages agricultural development programs in five
rural African countries including Camelia. He has had this
job for only three years now, but has over 15 years' experience with African food problems. He should be a mediating
force in the conference, but only if Camelia gets a fair
shake. He'll drive a hard bargain if they don't.

The U.S. State Department and the Department of Agriculture decided five years ago to join forces in coordinating policies about providing foreign agricultural assistance. This coordination is administered by Project Progress. The program hasn't won the hearts of Congress as yet, so funding for the organization hasn't been generous. It is thus a rather skimpy attempt by the State Department to respond to emergency situations such as the one which may be arising in Camelia. But it could act as a catalyst in marshalling U.S. technical assistance and in providing seed funds for international relief measures. It is headed by Allan Draper, an American who has been in Paris for several years. Draper is a diplomat with a background in economic planning. Although we met several years ago, I don't really know a lot about him. Project Progress could be of some assistance for drought relief, but they're really not big enough to do much.

I plan to include two representatives from Consolidated Produce Organization. As most of you know, Consolidated Produce is a multinational agribusiness corporation, which functions as a public consortium. It plays an important role in Camelia's economy (and other aspects of its culture as well) because it purchases and processes a significant portion of Camelia's crops for eventual resale in foreign markets. It also sells some agricultural products, such as seed and fertilizer, to the country. Given its importance and leverage in the Camelian economy, Consolidated Produce is always under close scrutiny by some quarter in Camelia and by those groups whose cause is the equitable development of the poorer countries. Relationships between the conglomerate and the Camelian government over the past five years, however, have been workable, although occasionally tense.

Consolidated Produce is represented in Paris by Jack Morris; I have invited him to participate in the meetings. Morris reports directly to George Clemmons, Jr., in Lincoln, Nebraska--the organization's international headquarters. Clemmons is a classic example of a successful international businessman. He is a sophisticated corporate leader and his Nebraska drawl is a powerful force around any conference table. (Incidentally, he is also a prominent member of the First Methodist Church of Lincoln--the same denomination as Bishop Ampleby.)

Two regional groups will be represented, the most cautious of which is the African Agricultural Board. Eduardo Ribera will be their representative and could assist in interpreting the discrepancies in the various data on the agricultural impacts of the drought. He is an outstanding economist, though he doesn't have a lot of international conferencing experience. As I indicated previously, the African Agricultural Board has demonstrated a willingness to give technical assistance, as well as favorable loans, to Third World nations hit by adverse climate conditions-- perhaps more a show of long-range self-interest than altruism, but important in our situation, nevertheless.

Helene Dubarieux of the Lutte Contre la Famine (LCF), will definitely be an important force in the conference. The LCF is an activist group with considerable legal sophistication; it has been a strong force for the rights of developing countries and has access to powerful press channels. They distrust Consolidated Produce, and they have argued against it as another "big business" conglomerate. Helene is one of the LCF's most articulate spokespersons; her conscientious and aggressive style as well as her unique viewpoint suggest that she will be a strong participant.

There is some question about how serious and extended the dry conditions in Camelia are likely to be. One group that has geared itself up over the past decade to help assess situations such as this one is the International Association of Meteorologists and Climatologists, of which Professor Glenn Pierson is an officer. He is Professor of Climate Studies at the University of Colorado, and has written extensively on food and climate problems. His background includes work with OXFAM in England, and he is an expert on crop-growing in arid lands. We have worked with him frequently before; while he is sometimes a bit shy in such gatherings, he should be an excellent resource person.

As you can see, this array of participants does not promise instant communication. On the other hand, I think all of them have some stake in a positive outcome--even though there will certainly be diverse points of view. Clemmons, Dubarieux, and Arume are perhaps the strongest personalities, but some of the others may surprise us.

Bill Owens
The Foundation

Abu Arume
Economic Minister
Camelia

Cyprian N'dolo
Camelian Weather Bureau

Francoise Mwanga
Camelian Office of Planning

Bishop Amplelby
Council of African Missions

Eduardo Ribera
African Agricultural Board

Jack Morris
Euro-African Representative
Consolidated Produce Organization

George Clemmons, Jr.
Chairman
Consolidated Produce Organization

Helene Dubarieux
Lutte Contre la Famine

Allan Draper
Director
Project Progress

Glenn Pierson
Professor of Climate Studies
University of Colorado

A video teleconference room, modeled after the
Picturephone® Meeting Service

PROJECT PROGRESS

Washington, D.C.

Allan Draper

April 13, 1985

Ms. A. Henley
Conferencing Unlimited, Inc.
2740 Kissinger Plaza
Washington, D.C.

Dear Ann:

As you requested, I'm writing this letter to record my reactions to the video teleconference on the Camelian situation. Since you and your colleagues at Conferencing Unlimited were so helpful in the preparation stages, the least I can do is take a few moments to tell you how it worked out. We have made good progress, with the Camelia problem just about solved now, and the draft of a relief plan is in its final stages. I think all of us in this conference were pleased with the interaction within the meetings, which was disciplined but friendly. Your colleagues in the visual communications trade are to be commended for the fine job they've done in training people for the subtleties of video communication. I was really struck by the general improvement in conferencing skills in just the last five years since training programs have been in full swing. (When were the first training programs begun? 1979?)

Before the meetings began, Bill Owens talked to each of us individually over the VideoCom system. These introductory sessions were very useful. We were able to check out the VideoCom rental equipment (no shorts in my system this time!) and to make sure our office arrangements were comfortable. During these sessions, Bill also went over the background of each of the other participants. We had received biographical information by electronic mail, but I'm sure Bill wanted to reinforce our similarities and downplay our differences so we could get off on the right foot.

After our individual meetings with Bill, we all traveled to Crete for a two-day weekend meeting. It was a fairly informal occasion, and the Foundation had arranged for a private villa which could accommodate everyone. We set some preliminary goals and scheduled the video meetings. We also got to know each other personally in the course of these preliminary sessions. I think if we hadn't met face to face, I might have had a very different impression of some of the participants. Like Jack Morris--in person, he was easygoing and friendly. But over the system, he came across like Mr. Cool Efficiency. On the other hand, Helene Dubarieux's personality seemed unchanged by the video medium; she was as warm--and as volatile--in the conference sessions as in person.

Once the video meetings began, it was apparent that Bill had really done his homework on the use of video conferencing. The weekly VideoCom sessions of the group were strictly limited to one hour. Agendas were sent the day before, and the meetings always began and ended on time. This schedule was great for me; the formality and the lights and the general tension can really be tiring if meetings go much beyond an hour. But I also know that the short meetings were a mixed blessing to Arume. He explained to me in a phone call one day that, while the time restrictions allowed him to keep on top of all of the immediate pressures in his office, they also made him uncomfortable because he felt some of the issues couldn't be discussed in such a short time and he hated to break off the discussion in the middle of a disagreement.

Actually, his comments helped me overcome some of my anger with him on a couple of occasions. It often seemed that he was trying to stall a discussion just when we were getting to a workable solution. Clemmons actually accused him of this once. Gradually, though, I realized that Arume wasn't stalling at all; he simply had a different perception of the problem than some of us did. He really had no doubt that we could feed several thousand starving Camelians, but he wanted to know what would happen to them after they were fed. Bill was quick to recognize this difference and occasionally arranged additional sessions so that we could pursue the special concerns which were not always on our agenda. I certainly never objected to an additional session with Arume. He's such an animated speaker. You can be sure no one ever falls asleep watching him on a screen!

In general, Bill encouraged a highly interactive conferencing style. At the very first video meeting, for example, he invited N'dolo to begin the discussion. Well, N'dolo was obviously uncomfortable and resorted to reading a prepared "speech." But Bill interrupted him right away with a question, asking Glenn Pierson to comment, too. His question broke the ice, and N'dolo, obviously relieved, responded casually to our questions. It has been my experience that once you break through that initial awkwardness of talking "for the camera," video conferencing seems to encourage everyone to participate.

As the meetings progressed, we tried to focus on the information exchange, discussion of ideas, and problem-solving aspects of our tasks, occasionally calling in outside resource people from various locations to help out. We definitely avoided video negotiations. For instance, George Clemmons suggested a change in the Camelia export tariff structure at one point. As you might guess, this was a highly controversial proposal, so Bill tabled it until a face-to-face meeting with Mwanga, Arume, Clemmons, Ribera, and Dubarieux could be arranged. The proposal was complex; the arguments were subtle; and the members wanted direct face-to-face discussions to deal with such concerns, although some background discussion of the proposal was carried out by teleconference and written papers. (Bill also used personal telephone calls to follow up meetings in which the tensions ran high.)

At a point in one of the meetings, just as it seemed that we were getting wrapped up in the immediate problems of communicating with each other, Bishop Ampleby requested that we take 10 minutes of group time to see a videotape he had on the current situation in Camelia. The tape was made by one of his colleagues, and it was not much of a film by Hollywood standards. But it did provide a good current image of the country. Also, since Clemmons hadn't been in

Camelia for several years, the film was really useful.
Later in the meetings, when particular areas of Camelia
were being discussed, Ampleby would dispatch his colleague
to get some more pictures, and we saw them as quickly as the
next day through another videotape. These tapes--there were
five in all--helped us to visualize the situation and gave
us a sense of perspective which injected life into even
the dullest of data-base debates. Incidentally, each
session was also videotaped and became an important record
to which we sometimes referred later, even though it is
difficult to access information stored on videotape.

Of course, Bill was also sensitive to the dangers of
the "visual channel." I recalled your little lectures on
how important nonverbal communication really is--that hand
movements, for instance, can come across so differently over
TV compared to face-to-face situations. When problems
in nonverbal expression occurred, either Bill or the translators would step in. The translators both watched and
listened and occasionally interpreted the gestures as well
as the words of a speaker. All participants, however,
pledged at the start of the meetings that no other observers
would be present off-camera at their locations.

There was one fascinating exchange last week between
Eduardo Ribera and Francoise Mwanga about the actual meaning
of some crop production data. I don't think the problem
could have been resolved if Mwanga hadn't been able to draw
from the resources of her department and some contacts at
the University of Camelia. In a face-to-face situation, she
would have lost the argument. Here, she just asked to
reschedule the afternoon session for the next day, and she
spent the evening with her colleagues, checking all the

calculations. The next day, they made a television presentation, using map overlays and graphs, which was the
turning point of the whole thing: they found that both
sides had been right all along, in a way. There had been a
decline in Camelian production before the drought (so Mwanga
was wrong), but it wasn't due to poor management of the
agriculture as Ribera had claimed. Instead, some correla-
tion analyses with other social indicators suggested that
rapid urbanization and industrialization in Northern Camelia
as well as its neighbors were to blame. This means that no
ad hoc program is going to provide a permanent solution.
There is an interesting diplomatic situation here because a
large part of Africa will have to face the problem in a
concerted fashion.

Anyway, our job is almost done, and we have drafted a
plan that should be signed by the middle of next week. If
all teleconferences went this well, I just might convince
the State Department that I could run the Embassy from
Washington! But since my job involves a wide range of communication activities, and VideoCom isn't appropriate for
all of them, I guess I'm still doomed to occasional jet lag
and high Paris prices.

Thanks again for your help.

                                        Best regards,
                                        Allan

MEMO TO: Headquarters, Council of African Missions,
          Nairobi (Kenya)
FROM: Bishop Ampleby, Timbalwe
DATE: 17 March 1985

SUBJECT: CONTINUING DROUGHT IN CAMELIA

It is with sadness and some bitterness that I must
report another failure of the "advanced countries" in
applying their resources to a real need in this continent.
This time, the Foundation raised high hopes of coming to
grips with the threat of drought in Camelia. But instead of
a working conference, all they have obtained for their money
is another example of "show business." Their decision to
hold the meetings by television contributed greatly to their
ultimate failure.

The Video Travel System was adopted as the official
communications medium by the Foundation--they told us--as a
response to several strong concerns:

1. The economic burden of continuous travel is be-
    coming oppressive.

2. Fear of crime and terrorism has mounted to the
    point where people of the calibre of Consolidated
    president George Clemmons travel outside the United
    States only at high risk; video conferencing allows
    everyone to stay home in guarded rooms.

3. Video Travel allows more control of the group since
    all the interactions are via the medium (usually
    taped), not in backroom meetings.

4. Much higher consistency in multilanguage communication is possible due to the translation of several
   languages simultaneously via a central switchboard
   in the Video Travel system.

The Video Travel brochures promise a "communications
intimacy found previously only in face-to-face contact."
Video Travel, they say, offers the warm familiarity of
face-to-face communication without many of its interpersonal
burdens--obligations to dine with conference participants,
for example. It means precision of communication without a
loss of emotional flavor, or so we thought.

The problems began with the conferencing equipment
itself. Video Travel normally provides all its participants
with the same equipment. But since Consolidated had a fully
equipped video conference room at all its major sites, it
was possible simply to plug them into the Video Travel
system. As it turned out, it was a mistake to let Clemmons
use his own conference room; it created an immediate gap in
communications. Clemmons sat magnificently behind a massive
oak desk with a bronze bust of Abraham Lincoln visible just
behind him. He apparently had assistants all around him,
feeding him information as he needed it. (The rest of us
wondered who he had sitting next to him; I almost always
felt like someone was watching us.) The sound and picture
quality from his room was impeccable--far superior to that
of the rented units from Video Travel. Thus, when Clemmons
spoke, he sounded like a stern parent allowing his squeally-
voiced children but a few minutes of his valuable time. His
voice boomed through the system, seemingly sucking the
decibels from the other timid microphones.

In contrast to Clemmons, the Camelians met together in
a governmental conference room equipped (temporarily) with
Video Travel hardware. The three of them invited me to join
them in the room as well, since I was in Timbalwe. I'm
afraid the conference room was chosen somewhat carelessly.
We were constantly distracted by various technical irrita-
tions, such as lighting problems requiring banks of video
lights rather than partial reliance on natural daylight.
Also, the soundproofing was inadequate, so we had quite a
bit of noise from the street below.

In Paris, Jack Morris had his own equipment at the
Consolidated regional headquarters; while not as imposing as
Clemmons' office, it did provide a higher quality image than
did the rental equipment. Helene Dubarieux of the LCF and
Allan Draper of the U.S. State Department were also in Paris
but shared a single site at the U.S. Embassy. Eduardo
Ribera of the African Agricultural Board had Video Travel
equipment in Lagos; Owens, the Foundation staffer who called
the meetings, was alone in Dayton; and Professor Glenn
Pierson was in Denver. Thus, six of us were in two conference rooms, while the other five were each by themselves.
Such an uneven distribution of participants proved particularly troubling. Abu Arume easily dominated our conference
room in Timbalwe; even I had trouble getting much in.
Arume's sense of presence in person is really awesome,
and it meant that the rest of us were subjugated to supporting roles. Arume's presence seemed to come through the
video medium all right, but he probably looked somewhat
comical in contrast to the stern elegance of Clemmons.
Also, it was easy to feel off by ourselves, the only ones
with real information, trying like hell to stuff our experience of the impending drought into that silly camera!

Clemmons' media superiority made that feeling even worse, and nobody was able to overcome it.

Bill Owens, though certainly well-meaning and likable, proved to be a weak leader because of his isolation from the others. It was as though he thought he could just hook us up through this video beast, add some film resources, and stand back while we automatically solved all the problems. Perhaps he was aiming for flexibility. He encouraged us to be spontaneous, so there was no regular schedule for the meetings; instead, they went on almost daily for three weeks.

One big problem was that none of us had ever met together as a group, and only a few had ever met individually. Obviously, there are ways for group members to get to know one another, but the stress here was more on presentation than interaction. A face-to-face preface to the video meetings might have been a big help. As it was, we didn't even get biographies of the participants in advance of the meetings. When the first video meeting started, we had only hints about the status and personalities of one another. (Incidentally, George Clemmons led the way in hints about *his* status, hardly revealing the best in Nebraskan Methodism.) In the full three weeks, we never really developed efficient communication procedures; we were just a collection of interested parties.

The meetings began on February 23. Owens began with a film about Camelia--a slick, 10-minute state-of-the-country report. These films became regular features, sort of like the opening prayer of the meetings. Kettering had commissioned a commercial news team to put the films together each day, so we could have a constant update on the Camelian

situation. I guess Owens thought that the "crisis mentality" of these films--with their reports on soil and weather
conditions, the fears of the Camelian farmers, and the
nutritional implications of the drought--would encourage an
atmosphere of sober cooperation. In fact, I think they
subtly undermined the entire conference. On one hand, they
gave us a false sense of confidence that we had the proper
knowledge to make decisions. I remember challenging the
American Pierson about one of his statements on climate
shifts in the Eastern Plateau before I realized that my
"knowledge" was really based on one 90-second summary from
one of the "Camelian Updates" a few days earlier. Those
films were so polished and neatly packaged, while Pierson's
hand-scribbled charts and diagrams were complex and hard to
read. I'm afraid it was easier for all of us to rely on the
visual impact of films as our common reality than to explore
the data before us.

At first, everyone played the "purity" of video communication to the hilt. The tapes of the first meetings
showed polite, respectful exchanges among all the representatives. But it didn't take long for antagonisms to
arise. Owens got us started on a monstrous first task:
negotiating the administrative structure for a food distribution plan in Camelia. Lots of bargaining was involved, and
it was hard to get down to the real issues. Looking back,
it is clear that we all had agendas and that they didn't all
fit together neatly. Some sorting process was necessary,
and it simply didn't occur. Each of us *presented* our own
ideas, but the structure did not encourage enough interaction among us to sort through the differences in our perspectives. When Owens saw us floundering, he shifted to

what he thought was a safer topic: the agricultural technologies for responding to the drought conditions. As it
turned out, this subject was more complicated than he had
realized. Pierson began with a professorial lecture and
gradually covered his display board with his hand-drawn
figures full of numbers which we could barely read on the
screen. When Cyprian N'dolo displayed the Camelian statistics, the numbers didn't agree! Each tried to persuade the
other that his figures were correct. Jack Morris of Consolidated seemed to have yet another point of view. We
struggled on; I *almost* prayed for a commercial to break the
tension!

Eduardo Ribera was a sad disappointment. He is a
leading world economist and was considered by the Foundation
to be one of the conference's biggest assets. But he
repeatedly failed to share his carefully prepared presentations of charts and tables; he is, after all, very nearsighted and his eyes are sensitive--it would have been
difficult for him, perhaps even embarrassing, to try to read
before the camera. At the same time, Pierson, Mwanga, and
N'dolo, who could have presented important technical information, hesitated to speak in front of Ribera. The result was
an ever-declining amount of technical input to the discus-
sions--and few challenges to what was presented.

As the communication deteriorated, tensions rose. At
one point in the discussion, Arume moved his arms dramatically, as he often does when he talks. Clemmons must have
been startled by this because he shouted, "Don't shake your
fist at me!" I was in the same room as Arume, and he
was clearly *not* shaking his fist at Clemmons or anybody
else. But it apparently looked like he was over the TV

screen! Clemmons ended up breaking the connection abruptly,
leaving all of us staring at a blank screen.

So we stumbled from one issue to another, with group
leadership juggled in the growing verbosity contest. Some
people were definitely more skilled in this contest than
others. Previous experience with this technology was
uneven. Within Consolidated, video travel is often used as
an official communications medium; most administrative
tasks--sometimes even important negotiation sessions--are
conducted by video conference. The representatives of the
other organizations generally had some degree of previous
experience with it, too. Unfortunately, many "training
sessions" for video teleconferencing are more like lessons
in theatrics than lessons in communication. The result is
the manipulation of meetings by the most skilled "actors."
In our case, I expected Arume to be a natural, but I was
struck by how Jack Morris consistently came out on top in
any discussion. Thanks to some investigative work by Helene
Dubarieux and the LCF, we discovered before too long that he
was actually an accomplished actor substituted for the
real Jack Morris. Many of his "spontaneous" speeches were
in fact prepared and skillfully read from hidden cue cards.
They even had a make-up kit for him! Of course, Consolidated claimed they only resorted to this tactic because the
real Jack Morris became ill at the last minute and they
didn't want to lose his vote.

I'm afraid that the promise of Video Travel and its
apparent ability to provide continuous "communication" led
the Foundation to rely too fully on this technology. Once
the trust among participants began to deteriorate, video
travel offered no channels for restoring communication.

For me now, it is back to the bush with the prospect of another long struggle to help the villagers survive. Once again, I will rely on Headquarters' support of our efforts in Camelia. I am afraid we will be very much on our own from now on.

ANALYSIS OF THE VIDEO
TELECONFERENCING SCENARIOS

If it is true that "a picture is worth a thousand words," video teleconferencing has some obvious advantages. Visual information—a smile, a photograph, a map—can be exchanged easily over video. Also, gestures are easily communicated, serving to lubricate group interaction. Yet, video conferences are not carbon copies of face-to-face meetings; they have their own set of rules and their own traps for the unsuspecting conference organizer.

The Hollywood Syndrome

New users of video teleconferencing often unconsciously associate video teleconferencing with Hollywood-style movies and television. Broadcasting words from the world of television often litter the operation of a new teleconferencing system: participants talk about the "program," the "studio," and the "director" (V57*). Such an association tends to make the group—especially new users—very self-conscious and can encourage *presentations* rather than *communication*. Such presentations dominated the Ineffective Scenario, as Bishop Ampleby noted:

> Each of us *presented* our own ideas, but the structure did not encourage enough interaction among us to sort through the differences in perspective. . . . Instead of a working conference, all they have obtained for their money is another example of "show business."

The association with television was subtly encouraged in this scenario by the Camelian Updates—"slick, 10-minute state-of-the-country reports." With weak empirical support (V53 is only indirectly related), we nevertheless speculate that video teleconferencing can potentially create a false sense of confidence in one's information. Just as television news broadcasts provide the illusion of total news coverage in a very short time (Consider TV newsman Walter Cronkite's closing message: "That's the way it is. . . ."), packaged programs such as the Camelian Updates might provide a false sense of being in control of the necessary information. In our opinion, such a mood becomes particularly volatile when complex topics arise, as was the case in the Camelian conference. Of course, the use of visual information does not have to be misleading. In the Effective Scenario, Bishop Ampleby made use of the visual capacity in a similar—but much less polished—fashion. He supplied amateur videotapes which were taken in Camelia and sent immediately to the teleconference. Without the ritual and the polish of the Camelian Updates, these films assumed a more humble, but probably more appropriate role in the conference.

In the extreme, the "Hollywood" qualities of video could encourage deliberate deception. Users of video will require some initial training in effective self-presentation via the medium, but the line between effective presentation and deception may be as difficult to draw as the line between effective and deceptive use of

---

*The codes in this analysis refer to the numbers of the "strengths" and "weaknesses" listed for each of the media in the Summary of Social Evaluations of Teleconferencing in Appendix A. Thus: V for video, C for computer conferencing, A for audio, and F for face-to-face.

television by political candidates. The make-up kit and the hired actor in the Ineffective Scenario, though probably extreme, illustrate the dark side of the same skills which are necessary to communicate effectively via the medium. Of course, comparable problems can arise with any communications medium, including face-to-face. However, with teleconferencing, we suspect that, because of the lack of social presence (V49, V50, V52), it will be particularly difficult to restore a sense of group trust once trust levels have deteriorated.

Video Personalities

Even with training, individual skills in using the video medium are likely to vary. Video teleconferencing has basic characteristics which lend themselves better to some interpersonal communication styles than to others (V55). The most obvious of these is the ability to communicate visually as well as orally. For someone who relies on expressive gestures to communicate, the visual channel promises to be an important plus. In the Ineffective Scenario, however, it didn't work out that way for Abu Arume:

> At one point in the discussion, Arume moved his arms dramatically, as he often does when he talks. Clemmons must have been startled because he shouted, "Don't shake your fist at me!" I was in the same room as Arume, and he was clearly *not* shaking his fist at Clemmons or anybody else. But it apparently looked like he was over the TV screen!

With no direct empirical support, we speculate that gestures which are acceptable over one medium may be perceived as hostile over another. This possibility is increased in a cross-cultural situation, where gestures may be misunderstood at the outset! In the case of video teleconferencing, we are guessing that gestures like Arume's arm movements might appear amplified and even violent when projected on a television screen. The example may be overstated, but we feel that situations similar to this one are likely to arise.

The visual channel also proved to be more burdensome than helpful to the nearsighted Ribera. He struggled with charts and figures, and it was difficult for him to read before the camera. The result was an embarrassing situation for everyone. Since Ribera's inability to develop a strategy for effective self- presentation is linked so closely to his nearsightedness, the problem is most likely Owen's fault for not predicting such an occurrence. Group leaders making choices among media will have to consider participant/medium matches as part of their planning.

Group leaders may have to invest extra care in participant/participant matchmaking, too. Video teleconferencing has not yet been demonstrated as an effective medium for getting to know someone or for meetings among strangers (V41, V43, V44, V49). While there is some debate on this point (e.g., V10), we think Bill Owens took a big chance by not scheduling a face-to-face meeting *before* the group began to use the video medium. If he were forced into this position, he should at least have provided biographical information in advance and focused on social issues as much as possible during the first meeting (by pointing out common areas of interest, for example). As it was, the group had "only hints about the status and personalities of one another." And evaluations of video conferencing suggest that confusion about status and roles can only create problems. (V7, V41, V42).

In the Effective Scenario, Owens gets a better score. Here, he held preliminary sessions with each participant over the VideoCom system: "During these sessions, Bill also went over the background of each of the other participants. We had received biographical information by electronic mail, but I'm sure Bill wanted to reinforce our similarities and downplay our differences so we could get off on the right foot." Notice that Owens also raised the issue of off-camera observers immediately, since video has been criticized for failing to convey a feeling of privacy (V54).

The Video Conference Room

Basic to the success of a video teleconference is the physical arrangement—the way in which the electronic conference room is created. Ill-conceived arrangements can have strong negative effects on the conduct of teleconferences. The most extreme example of this problem in the Ineffective Scenario is the imbalance between the conference arrangements for George Clemmons and those for the Camelians. Clemmons used his specially equipped room, which emphasized his strength in the proceedings: "Thus, when Clemmons spoke, he sounded like a stern parent allowing his squeally-voiced children but a few minutes of his valuable time. His voice boomed through the system, seemingly sucking the decibels from the other timid microphones." Meanwhile, the Camelians spoke from carelessly arranged temporary facilities and were immediately at a disadvantage.

This technical inequality was amplified by the unequal distribution of the participants among the sites. Multilocation video teleconferencing is technically difficult anyway, due to problems of showing all the participants on screen simultaneously. But when there are unequal numbers of people at each location, there is an especially high probability of "insider-outsider" feelings (V58)—sometimes leading to overt hostility. The people in one conference room are likely to feel "closer" to those in the same room and more "distant" from those in the remote location. Ampleby expressed the sentiments of the Camelians:

. . . it was easy to feel off by ourselves, the only ones with real information, trying like hell to stuff our experience of the impending drought into that silly camera!

Providing electronic links is only the first step in creating a communication "space." In the Ineffective Scenario, Owens did little more: "It was as though he thought he could just hook us up through this video beast, add some film resources, and stand back while we automatically solved all the problems." In the Effective Scenario, however, he paid close attention to details of scheduling, for example. Current results suggest, at least tentatively, that some sort of regular schedule is necessary for the use of video teleconferencing, particularly with a new group (V4). Having done his homework, Owens scheduled weekly sessions, strictly limited to one hour in length. He made sure that agenda were always available in advance, too.

The role of the leader *during* a video teleconference is open to some debate. A study on the use of the Bell Laboratories video system concludes that a regular committee-like structure is required (V4, V8). However, there is also evidence to suggest that formal organization of the meeting is not very important via video.

One field experiment indicates that the time spent maintaining group organization is lower by video than by audio, though higher than face-to-face (V28). Another study, based on a series of laboratory experiments, suggests that an "unorganized formality" develops in a video teleconference, eliminating the need for strong, overt leadership (V32). In the scenarios, we have adopted a moderate position: Owens was a strong (but not rigid) leader in the Effective Scenario, while he asserted no leadership in the Ineffective Scenario. We *do* feel that strong leadership will be necessary in this communication situation.

Video For What? No Simple Answers Yet . . .

By task analysis alone—which tasks are affected by which media?—video teleconferencing does not compare favorably with either face-to-face or audio at present. Short, Williams, and Christie (1976) conclude that video teleconferencing is difficult to justify by current criteria: it costs a lot and differs very little from audio in evaluation results. One task for which video currently ranks high is "giving information to keep people in the picture" (V14). In the scenarios, this potential of video to maintain friendly relations is linked to regularity of usage. In the Effective Scenario, regular meetings make it possible to feel "in touch." The Ineffective Scenario is characterized by irregularity and perhaps even an overreliance on video to perform this function.

The strongest negative evaluation of video teleconferencing concerns bargaining (V44). Actually, however, video systems have rarely been used for real-life bargaining. Thus, it is possible that this judgment may say more about the difficulty of bargaining than the unsuitability of video teleconferencing for bargaining. Based on current evaluations, though, it seems ill-advised to rely on video for this task. In the Effective Scenario, Owens carefully avoided such a situation by scheduling a separate face-to-face meeting to focus on negotiation. This strategy, of course, assumes that the group could get together face to face and avoids facing the difficult question of how to bargain if all you have is video. Anecdotal evidence from at least one operating video system suggests that effective bargaining by video *is* possible and that perhaps the experimental evidence is misleading. At any rate, our Ineffective Scenario still has Owens charging blindly into bargaining as his very first group task: "Owens started us on a monstrous first task: negotiating the administrative structure for a food distribution plan in Camelia."

In Summary . . .

While video teleconferencing was a glamour child of telecommunications not long ago, it now seems besieged by bad press. Evaluation studies have found few attributes of video which come close to justifying its cost. In our opinion, however, it is still too early to offer a final indictment of video as pure conspicuous consumption. Video has the potential for types of communication which can't be reduced to words or print, and such communication might be crucial in some situations. But video probably has been oversold. As in any other medium, there are communication hurdles here. Overcoming these hurdles may require more—not less—planning.

GEORGE CLEMMONS' TRANSCRIPT OF THE CAMELIA
COMPUTER CONFERENCE

GEORGE —
   As you suggested, I have noted
   MY REACTIONS TO THE CONFERENCE ON YOUR
   TRANSCRIPT. HOPE THESE ARE USEFUL!

[1] OWENS 5-APR-85 2:30 PM GMT   *Jack*

I would like to summarize our progress to date. I
think we would all agree that, in Part 1 of this
conference, we have taken several important steps   *Good*
toward the resolution of the impending crisis in   *OVERALL*
Camelia. First, we have agreed on the data re-   *SUMMARY*
quirements for an emergency monitoring program, and   *HERE*
I have now established a separate conference called
"Camelia Monitor" that will deal more specifically
with these technical issues. All of you will be
registered as participants in this conference.
Other participants will include scientists from
Consolidated, Camelia, and the African Agricultural Board, and three independent universities
who have agreed to perform monitoring functions.
I am sending their biographies to each of you. I
will be holding an "introduction" session from
12:00 to 2:00 P.M. (Greenwich time) on 10 April
and 11 April for any of you who want to get to
know these newcomers.

                                        YES! LETS KEEP
                                        THE TECHNICAL DETAILS
[2] OWENS 5-APR-85 2:37 PM GMT   *OUT OF HERE*

I have also established a parallel "Data Interpretation" conference. The entries in the Monitor
conference will be pretty cryptic to most of us.
For example, moisture content of soil will be

reported in AAB standard units, in the following format:

```
Date 4/07, 6/13, 6/20, 6/27
Plot 37E, 39D, 52, 38E
Map 321E, 321E, 321E, 321E
Moisture .337, .446, .366, .374
```

The purpose of the Interpretation conference will be to answer questions about the nature and meaning of the data.

[3] OWENS 5-APR-85 2:45 PM GMT

Second, we have agreed not to launch any immediate relief program unless the Monitor conference indicates a rapid deterioration in the Camelian situation. While this decision perhaps increases the pressure on us in this second part of the conference, the Camelians do not want to commit themselves to an emergency program which might threaten the chance of long-term recovery from the drought.

[4] OWENS 5-APR-85 2:51 PM GMT

Finally, in our lengthy debate over objectives, I think we have clarified the major issues which will have to be resolved before any long-term agri-cultural relief program can be implemented. Mr. Arume has summarized these in entries 514-519 of Part 1; Ms. Dubarieux added two more in entry 530. This conference, then, will focus on long-term relief proposals.

[5] OWENS 5-APR-85 2:54 PM GMT

I would like to hold a synchronous conference on 8 April at 4:00 P.M. (GMT). At this meeting, we should discuss whether to meet face to face to discuss the relief proposals. Any of you who would like to enter your thoughts before then should feel free to do so.

[6] MWANGA 5-APR-85 11:43 PM GMT

I've been on the plains outside of Timbalwe all day and have just returned. I was with Cyprian, and he will report on the installations for moisture testing today or tomorrow.

[7] MWANGA 5-APR-85 11:45 PM GMT

I talked with local officials about precautionary procedures now in effect in most areas of Camelia; they are worried but still hanging onto their optimism. I briefed several gatherings of local officials about our discussions in this confer-ence. They are glad that we are talking, but are puzzled about the role of Consolidated. They are also, of course, concerned about maintaining Camelian independence. It would be very help-ful if Consolidated could provide a summary statement of its interests in Camelia. George Clemmons or Jack Morris, what are the near future plans for Consolidated in Camelia, apart from the drought?

PRETTY CLEVER OF HER!

> PRIVATE MESSAGE FROM MWANGA TO OWENS
> 5-APR-85 11:48 GMT*
>
> I'm really glad I can visit local groups here
> during the day and still be an active par-

---

*These private messages would normally be seen only by their intended recipients. We include them here to show the reader what goes on "behind the scenes" in a computer conference.

ticipant in this conference. If I had to travel to Paris, I couldn't keep in touch with the feelings of our people here or discuss conference topics with them before they are finalized.

PRIVATE MESSAGE FROM MWANGA TO DUBARIEUX
5-APR-85 11:48 PM GMT

Est-ce que je pousse les choses trop loin avec la question que je pose à Clemmons en [7]?

TRANSLATION:
Do you think I'm putting Clemmons too much on the spot with my question in [7]?

PRIVATE MESSAGE FROM MWANGA TO CLEMMONS
5-APR-85 11:50 PM GMT

I'm not trying to put you in an awkward position with my question in [7] and certainly don't want you to discuss matters which you feel are confidential. I do think it is important, though, for you to give the whole group a statement of Consolidated's long-term interests in Camelia, and my question was merely intended to give you an opportunity to do so.

SHE PUTS US ON THE SPOT IN PUBLIC — THEN SHE NEGOTIATES IN PRIVATE!

[8] MWANGA 5-APR-85 11:56 PM GMT

I'll continue to join this conference regularly each evening, probably around midnight, my time. My office knows where I am during the day, but it's usually out in the field. Tonight, I have a

portable terminal at a base camp 105 miles south-
west of Timbalwe.

[9] CLEMMONS 6-APR-85 11:50 AM GMT

Re [7], our position on the relief program should
be clear to all. Our opening statement in Part I
of the conference set the stage for our involvement in a relief program that would preserve both
Camelian independence and the welfare of its
people. Our facilities would be made available to support this effort throughout Camelia,
and the contractual arrangements would spell out a
timetable and a favorable price structure. As for
our long-term interests, I think that they are
reflected in our general policy of reducing
the barriers to exchange of agricultural products
among all countries.

[10] DUBARIEUX 6-APR-85 2:30 PM GMT

M. Clemmons, je viens de me reporter à votre
déclaration en [192] dans la première partie de la
conférence. Dans ce paragraphe vous déclariez que
Camélia recevrait le statut de "nation favorisée"
parmi les clients de Consolidated après la fin de
la sècheresse, en échange de modifications des
tarifs d'exportation de Camélia. Une clarifica-
tion de vos intentions s'impose pour permettre à
la LCF et à l'opinion mondiale d'évaluer la
sincérité des efforts de Consolidated et le plein
impact potentiel de l'effort de secours qui
pourrait en résulter.

[10]   TRANSLATED

Mr. Clemmons, I've just been referring back to
your statements in Part I of the conference
transcript (entry [192]). In that entry, you
stated that you would give Camelia "favored
nation" status among the Consolidated clients
beyond the duration of the drought in return for
changes in Camelian export tariffs. Your intent
here needs to be clarified before the LCF and
world opinion can assess the sincerity of Consolidated's efforts and the full potential impact
of the relief program which might result.

SHE KEEPS DOING THAT!

[11]   CLEMMONS   7-APR-85   12:01 PM GMT

With due respect to Ms. Dubarieux, I believe she
is taking a passing reference which I made out of
context and inflating its importance. Certainly,
we are concerned about tariff structures, but I
would hope that the LCF would not threaten the
workings of these conferences by dwelling on this
issue.

CLEARLY, THEY HAD ALREADY DECIDED TO FORCE THE ISSUE.

>   PRIVATE MESSAGE FROM CLEMMONS TO MORRIS
>   7-APR-85   12:08 PM GMT
>
>   I wish I hadn't phrased my initial comment
>   the way I did; leave it to Dubarieux to dig
>   it up out of the transcript. Why do you
>   think the Camelians are being so cautious; I
>   thought with half of their people on the
>   brink of starvation, they'd be much more
>   eager to cooperate. I guess we've got to be
>   more careful on this point. Why don't you

come in here and reassure them that we are
not trying to be crass.

[12]   ARUME   7-APR-85 7:01 PM GMT

La suggestion par M. Clemmons de changements dans
la structure de nos tarifs représente certaine-
ment, à notre avis, une interférence politique si
elle est posée comme condition à la participation
de Consolidated dans un effort de secours.
La question de modifications des tarifs est à
l'étude par notre Gouvernement, mais je voudrais
qu'elle soit entièrement séparée de toute discussion de la sécheresse et des mesures à prendre.
Ce n'est pas ainsi que l'on influencera les
structures de tarifs Caméliens!

[12]   TRANSLATED

How can they be separated?

Mr. Clemmons' suggestion for changes in our tariff
structure does represent, in our view, political
interference if it is a condition for Consolidated's participation in the relief effort. The
question of tariff modifications is under consideration by our government, but I would like to
separate it entirely from any discussion of the
drought and our responses to it. Camelian tariff
structures will not be influenced in this manner!

[13]   MORRIS   7-APR-85 9:13 PM GMT

Tariff structures are but one of a series of
issues which are important to consider in a
comprehensive discussion of the Camelian situation. To elevate them in importance would be

destructive; to eliminate them from our discussion would be naive.

I WAS TRYING AT THIS POINT TO RECOVER SOME OF THE INITIATIVE VIA PRIVATE MESSAGES WITH MWANGA.

PRIVATE MESSAGE FROM MORRIS TO MWANGA
7-APR-85 9:20 PM GMT

I hope that Mr. Arume understands that we are just trying to be candid in bringing up the subject of tariffs. We have responsibilities to our stockholders and board, which would be much easier to uphold if we could report both a relief program to Camelia in the short run <u>and</u> a more desirable tariff structure in the long run. I think this is the sort of issue which you and I could negotiate privately without becoming immersed in the formality of the public transcript.

[14] RIBERA 7-APR-85 9:30 PM GMT

I may not make it to the synchronous conference tomorrow. Was finally able to get a meeting with the AAB planning committee tomorrow morning, and don't know how long it will last.

SYNCHRONOUS MEETING STARTS HERE

[15] OWENS 8-APR-85 12:02 PM GMT

I think everyone is online now except Dr. Ribera, who won't be able to join us today. But of course he'll see this transcript when he joins later this evening. As I indicated, our first order of business is deciding whether to continue negotia- tions via this medium or meet face to face. Or, of course, we could <u>consider other teleconfer- encing media</u>. Given the progress we have made via

IT WOULD HAVE BEEN DISRUPTIVE TO SWITCH

this medium, I think these alternatives may not be necessary.

[16] DRAPER 8-APR-85 12:04 PM GMT

I want to thank Bill Owens and the Foundation for mailing us the edited transcript of Part I of this conference. I think you did a fine job in a short time. In my opinion, the transcript is one good argument for continuing in this conference. *→ WHY DOESN'T THIS GUY EVER ADDRESS THE REAL ISSUES?*

[17] N'DOLO 8-APR-85 12:05 PM GMT

Les stations de mesure hygrométriques ont été établies dans sept emplacements dispersés en Camélia. Elles sont toutes équipées de terminaux pour l'envoi des résultats dans la conférence-moniteur. Nous avons commencé les mesures d'humidité quotidiennement à 7 heures (locales) aujourd'hui. Les donnees hygrométriques que nous obtenons sont pratiquement celles que nous attendions. L'analyse régionale sera finie cette semaine.

[17] TRANSLATED

The moisture testing sites have now been set up in 7 locations throughout Camelia. All are equipped with terminals for reporting results in the Monitor conference. We began sampling moisture content on a daily basis at 0700 hours (local time) today. The moisture data we're getting so far is pretty much as we expected. The area analysis will be completed this week.

[18]   OWENS   8-APR-85   12:05 PM GMT

I'm for the computer-based system as we've got it
now.   But I think we should try to avoid solving
interpersonal problems in this medium.   Remember
when we were having trouble with the LCF data base
and we attempted to solve it over the terminal?
We were trying to help, but each message came
out like judgments in a criminal court.   We all
rationalized that Helene misinterpreted our
statements because she was so protective of the
data.   But when I went back and read the transcript, I could see how our "helpful" statements
could be misinterpreted.

→ LETS
REMEMBER
THIS !

[19]   MWANGA   8-APR-85   12:08 PM GMT

I agree with Bill Owens that this conference is
working, but I think we should take it really
slow, with a minimum of synchronous meetings.
Those meetings invite trouble.   Someone puts out
an idea and by the time someone else responds,
three or four other ideas have been suggested.
While it may be helpful to have the ideas numbered
and written down for easy reference, I don't think
anybody can respond thoughtfully to all the
suggestions and ideas when they come at you in
such a disorganized fashion.

→ SHE MAY
BE RIGHT

PRIVATE MESSAGE FROM MWANGA TO MORRIS
8-APR-85   12:10 PM GMT

It has to remain clear that we don't have to
bargain away our economy in order to survive
this crisis!   This is where Mr. Arume needs

to remain strong. However, there is some negotiation room here if we are not forced into a public statement right away. Let me prepare the groundwork here, and I'll keep in touch through you. I think Mr. Clemmons and Mr. Arume should handle the public debate.

[20] PIERSON 8-APR-85 12:10 PM GMT

For accuracy's sake, I think it might be best to stick to computer conferencing. In other meetings, a lot of technical errors go unnoticed. There are transposals of numbers, missed numbers, misused technical names.

THOSE ACADEMICS!

[21] MORRIS 8-APR-85 12:12 PM GMT

Every possible error that can be made in a technical report has been made via audio teleconference. For example, I remember in one of the yearly reports, our people reported that some rice was infected with "Swollen Shoot" which is exclusively a disease of cacao trees.

MY FEEBLE ATTEMPT — I WAS TRYING TO RELIEVE THE TENSION.

[22] ARUME 8-APR-85 12:12 PM GMT

I'm willing to continue with this medium, as long as it is working. But I think we should keep the face-to-face option open all the time.

PRIVATE MESSAGE FROM AMPLEBY TO ARUME
8-APR-85 12:13 PM GMT

I just received our latest budget figures for agricultural development aid to Camelia from the major religious denominations: it looks

as if you will receive an increase of about
10 percent over last year. That should help,
but not much. These figures won't be made
public for at least another month. I'm
reluctant to mention them now in this conference because they might provide a false
sense that the extra money will end the
crisis. I'll follow your advice on whether
or not to quote it publicly, but I knew you
would want to know as quickly as possible.
Call me on the phone if that raises any
immediate issues.

[23]   PIERSON   8-APR-85   12:13 PM GMT

Let me just mention something else, while we're
all together. I've been thinking about the
crop/climate figures Eduardo and Cyprian entered
in the last week of Part I. I showed them to some
of my colleagues. Also, I finally dug out the   *THAT WAS*
paper from my files which I had relied on so   *UNEXPECTED!*
strongly in my arguments. Although I was very
skeptical at first, my reflection period and the
resources I checked have changed my mind. Your
figures seem correct, Eduardo, and I think they   *EXCELLENT!*
can be used as the basis for further planning.   *NOW WE*
I'm glad I was here in my university where I could *CAN GET*
double check my knee-jerk responses the other day. *DOWN TO*
If I was smart about using this medium, I would   *BUSINESS.*
have refrained from saying anything until I could
check over my thinking. I apologize for the quick
response and give my complete support to Eduardo's
figures.

PRIVATE MESSAGE FROM MWANGA TO DUBARIEUX
8-APR-85   12:15 PM GMT

Hélène, nous sommes heureux de votre support
et de celui du LCF dans la question des
tarifs, mais à notre avis il vaudrait mieux
ne pas forcer une confrontation avec Clemmons
pour le moment. Nous préférons conserver
une certaine flexibilité sur cette question
jusqu'à ce que les choses soient un peu plus
claires. Je vous tiendrai au courant de nos
opinions.

TRANSLATION:*

Helene, we appreciate the support of you and
the LCF on the tariff question, but I think
it might be a good idea not to force a
confrontation with Clemmons at this time.
We'd rather keep some flexibility on this
issue until the air clears some. I'll keep
you up to date on our thinking.

PRIVATE MESSAGE FROM DUBARIEUX TO MWANGA
8-APR-85   12:17 PM GMT

D'accord, j'attendrai que vous me fassiez
signe. Je crois que c'est un point où
Consolidated peut être vulnérable, mais je
n'insisterai pas, du moins pour le moment.

TRANSLATION:

I'll wait to hear from you, then. I think
it's a point where Consolidated might be

---

*In an actual transcript, no translation would be needed because both Mwanga and
Dubarieux speak French.

vulnerable, but I won't press it for the time being at least.

PRIVATE MESSAGE FROM MORRIS TO OWENS
8-APR-85 12:17 PM GMT

I'm glad to see Professor Pierson speaking up in this conference. He is really a strong thinker, but I know he is also very shy in meetings. A colleague of mine attended a large international conference in Montreal where he was also in attendance, but didn't say a word!

PRIVATE MESSAGE FROM CLEMMONS TO AMPLEBY
8-APR-85 12:18 PM GMT

AMPLEBY HASN'T DONE AS MUCH AS HE COULD HAVE TO MOVE US TOWARD A SOLUTION.

How long are you planning to stay in such out-of-the-way places? I hope we'll have a chance to meet in the States some day. With your talents, you could be doing some really important work back here in your own country. Chuck Davis, our minister here for the last five years, tells me you both were at Clare-mont Seminary together for a workshop several years ago. Chuck sends his best to you; he is doing a fine job here.

HAS AMPLEBY EVER RESPONDED TO THIS, GEORGE?

PRIVATE MESSAGE FROM OWENS TO ARUME
8-APR-85 12:18 PM GMT

How is your remote chess game with Allan going?

[24] N'DOLO 8-APR-85 12:19 PM GMT

La téléconférence fonctionne bien dans mon cas.
Je peux envoyer mes rapports à n'importe quelle

heure, en garder un enregistrement permanent, et vérifier la précision de ce que j'envoie. Cela nous permet de traiter avec objectivité une grande masse de données.

[24] TRANSLATED

Computer conferencing works well for me. I can file my reports at any time of the day, have a permanent record, and can check to see if what I am sending is accurate. It enables us to deal objectively with a mass of data.

> PRIVATE MESSAGE FROM ARUME TO AMPLEBY
> 8-APR-85 12:20 PM GMT
>
> We can certainly use the increased aid, but it won't be enough. I don't think it would be appropriate for you to mention the new budget in the public record, especially since it is not "official" yet [sic]. I appreciate your continued support, Bishop.

[25] CLEMMONS 8-APR-85 12:22 PM GMT

I don't think anyone will argue that this conference has been fine for dealing with the technical information. If we can keep the discussion focused for the negotiations, I think it will work. But if not, we'll have to try something else.   *I THINK YOU'RE RIGHT; LETS NOT CLOSE OUR OTHER OPTIONS.*

> PRIVATE MESSAGE FROM ARUME TO OWENS
> 8-APR-85 12:23 PM GMT
>
> He's got me in a tight spot, but I think I have a strategy to beat him. Thanks for telling me that he likes chess.

[26]   OWENS   8-APR-85   12:25 PM GMT

Well, it seems like a consensus, but I'll call for
a vote just to make it official.

[27]   [RE 25]   8-APR-85   12:30 PM GMT

Shall we continue the computer conference for
Part 2?
Number of votes:

        Yes: 10

         No: 0

   Abstain: 0

    Absent: 1

Reprinted from
THE FUTURIST

*Participants in a computer conference "meet" without regard
to time and space*

MEMO TO: Representatives to the African Agricultural Board

FROM: Eduardo Ribera

SUBJECT: THE CAMELIAN RELIEF CONFERENCE

   By now, I trust all of you have received the full
4-volume, 2,200-page transcript of the Camelian conference,
together with my official summary of the results. My
purpose here is to clarify the procedural problems which
plagued the conference.

   When Bill Owens of the Foundation first suggested to me
the idea of a computer conference to link the principals in
the Camelian controversy together with access to economic
and agricultural models, I was indeed optimistic. As you
know, our organization has been using integrated modeling/
conference systems to support internal decision-making for
a few years now, with some very satisfying results. The
Foundation proposal was to have been an extension of this
idea; representatives of several different viewpoints could
negotiate a common relief program with the support of the
best knowledge available. Online models could forecast the
possible impacts of alternative strategies as they were
introduced. And the discussions could be conducted over a
period of time which would allow careful consideration of
all of the alternatives. Unfortunately, my optimism proved
unwarranted.

In retrospect, I can see that the basic flaw in the
conference was the overemphasis on the value of information
in solving a culturally complex problem. With one or two
possible exceptions, we failed to acknowledge the importance
of the interpersonal aspects of the meeting--the building
and maintenance of alliances. We tried to ignore the kind
of interpersonal diplomacy--both delicate and dramatic--
which is the stock and trade of most of the people who
participated in this conference. As a result, alliances
were formed in private messages, when formed at all. There,
they were hidden from view, so none of us ever really knew
just what kind of a group we were. We debated with lots of
computer-printed words, but seldom with other people.

I think everyone approached the conference with the
same optimism as I did. Unfortunately, they also approached
it with very different perceptions of what the problem was.
I certainly viewed the problem as an economic one: some of
us needed food and some of us had it to "sell" at some
price. Of course, it was more complex than that, but I
thought we could probably model the economic consequences of
alternative relief proposals for Camelia, for the Board, and
for the farmers which Consolidated represents. However,
in reading over the transcript, I can see that Draper, for
example, wasn't really interested in economics beyond the
cost of delivering food to the hungry and delivering dry-
zone seeds to the farmers. On the other hand, Arume--and I
think this is quite typical of our African leaders--kept
probing cultural and social consequences five years down the
pike. Unfortunately, I didn't recognize these differences
until the last few days of the conference. It was structured so rigidly that we never had a chance to get basic
concerns out in the open.

Owens opened the conference with a series of questions which he thought should be addressed and then led us lock-step through each question in turn. The first few were climatological questions, and the troubles started here. The Americans had an online file of weather and crop data for Africa that didn't agree with the Camelian data. We ran the Foundation's model on both. Then Pierson spent two weeks arguing with N'dolo about the results. (Pierson actually resembled a tinker in a toy shop, perturbing the model this way and that and hardly acknowledging the rest of us.) Owens rescued us from that fire and tossed us into another--the economic consequences of the drought.

I must admit that I probably looked something like a tinker, too, when we ran the economic models. But I had some company. Francoise Mwanga and Jack Morris really did some fine analytical work in interpreting the results of the AAB model. But then Helene Dubarieux began questioning the model's assumptions--the most fundamental economic concepts in some cases. We tried to respond to her first few questions by altering some of the model algorithms, but we didn't really know what we were doing and the flood of new data from the revised model was overwhelming. I'm afraid we just ignored Ms. Dubarieux's questions after that (it's so easy to do in a computer conference), and she understandably became quite belligerent. We finally reached a complete impasse when there was more data than any of us could absorb! Owens then led us to the next question.

By now, the original high expectations of the partici-pants--soured by controversy over the data--had been trans-formed into distrust of the motivations of others. And several factors produced a further deterioration in trust.

One of the most serious was the unevenness of participation. Some people responded to new entries every day. Others responded only irregularly. I have seen this happen in other computer conferences, too. People are busy or not particularly interested, and they just don't log in. Since there aren't equivalents to a ringing telephone or even regular meeting times in computer conferences, there's really no way to get them into the conference. Then, when they do come in, they are so far behind that they have a lot of reading awaiting them. Faced with this burden, they enter some trite remark, log out, and then don't get back in for several days more. It really is frustrating for those who participate regularly.

In this case, the unevenness was more than just frustrating. This was a very political group, and nonparticipation in such a group is often interpreted negatively. Clemmons was the most serious offender. Looking back on it, I think he was probably speaking through Morris. But most of us felt that his lack of participation was a statement of his disdain for our "petty problems."

Another factor threatened the group's basic trust level--the private message mode. The public transcript of this conference was dominated by debates about resources and technologies which obscured the personal motivations and objectives of the participants. Owens spent all his time trying to reconcile the mathematical results, out of a mistaken belief that the other problems would go away if we could just agree on one set of numbers. But some of the others began to use the private message mode to pursue their personal objectives. Draper was one. From the very beginning, he sent me humorous notes about the heavy rain in

Paris and asked me about good places to eat in Lagos.
Frankly, those were about the only pleasant exchanges I had
during the whole conference. Of course, it became clear
during the voting that he was using it for more than pleasant exchanges. He had managed, in spite of Owens' obsession
with *data,* to build a coalition of *people.*

The voting. Here again, Owens' rigid structure inhibited any real communication. We were discussing the
roles of different agencies in a possible relief program.
We began with the LCF. Morris was bombarding us with messages about the technical expertise needed to oversee a
relief program, implying that LCF just didn't have that kind
of expertise. Dubarieux responded with mini-philosophies on
the ethics of the situation, accusing Consolidated of a
"food blackmail." Arume tried to facilitate the debate to
avoid polarizing the conference. But Owens grew impatient
with the confusion. He decided that we would spend only 30
messages on each agency, after which he would call for a
vote. If we had been meeting face to face, I think Arume
would have flown into a powerful rage. But in this medium,
his anger over being forced into a premature vote came
across only as a hopeless objection. He's a powerful
orator, but in computer conferencing even the best orator
can't keep the group's attention.

The final blow, of course, came from the series of
anonymous entries made by a person claiming access to secret
weather modification data. This user of the system--who
must have been one of the delegates--called himself (or
herself) Hungry Jack and accused the United States of having
accidentally caused the African drought in covert attempts
to alter climate patterns over large sections of Communist

Asia. All trust was gone then, and computer conferencing simply offered no suitable channels for recovery.

It was a disappointing failure. For all that computer power--all of the models and data--there was very little negotiation, very little change in the viewpoints of participants. I think the lesson here is that it takes more than technology to solve a problem like this. What was supposed to be the ultimate information system proved to be a disinformation system.

ANALYSIS OF THE COMPUTER
TELECONFERENCING SCENARIOS

Computer conferencing is an unfortunate label for this medium: the computer ideally should remain in the background, invisible to the user. Furthermore, "conferencing," too, may be a misleading designation; other types of communication can also occur through this medium. Essentially, computer conferencing is print-based communication which does not require all participants to be present simultaneously. And such *written, asynchronous* communication changes many of the rules for small group meetings.

Participation When You Want, *If* You Want

A major advantage of computer conferencing over other teleconferencing media is flexibility of participation time. Conference organizers can avoid all of the problems of scheduling usually associated with "meetings." Participants can maintain their normal routines and participate at their own convenience. This flexibility may be more than convenient; it may improve the quality of the meetings, as Francoise Mwanga observes in her entry in the Effective Scenario:

> I'm really glad I can visit local groups here during the day and still be an active participant in this conference. If I had to travel to Paris, I couldn't keep in touch with the feelings of our people here or discuss conference topics with them before they are finalized.

Unfortunately, the leader cannot just invite the participants and expect them to carry the ball. The self-activated nature of the medium means that participation may be irregular (C34*), particularly if the need to communicate is not clear. Computer conferencing has no equivalent of a ringing telephone, no gavel to bang to call the group to order. Thus, the group may feel frustrated by the lack of immediate feedback, which can give computer conferencing an impersonal quality (C46, C45). Questions may go unanswered (C30, C47) as did Helene Dubarieux's questions about model assumptions in the Ineffective Scenario. In the extreme, irregular participation may threaten group trust. When George Clemmons was inactive in the Ineffective Scenario, for example, the group felt that it was "a statement of his disdain for our 'petty problems.' " An organizer of a computer conference needs to begin with a strong commitment from each participant and then consistently shepherd those who lag behind. Thus, in the Effective Scenario, Owens sent a discreet private message to Clemmons, asking him to urge Morris to participate more regularly.

The Written Word

Of course, the key to the flexibility of this medium is the existence of a printed transcript, always available for review. Aside from the convenience of having an ever-current record of the conference, we assume that it may provide a tool for

---

*The codes in this analysis refer to the numbers of the "strengths," and "weaknesses" listed for each of the media in the Summary of Social Evaluations of Teleconferencing in the Reference Mateials. Thus: C for computer conferencing, etc.

manipulating the communication in either good or bad ways. Dubarieux seems particularly skilled in this use of the medium, challenging Clemmons with one of his earlier statements:

> Mr. Clemmons, I've just been referring back to your statements in Part I of the conference transcript (entry [192]). . . . Your intent here needs to be clarified before the LCF and world opinion can assess the sincerity of Consolidated's efforts. . . .

Dubarieux is effective in pressing Clemmons on this point. However, this situation demonstrates why potential participants may be reluctant to use computer conferencing in a situation such as this. They may *not want* people to refer verbatim to their earlier statements (C32).

Information, But Not Too Much

For some tasks, though, the written word makes computer conferencing a hands-down winner. The management of technical information is such a task (C14, C15, C17, C20). In the Effective Scenario, for example, Owens establishes a parallel data collection conference, and Pierson testifies to the superior accuracy of the medium for communicating technical information. Also, since computer conferencing allows more time for deliberate, reflective responses (C3, C17), the quality of the information exchange is likely to improve: Pierson first disagrees with N'dolo's crop/climate figures in the Effective Scenario, but after checking his resources, confirms N'dolo's report, and the group is able to move on.

Carried to a logical extreme, the ability of computer conferencing to deal systematically with large amounts of information suggests that it might be very effective in solving global crises as they develop (C18). However, the Ineffective Scenario portrays an abuse of this hope: an over-reliance on the value of the information accessible via computer conferencing and an underemphasis on interpersonal communication:

> Owens spent all his time trying to reconcile the mathematical results, out of a mistaken belief that the other problems would go away if we could just agree on a set of numbers.

Owens appeared determined to "structure out" interpersonal communication in this scenario. He rarely used the private message mode, where we suspect much less formal communication occurs, and led the participants lock-step through question after question, calling for votes with little opportunity for debate or discussion. Furthermore, he allowed the volume of information to get completely out of hand. A four-volume, 2,200-page transcript is surprisingly easy to produce, but may be impossible to decipher. It's hardly surprising then that one participant, frustrated by the inability to communicate, resorted to a destructive anonymous attack: Hungry Jack, with his accusations against the United States, dealt the death blow to the conference. Thus, computer conferencing, overstructured and overwhelming, proved its potential as a disinformation system.

In contrast, the successful Bill Owens used structure moderately and encouraged interpersonal communication, even laying the groundwork for a remote chess game between Arume and Draper. There is a real question whether computer conferencing *alone* can provide the opportunity for delicate interpersonal diplomacy. There is some evidence that written messages are more persuasive than those transmitted orally (C1, C2). However, it is obvious that voice media allow more messages to be exchanged and more flexibility in the interaction (C28, C29, C31). A blend of public and private messages, with other media used occasionally, seems crucial in a situation such as this.

Both Public and Private

In the Effective Scenario, Owens encouraged a dynamic use of both the public and private modes, revealed in the synchronous meeting. Public and private communication were occurring simultaneously—the latter being of prime importance. In the private mode, Morris and Mwanga were negotiating, with Dubarieux assisting Mwanga. Ampleby and Arume exchanged information about the latest aid figures and decided not to make the information public. Meanwhile, on top of the table, business was proceeding, too, as the group decided to postpone a decision on a face-to-face meeting. While the private negotiations were hidden, we believe that they were probably reflected in the public interaction. Furthermore, we suspect that, while the group didn't know *how* alliances were being formed, they at least recognized that they *were* being formed.

Owens' approach in the Ineffective Scenario allowed no such group sense of alliances. And his indifference toward the private message mode opened the door for its manipulation by Draper. As Ribera explained:

> From the beginning, he sent me humorous notes about the heavy rain in Paris and asked me about good places to eat in Lagos. Of course, it became clear during the voting that he was using [private messages] for more than pleasant exchanges. He had managed to build a coalition.

Meanwhile, in the public mode, most of the group members were simply struggling with presenting their viewpoints in a straitjacket structure.

Self-Presentation in Print

In computer conferencing, all of the splendor of self-presentation is funneled into the single channel of print. Some people respond gloriously to this concentration of communication and fully exploit the printed word. Shy Glenn Pierson, for example, adapts well to this medium in both scenarios (although the emphasis on data encourages a "tinker in a toyshop" image in the Ineffective Scenario). Others, like Arume, may find computer conferencing inherently limiting: "He's a powerful orator, but in computer conferencing, even the best orator can't keep the group's attention."

There is evidence that computer conferences encourage more equal participation than other media (C23, C24). This observation is speculative, but we feel confident that people who are socially uncomfortable and easily dominated in other media can play a more dynamic role in a computer conference. Mwanga is a case in point. She participates aggressively in the public conference and probably has more impact in the private mode than we can imagine in any of the other media.

Some personal skills seem to have surprisingly little effect in computer conferencing. The ability to type does not seem to be as large a barrier to participation as one would at first assume; nor does computer expertise (C25, C26, C27). While such skills might add to a participant's abilities via this medium, there is no evidence to suggest that they are major inhibitors. And as computer conferencing systems become more simple, this situation can only grow better.

In Summary . . .

Computer conferencing provides potentially effective technical structures for controlling group interaction, but few of the familiar social structures. Training people to use the system will be technically easy but socially difficult. We believe it would be a mistake to rely on the technology to direct the communication process—either by imposing highly structured formats or simply using it as an open forum. Leadership is no less important in a computer conference than in face-to-face communication. Strong but subtle leadership appears most appropriate.

MEMO TO: Human Relations Office, Project Progress

FROM: Allan Draper

DATE: 13 March 1985

SUBJECT: CONCLUSION OF THE CAMELIA FACT-FINDING
           TELECONFERENCES

You have each seen my final report on the Camelian
Fact-Finding Teleconferences by now, but we can learn some
lessons from the techniques that were used to deal with this
potential crisis, and they deserve a separate, informal
note.

When Bill Owens of the Foundation organized these
meetings, he decided wisely to use a mix of face-to-face
meetings, audio conferences, and one-to-one telephone calls.
Early in January, we all met for a two-day face-to-face session on the north coast of Africa to develop an inventory of
relevant information and establish a preliminary agenda.
This meeting also gave us a chance to get to know all of the
participants. Owens had done some fine work researching the
mythology of food in different cultures and presented it as
part of an opening statement. This presentation, together
with the attractiveness of our host culture, set the tone
for a cooperative initial meeting. There was no pressure to
solve the problems here; instead, we discussed in some
detail the protocols and schedules for a series of audio
meetings. And we emerged with a set of reasonable goals.

The audio teleconferences were well orchestrated; there was careful preplanning, but informal exchanges were also encouraged. At the start, Eduardo Ribera, Glenn Pierson, and Cyprian N'dolo attempted to resolve the differences in information about the drought. They conferred intensively over the telephone for two weeks, occasionally bringing together some of their colleagues for four- and five-person teleconferences. Ribera and Pierson certainly made good use of the facsimile capability for exchanging charts, graphs, and sections of reports. They weren't completely successful in resolving the discrepancies, but they did close the gaps considerably.

Then, as our leader, Owens decided that it was time for the rest of us to go to work. Our task was to determine the consequences of the drought. None of us wanted to leave this task to a pair of "objective" experts. We had agreed at the face-to-face conference to divide into committees to do this work, since 11 people trying to assess the whole range of economic, political, and agricultural impacts of drought would likely prove too complex and unmanageable for an audio conference. I spent two weeks in regularly scheduled teleconferences with Cyprian N'dolo, Jack Morris, and Helene Dubarieux discussing the economic consequences of the impending drought, based on the forecasts developed by Ribera and Pierson. We "met" every two days to pool our individual interpretations. At the end of two weeks, we had a general statement of the likely impacts for Camelia, for the African Agricultural Board, and for Consolidated. (If the frequency of these meetings seems burdensome, imagine the amount of time that might have been consumed in a face-to-face meeting. These were discussions which required

*An audio teleconference room, modeled after the Remote
Meeting Table*

a lot of preparation, and I am not at all sure that they
could have been carried out so quickly if we had met face to
face.)

I learned at least one important lesson during these
subcommittee meetings. One problem that was upsetting to me
was N'dolo's frequent interruptions. At one point, he cut
off an important presentation by Morris to launch into a
largely irrelevant discourse on local affairs. In an audio
teleconference, of course, all the communication is funneled into voice exchanges, so I had difficulty telling
whether the frustration I was feeling was related to the
medium or to N'dolo himself. I had a lot of trouble
listening to what he was saying because he annoyed me so
much. I was on the verge of shouting at him when I remem-
bered my training in cross-cultural communication and
started thinking, "Why am I upset?" I soon began to
realize that N'dolo didn't know the cultural intricacies of
arguing in English. I had to get over the idea that the guy
was being crude and remind myself that in most African
cultures the etiquette for interaction with strangers is
very different. Perhaps I appeared crude to him. I began
to understand how his standard of etiquette was coming
across via this medium. Gradually, I found that I could
listen to what he was saying and agree or disagree on the
basis of the data instead of on the basis of my reaction to
what (in my culture) would be his rudeness. The translator
Owens had arranged for was a big help in this process, since
she also had training as an anthropologist and did more than
mechanically translate the words of the participants. On
several occasions, I asked her advice privately.

After we had all had a chance to review the reports of each committee (which were limited to 10 pages), we met as an entire group for a series of information exchange meetings via telephone. These audio conferences were scheduled for 45-minute periods every other day at 7:00 p.m. Paris time. The meetings were formal and efficient. The experts served as a panel for the first three sessions. The rest of us were called upon by Owens (in varying order) to ask any questions we might have regarding the first committee's report. Translators were again present, and we also recorded all of the sessions. In addition, our graphics capability helped us avoid some of the communications problems since visual aids are more universal than language. We then went on to the other two committees. Meanwhile, all of us were trying to formulate in our own minds the best strategies for coping with the Camelian predicament.

We gradually realized, however, that "coping with the Camelian predicament" meant different things to different people. I kept pressing for an immediate relief program and found it initially perplexing when Arume went on and on about what would happen *after* we succeeded! With the help of Owens, the translators, and Francoise Mwanga, I came to understand that there were different cultural perspectives here and that it was important not to press for an immediate solution before the Africans had discussed all the social implications of the plan. Mwanga, in particular, served as an integrator since she had exposure to both perspectives. At the initial face-to-face meetings, she was so retiring in the presence of Arume that I barely noticed her. But over audio, where people listen more to what you say than how you say it, she made significant contributions to our understanding of the Camelian cultural perspectives. If this understanding had not developed, the meetings would have been a failure.

George Clemmons of Consolidated also seemed disturbed by the apparent slowness on the part of the Camelians, and at one point, it was obvious that he was beginning to lose his patience. Meanwhile, Helene Dubarieux of LCF made some piercing statements about similar situations in other developing countries and the programs which had been implemented there. These statements only made Clemmons more uncomfortable, since Consolidated was sometimes presented as less than well-intentioned. I remember at one point, just when Clemmons seemed on the verge of exploding, Owens adjourned the teleconference. I'm sure he called Clemmons on the telephone afterwards to calm him down and hold the meetings together. The audio medium did little in itself to keep the diverse perspectives together; the important element was Owens' leadership and sensitivity to the roots of conflicts as they emerged.

On the other hand, some people seemed perfectly comfortable with this medium. Eduardo Ribera, for example, shined in the meetings. He is extremely nearsighted and cuts a rather pitiful figure in face-to-face meetings; but he has an impressive range of expertise, and he was able to utilize it fully over the audio system. There was a brilliant exchange of scientific arguments between Ribera and Pierson during one session; it eventually led to a timetable for setting up a monitoring program with the help of Consolidated field personnel and the missionaries.

After the discussion of consequences, there was a lull in the audio meetings while we all worked on developing strategies for relief. Owens encouraged us to communicate

with each other individually during this period. I really
thought this approach was dangerous; I fully expected some
"hidden" negotiation and bargaining, but Owens emphasized
the importance of keeping in touch with everyone. The plan
was to have a statement of goals as well as written strategy
documents circulated to all participants by March 15, when
we are to meet again face to face.

As the audio meetings came to a close, I met Owens for
dinner in Paris, and we talked about them. We both agreed
that the initial face-to-face meeting had been crucial to
whatever success we had achieved. For one thing, it
provided the group with a manageable set of goals. It also
allowed the participants to get to know one another, to get
a sense of themselves as a group. Such a feeling would have
been difficult to achieve otherwise, given the impersonality
of audio and the fairly rigid social protocol which the
audio system demands.

Then, too, the teleconference meetings offered some
important advantages over face-to-face meetings. They
served as an equalizer, reducing the impact of the more
dominant personalities which had asserted themselves earlier. Everyone had the opportunity to express himself or
herself in a disciplined fashion, either to the group as a
whole or to individuals. The formality of audio conferences
had its drawbacks, but it allowed participants to prepare in
advance and remain on their "home turf," so they were
both more competent and confident. It was interesting to
learn from Owens that he had been prepared to switch, at
any point, to another conferencing medium. He confessed
that he was indeed worried about the formation of coalitions. Had any breakdowns in communication occurred, he

said, he would have attempted to call us together face-to-face as quickly as possible or would have taken off on his own rounds of "shuttle diplomacy."

March 10, 1985

Dear Amy,

I have been reviewing the tapes of my recent meetings on the Camelian crisis and thought I should share my reactions with you. I wanted to figure out why the meetings failed so miserably and to see if there weren't some clues there about strategies for the future. And since you may face similar meetings in the future, you might benefit from my experience.

It is truly amazing to consider how much time we spent arguing over protocol. I have been to many conferences in which there were procedural debates, but never have I participated in a group which spent so much of its time trying to organize itself--and with so much unrelieved confusion. There are explanations, of course. For an audio conference, there were too many people for the flimsy structures we had to guide us. Do you know how many goals Bill Owens presented to us at that first session? I counted 10 when I reviewed the tape. Unfortunately, his "democratic" style of leadership left us with collective responsibility for setting up the agenda. Thus, we not only had to argue over how bad the situation in Camelia really was and whether Project Progress should administer the relief program, but we had to argue over whether we were going to discuss how bad the situation was and how a relief program should be administered.

Even when we seemed to agree on an issue, there was something which was not quite right. It was as if the differences in cultures and world views of the participants would not allow us to get down to the real issues. Clemmons--and some of the rest of us, too--thought we might be able to sidestep the cultural differences in order to work more quickly toward a resolution. When Abu Arume or others resisted, Clemmons just kept pushing his ideas for quick action. Owens stayed in the background, as if he were afraid to get involved. Looking back on the meetings, it seems that each of us was interpreting what was happening in different ways. There was no structure to help us sort through these varied perceptions. Without such assistance, the audio medium invited us to ignore those cultural differences and press on in our own scattered directions.

In the end, I guess we chose the wrong goals. Trying to negotiate a joint strategy for agricultural development of Camelia was just too complex. We were glutted with cultural, political, economic, and technical problems but badly in need of usable information about those problems. I remember being truly confused in trying to sort out all of the points that different people were making--not to mention separating fact from rhetoric. It just goes by you too fast over audio.

Another problem was that many of us had never met before. This made it really hard to get a sense of who our allies were, so sometimes we fumbled terribly in the strategic debates. I must confess that I suspected all kinds of secret coalitions against me, especially when I overheard parts of side conversations at other locations. And the audio medium seemed to give me an uncommonly defensive feeling toward just about everyone. I don't think that would have happened if we had met face to face at least once. I also think part of my feeling was due to the "impersonal" character of audio. I never had the sense that

I was communicating with real people; they were just ideology machines. As people, we might have had a chance, but as isolated ideologies, we definitely did not.

The meetings themselves were almost painful. Two hours of audio teleconferencing is tiring when only two people are involved. But when 11 people are engaged in an emotional debate, the attention demanded by that electronic box is just too much. It's almost impossible to concentrate that hard for that long. And the language problem only made things worse. Several times, the translations actually introduced misunderstandings. At one point, Jack Morris responded to my appeal to consider the ill effects of the Consolidated warehousing system in West Africa. Through the translator, he said: "Nous n'en sortirons pas sans une nouvelle conference mediatisee." Because I understood his English, I knew that he was suggesting an additional teleconference to resolve the problem. But Arume believed him to say that we couldn't solve the problem without a mediator, which he felt was an insult. It took me almost 10 minutes to convince him that the problem was a linguistic one. There simply is no direct translation for teleconference in French, and the translator had expressed it, rather insensitively, as a "mediated conference." In addition to the ill feelings created, the translation problem placed me in the awkward position of having to give the Camelians a French lesson in front of all the others.

Even when the translations were accurate, they were tedious. I don't know how long we sat through the translation of Pierson's technical report on climatological changes. The translators had to keep asking him to repeat to make sure they had the details right. (He was a strange person

anyway. He seemed almost uninterested in the conference.
Do you suppose he was just terribly shy? Since there was no
formal structure enabling him to be recognized, he may have
been reluctant to speak up if he didn't feel confident using
this medium.)

Now that I think about it, the notion of being simply
"on call" for three weeks was absurd. It just added to the
hostility to have to wait when someone couldn't be reached.
We certainly needed better scheduling. For example, on the
15th of February, I was notified at 8:00 a.m. that there
would be a conference at 11:00 a.m. At 11:55, Bill Owens
called to say that 3 of the 10 participants could not be
reached. I asked who they were, but he declined to tell me.
He rescheduled the meeting for 4:00 p.m. At 4:00, everyone
was on except Francoise Mwanga, the Planning Director from
Camelia. Arume apologized for her, explaining that she had
felt it necessary to miss this meeting. I think we were all
irritable and a little distrustful since we didn't know who
had been missing earlier, and we weren't sure now that Arume
was telling the truth about Mwanga. So when N'dolo mentioned the impending allocation of new funds--the Americans
clearly knew about these, but I certainly didn't--I demanded
to know the details. Clemmons apparently felt I was trying
to delay the discussion and literally shouted me down before
hanging up! I was so insulted that I, too, hung up, vowing
an end to my participation. I am sure Owens still feels
that the failure of the conferences was my fault. He claims
that Clemmons was inadvertently disconnected. I am still
not sure that I believe that.

I do know that the meetings never really recovered from
that breakdown. When we finally went along with Owens'

urging to reconvene a week later, it was hard to know where to start. I think there is more awkwardness and hesitation on those tapes than on any of the others. Slowly, we began raising all the old issues of the seriousness of the drought and whether we should attempt a full-scale relief program or simply a stop-gap measure. But with the specter of another breakdown, we all seemed unwilling to risk sustained debate. Even when we did seriously attempt to pick up the main discussion threads, our recollections of what had been said earlier differed. The discussion jumped from topic to topic, now characterized more by disinterest than by hostility. I don't think any of us saw opportunities for arriving at a joint strategy at that point. And without such an objective, there was little motivation to communicate. An interlude of personal communication might have helped, but it wasn't possible. After all, we did not really know each other as persons. Clemmons and Morris were the first to withdraw, explaining that they had urgent matters to attend to. Owens struggled to schedule a meeting again two weeks later. I told him it wouldn't be possible for me. Several others said the same. We ended as strangers.

I know that Owens will have a hard time reporting his results. He'll probably say that the meetings opened a dialogue among the important parties. That's a nice way of saying nothing was accomplished. Furthermore, no "dialogue" has been opened! I am tempted to blame this failure on the audio medium, but we didn't really make very intelligent use of it.

So the crisis in Camelia continues. But I refuse to accept the monotoned refusals of Clemmons. (I can imagine what that guy must look like in person!) I believe the LCF should continue to place first priority on the struggle to meet the demands for the health and dignity of the Camelian people! I am arranging a lead article exposing Consolidated in the next issue of ACTION ET PENSEE, and LE MONDE has decided to publish my letter to the editor pleading for a diplomatic intervention by the French Government in this whole issue. Please let me know if you have any ideas about how we should proceed.

Sincerely,
Helene

ANALYSIS OF THE AUDIO
TELECONFERENCING SCENARIOS

Audio teleconferencing is a voice-only medium. While it can include a graphics-sending capability, most of the communication occurs through a single, audio channel. This essential feature of the medium means that many of the nonverbal signals assumed in face-to-face meetings are missing in an audio teleconference. Such lack of visual information does not necessarily inhibit communication (A1–A10*); in fact, for some kinds of communication, an audio-only channel may offer subtle advantages (A17–A23). However, for complex communication situations, organizers of audio conferences will have to guard against an increased potential for misunderstanding.

Who's Out There?

With no visual clues, speaker recognition and order of speaking create a "who's-out-there?" problem in audio teleconferencing. It is not surprising, then, to learn that audio works best when participants have met face-to-face before they begin the teleconference (A8, A39–A42). In the Ineffective Scenario, Helene Dubarieux experienced this finding:

> Another problem was that many of us had never met before. This made it really hard to get a sense of who our allies were, so sometimes we fumbled in the strategic debates. I must confess that I suspected all kinds of secret coalitions against me, especially when I overheard parts of side conversations at other locations.

Furthermore, if current studies are to be believed (A60, A61–A63), most people are initially negative toward audio teleconferencing. Thus, as organizer of the Camelian conferences, Bill Owens had to overcome these initial hurdles *before* the teleconference began. In the Effective Scenario, he chose to hold a two-day face-to-face meeting prior to the audio meeting—an opportunity for participants to get to know one another without immediate pressures to solve the problem. He also talked with the participants individually by telephone. Such mixes of media seem particularly important in audio teleconferencing.

The "who's-out-there?" problem is also reflected in the feeling that audio lacks a sense of interpersonal contact; it is often seen as impersonal (A43, A44, A47, A49). If this impersonal potential is not countered (in the Effective Scenario, Owens encouraged private phone calls among group members), it will not be surprising to find that the participants feel isolated from one another. Or, as Helene explained, they all may become mere "ideology machines."

We speculate that the impersonal quality of the medium may also increase the potential for cross-cultural misunderstandings. Thus, in the Effective Scenario, Draper discussed his reactions to N'dolo: "I had a lot of trouble listening to what he

---

*The codes in this analysis refer to the numbers of the "strengths" and "weaknesses" listed for each of the media in the Summary of Social Evaluations of Teleconferencing in the Reference Materials. Thus: A for audio, etc.

was saying because he annoyed me so much. . . . I soon began to realize that he didn't know the cultural intricacies of arguing in English."

In general, audio conferees will probably spend a lot of time organizing themselves (A56): "Never have I participated in a group which spent so much of its time trying to organize itself—and with so much unrelieved confusion," Helene reported. And the confusion may be more inhibiting for some than for others. For Glenn Pierson, the audio medium made it even more difficult than usual to overcome his inherent shyness. It was easy for him to feel off by himself and cautious about participating in the Ineffective Scenario. It was no surprise that Helene found his behavior confusing: "He was a strange person anyway. He seemed almost uninterested in the conference. Do you suppose he was just terribly shy?" In contrast, the preplanned group structures in the Effective Scenario were intelligent counters to these kinds of problems.

Of course, the lack of a visual channel may be a boon to some participants. In the case of Eduardo Ribera, audio teleconferencing was a good match for his communication abilities: "He is extremely nearsighted and cuts a rather pitiful figure in face-to-face meetings; but he has an impressive range of expertise, and he was able to utilize it fully over the audio system." Ribera's nearsightedness would be an obvious problem via visual media, but he shone in the voice-only mode. He had more control over his environment and that part of himself which he presented to others. He was an effective speaker who was well prepared, and these strengths carried him through.

Efficient . . . As Long As It's Simple and Short

The key word in planning audio meetings is *brevity*. The concentration of communication into the voice channel means that the participants focus their energies, and it seems that they tire easier than when using visual media (A20, A24, A26, A27). Thus, Draper claimed that: "These audio meetings are just exhausting if they go much beyond an hour." A smart leader will schedule short meetings, increasing their frequency if more time is needed. Long meetings, usually a mistake in any medium, are deadly over audio.

If brevity is critical, so is *regularity* (A27). Like most other conferencing media, audio requires that all participants be present simultaneously. The scheduling problems inherent in this requirement range from substantial to nonnegotiable. In the Ineffective Scenario, they contributed to the breakdown of trust: "At 11:55, Bill Owens called to say that 3 of the 10 participants could not be reached. . . . I think we were all irritable and a little distrustful since we didn't know who had been missing. . . ." Bill Owens made a wiser choice in the Effective Scenario, scheduling regular, short meetings.

Simplicity is also an important guideline. The general wisdom from the evaluation literature is that audio teleconferencing is effective for information exchange, discussion of ideas, simple problem-solving, and similar tasks (A6–A8). The key here seems to be this: audio is very effective for simple tasks but becomes less desirable as tasks become more complex (A36, A53). In the Ineffective Scenario, Helene felt that:

> Trying to negotiate a joint strategy for agricultural development of Camelia was just too *complex*. We were glutted with cultural, political, economic, and

technical problems but badly in need of usable information about those problems. I remember being truly confused in trying to sort out all of the points
that different people were making—not to mention separating fact from
rhetoric. It just goes by you too fast over audio.

Again, an effective Bill Owens unscrambled some of the complexities by dividing
the group into subgroups with more narrowly defined tasks.

Negotiation: Maybe, Maybe Not

A crucial uncertainty in audio conferencing is negotiation. A series of laboratory
experiments with negotiation simulations have concluded that audio may have
distinct advantages over visual media. In particular, the findings suggest that audio
may allow conferees to concentrate on the substance of the negotiations rather than
the interpersonal dynamics (A17–A21). Also, people do seem able to sense the other
participants accurately—for instance, to detect lying—although they may not be as
confident in their assessments (A22, A23, A32, A64). Thus, Bill Owens *did* make
careful use of audio for negotiation in the Effective Scenario—while ensuring that
the subject matter was not overly complex. On the other hand, the Ineffective
Scenario involved full-scale negotiation which, we expect, will not be effective via
audio.

While audio may offer some unique strengths for negotiation, the same experiments also reveal a ghost in the attic: there seems to be a higher probability of
total breakdowns in negotiation via audio than via visual media (A38, A48). Thus,
the limited results to date suggest that audio for negotiation is a risk of extremes: if
the negotiations don't succeed, they may break down completely. Such a finding is
clearly speculative at this point, but a prime reason behind the conservative use of
audio for negotiation in the Effective Scenario.

In Summary. . .

The inherent characteristics of audio teleconferencing underscore the need for
leadership. In the Effective Scenario, Bill Owens was a strong, organized leader; the
meetings were "formal and efficient." Of course, these highly organized meetings
could become *too* organized, but an overly "democratic" leadership is likely to produce confusion more than communication in an audio teleconference.

MEMO TO: Camelian Office of Protocol

FROM: Francoise Mwanga

SUBJECT: CAMELIAN RELIEF CONFERENCE

     Several of you have asked for a summary of the two-week
meeting which produced the drought relief plan we are now
implementing. I am happy to provide such a summary in this
memo.

     As you may recall, Bill Owens of the Foundation first
approached Abu Arume about the drought situation in January
of this year. At that time, several of our staff were
engaged in a discussion with other scientists around the
world about the extent and causes of the drought. Since
there was a disagreement over facts, Owens apparently
recognized that any international relief program would
involve some conflict and considerable negotiation. He
therefore proposed the series of face-to-face meetings which
have now become known as the Camelian Relief Conference.

     Before the meetings, Owens met with each of us indi-
vidually. He explained to me that the meetings could take
several weeks and wanted to be sure that I would be able to
devote the time without a lot of pressures. He also spent
considerable time on my personal background and goals for
this conference. In the course of the conference, I realized that these questions were part of a deliberate--and

very successful--strategy to build alliances among all of
the participants. For example, at our very first coffee
break, Owens introduced me to Jack Morris of Consolidated
Produce, stressing my education at Berkeley. Afterwards,
Jack and I had several friendly dinner debates. These were
really helpful in sorting out our different perspectives. I
realized that Morris would be judged at Consolidated by how
well he was able to coordinate a relief program. So
naturally he was interested in feeding the most people at
the lowest cost to Consolidated. And he was understandably
impatient with our caution and concern about secondary
implications of his "efficiency." It took me some time to
make him understand that Arume and N'dolo both have strong
tribal loyalties and that they would want to be sure that
Consolidated's involvement in Camelia wouldn't jeopardize
the present tribal coalition. Once we understood each
other, we were able to move past political rhetoric in the
conference.

The meetings began on February 16 in Lagos. Owens felt
it was important to get all the participants out of their
usual cultures--to get Clemmons out of his air-conditioned
office and Arume away from the tensions of Timbalwe. Lagos
qualified well in this respect. It was actually quite
ironic (and funny) that it rained so hard several times
during the conference. From the very first meeting, we
joked about weather modification and saving some of the rain
to take back to Camelia with us. I think all those jokes
and the soggy handshakes made us feel like a group with a
common adversary--the weather. And this attitude carried
over into our formal meetings.

The formal meetings were always intense. There were
different world views here, which made it hard to know when
someone could compromise. But being together face to face
helped. We weren't just exchanging "data." We were exchanging feelings--smiles and handshakes, dissatisfied
frowns, and private glances with one participant or another.
All of these helped us to see one another as individuals
rather than ideologies. Jack Morris looks like cool efficiency personified on a television screen; but in person he is quite approachable and even quietly cynical about
Clemmons' sermons on economic efficiency. That's not to say
that everything was sweetness and light. There were some
loud confrontations between Clemmons and Arume and between
Allan Draper and Helene Dubarieux of the LCF. Even Arume
and I occasionally differed in our responses to Consolidated's proposals. (His point of view generally prevailed
in these cases.) But we always had our less formal, social
relationships to dissipate some of the hostility.

The problem that had brought us together--the discrepancies in the various data about the drought--was first
discussed even before face-to-face meetings. Owens had
arranged a computer conference with representatives
from the African Agricultural Board, the U.S. Food and
Climate Institute, and the Camelian government. Three of
the participants in this conference--Ribera, Pierson, and
N'dolo--attended the face-to-face meetings. But the
computer conference allowed them to involve their colleagues
at home, while interpreting the data based on our discussions of cultural and political problems. This input was
crucial in modeling the impacts of alternative relief
strategies, for without a channel for discussing the

underlying assumptions, they would have had a barrage of
numbers with no way to interpret the discrepancies between
the U.S. model and the AAB model.

I think that the key to the success of the conference
was a discussion which took place late in the second week of
the conference. We had been following our prepared agenda
fairly closely up until then; it had been demanding, but we
had managed to make several minor decisions about what to
monitor. At this particular session, we were going to begin
a discussion of the agricultural technologies which might be
applied to the problem. Clemmons began the discussion with
a glowing report of Consolidated's production records in
several countries. Not surprisingly, Helene responded
with some of her own reports about living conditions in
those countries. As the debate grew, Clemmons became
increasingly defensive about the social obligations of
Consolidated while some of us grew increasingly hostile
to his "economic efficiency." In the midst of all this,
Arume jumped up from his seat and began to tell an old
fable--which I'm sure most of you know--about the magical
mango. He walked about the room as he told his own richly
embellished version of the story and, as luck would have it,
the side table was set with a bowl of fruit for our afternoon break. He began passing the fruit around as he talked,
relating each piece to his story. By the time he was
through, we were all munching fruit and laughing at the
old farmer in the story, and the anger was gone. In its
place was the recognition that we had hit upon one of the
major differences in our world views. We all agreed to
depart from our original agenda to explore this cultural
difference in more detail.

Of course, incidents such as that didn't find their way
into the mass media. We all agreed that, in the best
interest of the negotiations, we should provide a single
daily statement to the press. Bishop Ampleby usually
drafted this statement. In fact, he proved to be a major
mediating force in the conference. It seems that Clemmons
is a Methodist, too, and while he didn't share Ampleby's
views about Third World development, he did seem to have an
inherent trust in the man. On several occasions, I know
that he consulted with Ampleby during lunch or coffee breaks
and then modified his stand.

Of course, a lot of things contributed to the success
of the meetings which will never appear in a formal report--
things like sharing umbrellas, admiring someone's coat or
pen or briefcase. Things like the wall charts prepared by
Foundation staff for all of our presentations--I think they
gave us a sense of equality about our information, and I
know they saved us all the embarrassment of watching Ribera
fumble through his notebook looking for his own small
charts. (He's very nearsighted.) Helene Dubarieux's warm
but analytical approach to the meetings was constructive,
too. The important thing to the world is that we have
arrived at a common plan for Camelian relief. But I can
assure you that it was due, in large measure, to some
careful planning by the Foundation and to the insight of
Bill Owens, who created the tone of the conference.

SPEECH FROM GEORGE CLEMMONS TO THE BOARD
OF DIRECTORS, CONSOLIDATED PRODUCE, INC.,
DRAFTED EN ROUTE FROM PARIS TO NEBRASKA

Before we begin discussing possible responses to this grave situation, it is important for each of you to understand as accurately as possible the events which preceded the kidnapping of Foundation official Bill Owens and our Paris representative, Jack Morris, by the Camelian terrorists who are now demanding that we set up a special food relief program.

Let me begin, ladies and gentlemen, by expressing my extreme sense of frustration following the Paris meeting which ended so tragically. Such tragedy, however, is in strong contrast to the spirit of hopefulness with which the meetings began. In fact, I can now see that we--and I mean all the participants--invested too much faith in that single four-day meeting, only to have it explode in our faces. It didn't, of course, explode immediately. We began by smoldering through two days of ~~political rhetoric from~~ verbal sparring by all sides (yes, I'm afraid Consolidated must share a bit of this guilt as well).

Bill Owens of the Foundation had organized the meetings in a sincere attempt to develop some accurate assessments of the supposed drought in Camelia and--if there really is a drought--the precautions which ought to be taken. Owens identified 10 of us as participants in the meetings, based on his perception of the key organizations involved. He visited each of us to discuss the problem and then called the Paris meeting.

The decision to hold a face-to-face meeting was probably not as bad as the decision to hold <u>only</u> a single face-to-face meeting, with sessions scheduled so tightly that there was little opportunity for informal interaction. Owens did distribute "position papers" before the meeting, but these only underscored our initial differences. Anyway, I wasn't at all sure that all the participants even read the position papers! I read them all, but didn't find them very enlightening. I also had my staff do biographies on each of the participants since I hadn't met any of them (except Jack and Bill Owens) and had only the most basic of information about them.

So, Owens was our only common contact before the Paris meeting, and he certainly did a lot to make me hopeful. I remember calling him several times about issues which concerned me; each time, he gave me a "wait until Paris, George" answer. It was obvious that he was banking on one very good meeting, and he encouraged us to do the same.

The Paris meeting was to have lasted only four days--an attempt to fit it into all of our personal schedules. The agenda was very imposing, including both highly technical and interpersonal topics. Actually, the technical topics were enough to bog us down by themselves, since the African expert Ribera was arguing on the side of Camelia with weather and crop data that didn't agree either with Foundation information or with our own! All of the experts were away from their sources of information, and the rest of us were oppressed with the burden of dealing with all these issues in a single meeting. It was downhill from there.

We struggled to get at the facts. But we didn't seem to be able to focus on the important facts. Abu Arume was completely preoccupied with local issues like Camelian "national integrity" and a bunch of tribal problems, while Draper kept asking about the number of ships that could be mobilized for food transport. I think only a few of us recognized the real economic implications of the crisis, and we couldn't agree on how to measure them. Eventually, there was so much information being tossed about that it became impossible for all the participants to absorb everything at anywhere close to the same rate. And the technical discussion was supposed to have formed the _foundation_ for our negotiations! It was like building a cloud on a swamp, and pretending we had a firm program.

In addition to all of our problems with contradictory information, there was very little time and no structure for small subgroup meetings. Our proceedings remained very formal and grew increasingly tiring as the hours wore on. We met all day and into the night, racing to finish our appointed tasks in the appointed time. As it became clear that we would <u>not</u> finish, a seed of hopelessness was planted in the group and obviously spread to the world outside the hotel.

Such a spread of despair is not surprising since we were quite visible as a group. The press demanded interviews from each of us, and some of the participants appeared to use these interviews deliberately to place pressures on Consolidated and the State Department. ~~That woman~~ Helene Dubarieux was quoted in LE MONDE as saying: "The lives of one or two million people are at stake, and it appears that the conference may have been carefully manipulated by the corporate giants. It raises questions about the sincerity of the other participants and the seriousness of the meetings themselves." She carefully avoided me the next day, but it was obvious what she was trying to do.

I took Bill Owens aside and told him that such press reports, coupled with the confusion about actual data on the so-called drought, were threatening to destroy the conference. Just as we were talking, Arume--the Camelian leader-- came up and began debating the agricultural management issue. (Actually, Arume had an apparently insatiable desire to be at the center of things!) Owens never responded to my concerns, and Arume continued to burden the proceedings with his dogmatism.

In the final analysis, the conference probably would have benefited from less speech-giving and more listening. Arume was the worst offender, of course; I never figured out why he bothered to bring the other two Camelians with him. He completely dominated Francoise Mwanga, who might have contributed an economic perspective to the Camelian position. In fact, he never gave her a chance to speak. Dubarieux, ~~was hysterical much of the time,~~ too, tried to dominate the conference with and our own emotional speeches State Department representative, Allan Draper, was actually fairly parochial in his view of U.S. involvement--when he wasn't asking about ships, he was talking about the obligations of Project Progress! Ribera, the supposed expert from the African Agricultural Board, fumbled through his presentations, and Professor Pierson, supposedly a key source of objective information, hardly got to say a word. Even

Bishop Ampleby was a disappointment. I was hoping he could help us understand the Camelian objectives, but I never really got much chance to talk with him. In short, if the meetings had not been so tragic, they could easily be called a comedy of errors.

This description of the Paris meetings should give you some feeling for the frustration which preceded the kidnapping of Morris and Owens. In fact, as I am acutely aware, I could easily have been the one who was kidnapped. When I left Paris, the front page of every newspaper had a photograph of the large, silent crowd that attended the burial ceremonies for the two French policemen killed Friday in the exchange of gunfire with the terrorists. We now have to make some decisions, and we must make them quickly . . . .

ANALYSIS OF THE FACE-TO-FACE
CONFERENCING SCENARIOS

Perhaps the most fundamental characteristic of face-to-face communication is also its most obvious: participants share the same location simultaneously. This commonality of experience provides the basis for both planned and unplanned communication opportunities, like rain. . . .

We joked about weather modification and saving some rain to take back to Camelia with us. I think all those jokes and soggy handshakes made us feel like a group with a common adversary—the weather. And this attitude carried over into our formal meetings.

Such shared experiences may seem trivial, but they will have an impact on a face-to-face conference. The *kind* of impact—beneficial or destructive—will depend a lot on the choices of the conference organizer.

"Friendly" . . . But Lots of Time Pressures

Experience to date suggests that face-to-face communication is perceived as more "friendly" than communication through any of the teleconferencing media (F11–F13*). In fact, most people respond more positively to face-to-face meetings (F16, F17, F21) and are more confident in their communication when they meet in person (F19, F20). A major reason for these perceptions is probably the opportunity for informal and unplanned meetings. These meetings are likely to be more personal; they are likely to build a sense of intimacy among the participants. And, as in the Effective Scenario, they are likely to shape the more formal communication:

It seems that Clemmons is a Methodist, too, and while he didn't share Ampleby's views about Third World development, he did seem to have an inherent trust in the man. On several occasions, I know that he consulted with Ampleby during lunch or coffee breaks and then modified his stand.

Owens made a real effort to encourage such alliances. Again, from Mwanga's point of view:

He also spent considerable time on my personal background and goals for this conference. In the course of the conference, I realized that these questions were part of a deliberate—and very successful—strategy to build alliances among all of the participants.

Of course, the initial openness to face-to-face communication can be short-lived if it is not cultivated. In the Ineffective Scenario, Bill Owens failed to bring the group members together. He did distribute position papers, but as Clemmons noted, "These only underscored our initial differences." Furthermore, we suspect that the original optimism made the failures even worse. Thus, Clemmons admitted

---

*The codes in this analysis refer to the numbers of the "strengths" and "weaknesses" listed for each of the media in the Summary of Social Evaluations of Teleconferencing in the Reference Materials. Thus: F for face-to-face, etc.

that they had "invested too much faith in that single four-day meeting only to have it explode in our faces." Finally, the same intensity of communication which creates intimacy can be perceived as pressure; in a short meeting with too many tasks, we suggest that this pressure can destroy the communication.

In the Ineffective Scenario, for example, there was an overemphasis on a single meeting to accomplish *all* of the group's goals. Clemmons said it well: "The decision to hold a face-to-face meeting was probably not as bad as the decision to hold *only* a single face-to-face meeting." The result was a highly structured and intense meeting which allowed few opportunities for the informal contacts that are a basic strength of face-to-face communication. On the other hand, in the Effective Scenario, Owens relied on a *series* of face-to-face meetings. The increased time, together with a less structured conference format, played a crucial role in allowing the participants to explore the cross-cultural differences revealed by Arume's tale about the farmer and the magical mango. Such a "digression" would have been impossible in a more rigid, harried meeting.

Save the Complex Tasks for Face-to-Face

Comparisons of face-to-face with audio and video have concluded that face-to-face is superior for more complex tasks, particularly those involving conflict and negotiation (F1–F4, F18). At the same time, other evidence suggests that more messages are exchanged face-to-face, and more options discussed (F6–F10). We guess that time is again a critical variable here: in the short, formal meeting of the Ineffective Scenario, the participants managed to raise all of the complexities of the Camelian problem but were unable to move beyond "verbal sparring." Another problem was the overemphasis on information. If teleconferencing media are better than face-to-face for information exchange, we suspect that discrepancies in data will be troublesome in Owens' four-day Paris meeting, particularly since participants have varied levels of expertise. Thus, Clemmons reported, "There was so much information that it became impossible for all the participants to absorb everything at anywhere close to the same rate." Owens' response to this problem in the Effective Scenario is the preconference computer conference.

A major question in this division of labor among conferencing media is raised by the negotiation experiments which imply that visual communication can actually serve as a distraction from substantive concerns (F23–F25; also A17–A21). Such findings are intriguing but don't seem convincing enough to change the focus of the scenarios. The Camelia meetings illustrate the dominant view in social evaluations of teleconferencing: complex tasks should be reserved for face-to-face communication.

A Medium for Great Orators

If social presence is important to group communication, face-to-face is clearly the richest of the communications media considered here. However, richness does not guarantee everyone an equal hearing. In fact, the current evaluations suggest that all three teleconferencing media promote greater equality of participation than face-to-face (A35, C23, C24, V30, V31). Some people, like Arume, will dominate this medium. Arume is a natural orator; he can take command of a meeting and have a profound effect on its outcome:

In the midst of all this, Arume jumped up from his seat and began to tell an old fable—which I'm sure most of you know—about the magical mango. . . . By the time he was through, we were all munching fruit and laughing at the old farmer in the story, and the anger was gone.

While productive in this example, too many orators out of control can be disastrous, as Clemmons noted in the Ineffective Scenario. There, Arume was the worst offender; he never gave the other Camelians a chance to speak. Dubarieux, too, was accused of dominating the medium, while Pierson, a "key source of objective information, hardly got to say a word." A group leader may thus have to consider individual traits more carefully for face-to-face meetings, balancing them with the needs of the group.

In Summary . . .

The communications richness of face-to-face is unequalled by teleconferencing media. The important question for a conference organizer is: When can this richness be used most effectively and when is it unnecessary or even misleading? A face-to-face meeting seems a wise prelude to any teleconference. In addition, it would also seem prudent to relegate complex communication tasks to face-to-face, although teleconferencing media might be used in a supporting role. However, while face-to-face will remain the most "natural" medium to most people for some time to come, it is not necessarily the most efficient for all situations—nor even the most "human."

UNANSWERED QUESTIONS

The evaluations of teleconferencing focus on such variables as how frequently each member of a group speaks in an electronic meeting or how many of the exchanges concern learning or how confident group members are that the others have understood them. Such findings provide insights into the way people might behave in electronic meetings; they suggest possible collisions between the sensitive zones of the communication process and the characteristics of the medium.

However, the media evaluations—and thus the Camelia scenarios—leave two kinds of questions unanswered. First, what will be the effect of the media beyond the conference room? How will the media alter organizations and governments and lifestyles of future users? Second, what are the practical day-to-day choices to be made in using the media? And what are the most important criteria for making those choices?

Chapter Five begins to explore the first set of questions. It is speculative and full of questions which have no clear answers at present.

Chapter Six then provides a narrative checklist of important choices in selecting and using electronic media. Although it does not provide absolute guidelines for making these choices, it does provide a foundation for informed decisions.

FIVE

In the future world of the Camelia conferences, the technology for holding electronic meetings was widely available. By stepping into this world, we were able to explore the impact of the new technology on a meeting among people from several organizations and several nations. The focus of this extrapolation was the *meeting*. The society around the meeting remained much as it is today, except for the ease of access to teleconferencing media.

In reality, the widespread use of electronic media could alter the organizations and social structures of the world as well as protocols for meetings. The CPO and the LCF could assume very different forms, and the types of meetings which they hold might not resemble our scenarios at all.

It would be a mistake, then, to project future societal effects of teleconferencing media from the Camelia scenarios. For example, computer conferencing's flexibility of participation times does not mean that all organizaions will adopt flexibility in working hours. Nor does audio's apparent emphasis on substance mean that charisma will cease to play a role in politics. But questions about societal impacts will arise as policy makers and investors, consumers and social change advocates make choices about if, when, and how to use the new media.

At present, the sources for exploring these questions are limited. Actual "tests" of societal impacts are difficult to engineer. Since the media are not widely available today, direct observations are seldom possible. There are focused applications of the media which certainly will serve as "trial balloons." Telemedicine, services for the handicapped, and office automation are examples. But these applications are seldom based on encompassing visions of societal reform. Telemedicine has not been linked to a proposal to revolutionize health care. Office automation has not been presented as a proposal to reorganize the corporate world. And the results of these early applications are still too isolated to suggest major organizational and societal impacts.

Most of the information about long-term effects of interactive electronic media is thus speculative and impressionistic. Visions abound. And visions will influence many of the choices about teleconferencing media over the next few years. These visions, then, might provide the best starting point for critical judgments about organizational and societal potentials of teleconferencing media.

THE UTOPIAN TEMPTATION

Whenever a new technology emerges, it is tempting to predict that it will lead to a new and better form of society. The technology for electronic meetings is no excep-

tion. The new media invite a look at alternative organizations and alternative societies. Combined with current social concerns, they also encourage utopian[1] visions
of what could be.

Ecotopia[2] is one such vision. Ecotopia is a nation of 1999, formed when
Oregon and Washington join Northern California in seceding from the United
States. The residents of this society hold ecological living as a primary value. To implement such a lifestyle, they have chosen social structures and technological aids
which reduce wear and tear on the environment. The suburban sprawl of the San
Francisco Bay Area has been converted to a decentralized society with "minicities"
which are compact, with plenty of room for trees and animals between them. Cars
have been all but abandoned in Ecotopia, while electronic media are called upon to
take their place:

> Feeling that they should transport their bodies only when it's a pleasure, they
> seldom travel "on business" in our manner. Instead, they tend to transact
> business by using their picturephones. These employ the same cables that pro-
> vide television connections; the whole country, except for a few isolated rural
> spots, is wired with cable. (There is no ordinary broadcasting.)[3]

The decentralized society described in *Ecotopia* is a society which makes
heavy use of teleconferencing-like media, although only within the borders of
Ecotopia. In fact, communication with those outside of the new country is
restricted. Thus, the potential of teleconferencing has been socially limited; it is a
tool for decentralization of work and regular communication among Ecotopia's inhabitants.

In contrast to the isolationist vision of Ecotopia is the possibility of the
"global village":

> The Earth for the first time will be knit together on a personal and not govern-
> mental level. There will be a kind of immediacy possible over all the world as
> has hitherto existed only at the level of the village. In fact we will have what
> has been called the global village.[4]

In this vision, electronic media create a sense of community and commonality
among all people of the world, from the inner city of New York and suburbs like
Pasadena to remote villages in Africa or communal farms in the People's Republic
of China. The vision is one of instant connectedness and mobility. Esfandiary, in his
Futurist Manifesto,[5] carries the vision to its extreme. He calls for "instant com-

---

[1]We are not using the term "utopian" in a pejorative sense; a utopia is an ideal condition. As such, it is a source of direction, if not a blueprint for society.

[2]Ernest Callenback, *Ecotopia*, Berkeley, California: Banyan Tree Books, 1975.

[3]*Ibid.*, p. 38.

[4]Isaac Asimov, "The Fourth Revolution," *Saturday Review*, October 24, 1970, p. 19;
"global village" is Marshall McLuhan's term.

[5]F. M. Esfandiary, *Up-Wingers, A Futurist Manifesto*, New York: The John Day Company, 1973.

munities" of over 100,000 people to be set up in less than six months, then dismantled after a few months or a few years. Wired for global communication, these communities create planetary citizens:

> The Instant Community is Universal. The sense of community exists not only within the community but more and more within the whole planet. The individual does not belong to a specific community but is part of many communities—part of the whole planet.[6]

In the electronically shrunken world of the global village vision, cultural barriers are diminished. As a result, so is fighting. Third World nations share a more equal footing with Western countries. World government becomes feasible, and national boundaries become absurd. There is the possibility of a global crisis response network, combining people and various computer-based resources.[7] Esfandiary sees in the new media an "unsung instrument for peace."

Many who find Esfandiary's optimism overstated nevertheless believe that new communications media will encourage more direct participation in government: "the world's town meeting is now a conceptual, and may soon be a physical, global reality."[8] Cable television combined with interactive computers and home terminals could provide an electronic structure for greatly increased citizen participation in government. Satellites dramatically increase the number of potential participants in such a network. And even if coordinated world usage does not develop, local communities might benefit from an electorate closely tied to the daily operations of government.

Electronic media suggest still other utopian possibilities: with more effective use of information, it will become reasonable to expect increases in productivity with fewer resources and less pressure on the environment;[9] there will be the possibility of solving major social problems by more direct communication between the "world's key synergetic thinkers"[10] and by increased access to "voluminous and up-to-the-minute"[11] information for decisionmaking. Worldwide networks might respond not only to crises but also to general educational needs. Learners could be connected to high-quality educational resources, learning at their own pace in an

---

[6]*Ibid.*, p. 65.

[7]A specific proposal for the use of computer conferencing to create a crisis response network is contained in: Robert H. Kupperman, Richard H. Wilcox, Harvey A. Smith, "Crisis Management: Some Opportunities," *Science*, February 7, 1975, pp. 404–10. See also the response to that article by Vallee, Lipinski, Johansen, and Wilson in *Science*, vol. 188, April 18, 1975, p. 203.

[8]John McHale, *The Future of the Future*, New York: George Braziller, 1969, p. 145.

[9]This is the vision of the "communications era" in Robert Theobald's *Habit and Habitat*, Englewood Cliffs, NJ: Prentice-Hall, Inc., 1972.

[10]Robert Theobald, *An Alternative Future for America*, Chicago: Swallow Press, Inc., 1968, p. 139.

[11]Brenda Maddox, *Beyond Babel: New Directions in Communications*, Boston: Beacon Press, 1972, pp. 254–5. Maddox speculates that "the worldwide sharing of information at enormous speeds will actually raise the collective potential of the human race."

"electronic world university."[12] Such a use of electronic meetings promises to redefine the teaching-learning process and perhaps even the nature of knowledge itself.

THE PROMISES—AND PITFALLS—OF UTOPIA

Visions such as these are valuable sources of ideas about the ways in which teleconferencing media *might* be used. The promises are attractive: the media might promote decentralization; they might reduce travel and therefore energy consumption; they could reduce cultural barriers, increase citizen-government interaction, and revamp education. However, each promise carries with it hidden problems of implementation, as well as potential surprises. For example, the vision of the global village raises questions for many in Third World countries and even in developed countries where cultures are highly fragmented. Will "this instrument of peace" be applied through a forceful takeover by the dominant technological culture, amplified by satellites and communications networks? Is such a massive vision only an American technocrat's oversimplification of international realities?

The promises of utopia are more like armchair glimpses of possible futures than active prescriptions for reform. Any prescription for reform must take into account the complexity and frequent nonrationality of social change. It should also reflect lessons learned from early attempts to implement some of the utopian visions. Most important, the potential misuses of the new technologies must be weighed against each of the promises.

The Promise of Decentralization

One need not go all the way to Ecotopia in 1999 to discover attempts to decentralize society using electronic media. In the Windham Planning Region of northeastern Connecticut, for instance, the New Rural Society Project has been exploring the potential of electronic media to "establish a more balanced rural-urban population distribution pattern as a response to the interdependent rural, urban, and energy crises."[13] Inspired by opinion polls which suggested that a large proportion of the commuting population might prefer employment close to home and that many people would prefer more rural lifestyles, the staff of this project tried to develop a model for decentralizing business and government operations to rural areas.

As a starting point, the staff of the project surveyed 16 businesses which had recently relocated to Connecticut. Their purpose was to identify the major considerations in moving to a rural area. Highest on the chief executives' list of concerns were land and building costs, labor supply and wage rates, and local property taxes. Considerations of communications ranked 11th on this list.

---

[12]While we are not certain of the exact origin of this term, we think that it was first used by Stuart Umpleby, now at George Washington University. He wrote a number of limited circulation papers on this topic while he was at the University of Illinois during the late 1960s and early 1970s.

[13]*The 1972/73 New Rural Society Project*, Report to the Department of Housing and Urban Development, Fairfield University, May 1973, abstract.

The staff offered the following explanation for their finding: while decisions regarding capital investments and labor problems are made by top executives in the organization, communications is often treated as a utility and may be the responsibility of a lower-level manager. Thus, decisions to move or not to move may be made without exploring the communication issues and opportunities thoroughly. In fact, the problem of "patching together some communication system that works" is sometimes addressed only after the organization has made its decision based on other considerations.[14]

If communication opportunities are not a sufficient motive for relocation, communication constraints are a sufficient reason *not* to relocate. The New Rural Society Project found that, among businesses which had considered relocation but decided against it, communication issues did indeed loom large. Particularly important were concerns that "valuable person-to-person relationships existing in the city would suffer."[15] This is a political concern. A business manager may gain an important advantage over his competitors by having lunch once a week with a major contractor. Similarly, the status of a public relations official in her organization often depends on the effectiveness of her contacts with people in several outside organizations. Threats to such contacts may not be the most important concerns of the organization, but they could be a threat to her position and her ability to carry out her role responsibilities.

Part of the New Rural Society project was a field test of an audio conferencing arrangement between the Stamford and New Haven offices of Union Trust Company.[16] The purpose of this test was to determine the acceptability of teleconferencing as an alternative to travel for face-to-face meetings among senior management personnel. This particular teleconferencing system is still in use. However, the project has now closed its offices, and the vision of the New Rural Society remains far from complete.

The experience of a French bank illustrates both the organizational and political problems which may be encountered in attempts at decentralization. The bank sought to move some of its international operations from Paris to the regional capital of Lyons. It encountered five major obstacles:[17]

Foreign-language information was stored in Paris, while only translations were available in Lyons;

Minutes and transcripts of meetings had to be preserved for review and approval by a supervising committee of top managers, all located in Paris;

Most experts on foreign investments currently live in Paris;

---

[14]*Ibid.*, p. 47.

[15]*Ibid.*, p. 48.

[16]Kay Kohl, Thomas C. Newman, Jr., and Joseph F. Tomey, "Facilitating Organizational Decentralization through Teleconferencing," *IEEE Transactions on Communications*, October 1975, pp. 1098–1104.

[17]"Decentralisation des activites Tertiaires: Lyon place Bancaire," *La Documentation Francaise*, February 1974.

French government agencies are not decentralized. Thus, local bankers still had to go to Paris for permits and visas;

Some investment risks involve political considerations and require the attention of the government (for example, should a particular investment be made in Tanzania or the Sudan?).

Could improved teleconferencing facilities help in this situation? The first problem, the availability of translations of foreign-language texts, probably could be remedied without teleconferencing. A simple facsimile link would suffice. Minutes of meetings, too, could be transmitted via facsimile; but it might be more desirable to appoint a Paris representative to "sit in" on the meeting via teleconference, and such a solution would probably require some personnel changes.

The need for expert information could be fulfilled, in part, by teleconferences. However, we suggested in Chapter Three that experts play a variety of roles. The "facts and figures" role may be well-suited to electronic meetings. But those who are experts by virtue of their contacts with the "right" people or their skills in mobilizing groups of people may not be able to function as effectively at a distance. They are more likely to be enmeshed in organizational structures which create concerns about privacy and confidentiality. Also, it may be difficult to "locate" such experts electronically; they are usually identified through continued associations with a variety of organizations. This problem is the same as the one which the New Rural Society Project found: there often will be a political advantage to person-to-person contacts, at least until many more people have gained a lot more experience with electronic media.

Finally, there are the problems of a centralized French administration for both government services and political decisions. To extend government services to the regional capitals—even by means of electronic media—would require the establishment of a new bureaucratic structure. Such a structure would, in itself, produce political conflicts. As a result, it is even possible to imagine that the new electronic procedures for obtaining permits and visas could be more inconvenient than travel to Paris.

Electronic meetings *could* allow people to work from remote office centers or even from their homes. Government agencies or companies *could* relocate away from large urban centers and even become more integrated in small-scale, local economies. The result might be less alienation; individuals might have more control over the institutions surrounding them. But the availability of electronic meetings does not, by itself, ensure effective decentralization. Successes have been rare. Furthermore, electronic media might even increase centralization, making it possible for a very small decision-making body to control an ever larger organization remotely. *People* might be decentralized, but *power* might not.

Substituting Electronic Meetings for Travel

The promise of electronic meetings as a substitute for travel is alluring. If business air travel were reduced by only 20 percent, Americans would save 50,000 barrels of jet fuel per day; a 20 percent reduction in business travel by auto would save another 80,000 barrels per day. If half of the office work force adopted "telework," savings from reduced commuter traffic could be between 470,000 and 640,000 barrels of gasoline per day by 1985.[18]

But the possible benefits of substitution go beyond energy savings. For organizations, they might include reduced costs, improved organizational response time, more flexible choice of location and organizational structure, and improved productivity. Furthermore, advocates of substitution point to opportunities for reducing growth-related problems in large cities and providing job access to the handicapped. Findings that 31 to 49 percent of existing business meetings could be conducted via audio while video would replace another 23 percent[19] lend further support to the vision of a society in which travel is reserved for pleasure.

However, the argument for substitution is typically based on the questionable assumption that an electronic meeting can substitute for face-to-face meetings (and therefore travel) without altering the nature of the communication. Unfortunately, there is little evidence that direct substitution can occur—except in the simplest cases. In 1974, Kollen and Garwood at Bell Canada surveyed nearly 10,000 Canadian business travelers to explore the substitution concept. They concluded that electronic communication might have replaced about 20 percent of business trips had the media been available. They note, however, that "the phrase 'substitution' is used here as a shorthand expression that refers to a very complex, mostly unknown (to date) relationship between the transportation and communications sectors of our society."[20] Furthermore, they found no consistent factors which distinguished the "substitutor" (the person who would substitute communication for travel) from the "nonsubstitutor."

Arthur Clarke's plea of "Don't Commute, Communicate"[21] is appealing in its simplicity but easy to take too literally. The reality is that simple substitution of new communications media for travel is a shallow hope indeed. In fact, new media could even *stimulate* travel by encouraging people to visit their new electronic friends far away.

In considering the potential of electronic meetings, redefinition may be a more useful concept than substitution. For example, one member of an organization may still travel to a face-to-face meeting while using teleconferencing as a way to involve other participants who are at the home site or traveling to their own meetings. The traveler would be free to make all the informal contacts at the face-to-face meeting, calling on his colleagues as needed. Thus, the face-to-face meeting would

[18]These statistics are reported by Richard C. Harkness in *Technology Assessment of Telecommunications/Transportation Interactions*, a three-volume report to the National Science Foundation, 1976; available from National Technical Information Service, Nos. PB272–694, PB272–695, and PB272–696.

[19]From a survey by the British Civil Service, quoted in Roger Pye, Michael Tyler, and Brian Cartwright, "Telecommunicate or Travel?", *New Scientist*, September 12, 1974, pp. 642–4.

[20]James H. Kollen and John Garwood, *Travel/Communications Tradeoffs: The Potential for Substitutions among Business Travelers*, Bell Canada, Business Planning Group, 620 Belmont, Room 1105, Montreal 101, Canada, pp. 1–2.

[21]Arthur C. Clarke, "Communications in the Second Century of the Telephone," *Technology Review*, May 1976, pp. 33–41.

be redefined. Perhaps it would be smaller, but travel would not necessarily be reduced. Those who didn't attend one meeting might now be free to attend others.

There is no organizational structure currently in place to reduce or restrict travel. On the contrary, there is a mesh of institutions and organizations to facilitate travel, organizations which have a stake in maintaining a growing transportation sector. Consider all of the groups who profit from travel: the automobile and airline industries, the highway construction industry, transportation services such as bus and taxi fleets, not to mention roadside services, hotels, and other travel accommodations. It is far easier to imagine that society will find new travel needs to support these industries than to imagine that they will be seriously downgraded—at least barring a much more severe energy crisis than any experienced so far.

Electronic meetings have a real potential to reduce the frequency of travel *if there are social structures to encourage such a reduction.* But will such structures emerge without the impetus of a crisis? And if they do emerge, how acceptable will they be to people who value mobility as a personal freedom?

Expanding Cross-Cultural Communication

As the Camelia scenarios illustrate, teleconferencing media offer no direct avenue to cross-cultural understanding. In fact, electronic meetings introduce new potentials for misunderstandings in international meetings. Furthermore, attempts to connect the global village will likely introduce their own set of misunderstandings, as specific groups defend their territories against electronic invasions.

There is already a complex international structure for providing conventional communication services. It includes private and public corporations as well as regulatory and defense agencies. In countries like the United Kingdom, a single public corporation may have complete control over all person-to-person communication. Such a corporation can block any new technology simply by refusing to adopt it or regulating against its use. The one international coordinating agency, the International Telecommunications Union, performs only advisory functions and is, itself, compartmentalized. Its work is thus complicated both by problems of coordination among its branches and by competition among national interests.

To illustrate the difficulty of achieving unified international development of a communications technology, Maddox notes the problems involved in establishing a policy for the management of satellites. She states that Intelsat, for example, represented an opportunity

> to use the new technology of satellites to create an organization in which governments not particularly friendly toward one another might have worked together. Instead, Intelsat, by its commercial orientation and American dominance, has encouraged the proliferation of other satellite systems and has created the real possibility that there may some day be international disputes about places in the synchronous orbit.[22]

Multinational corporations are perhaps the most likely pioneers of the global village. Satellite Business Systems (SBS), created in the mid-1970s as a joint venture

----

[22]Brenda Maddox, *op. cit.*, p. 14.

between IBM, Aetna Life & Casualty, and COMSAT, is an illustration of the corporate world's vision of global connectedness. It will equip its clients (the major industrial and government users of information) with the ability to expand their telephone network dramatically to include conferencing, facsimile transmission, data handling, and television transmission. Organizations like SBS will not necessarily emphasize cross-cultural understanding, however; their operational decisions will be guided by practicality and profitability.

For the near future, electronic meetings will rarely be accessible for international meetings. To be sure, government and large corporate uses between "developed" countries will gradually increase, spurred by such satellite ventures as SBS. But this is not the vision of an ordinary American talking to an ordinary Moroccan as though they were neighbors. It is a vision filled with questions about differing administrative protocols and conflicting perceptions of goals and objectives. Thus, even as global electronic meetings become typical, cross-cultural communication may remain elusive.

Citizen-Government Interaction

In the United States, representative democracy has typically been viewed as a practical necessity because fully participatory democracy has been impossible. Now, electronic polling devices and "town meetings" suggest that citizens *could* be involved directly in a great many more government decisions. They promise electronic community building, and their promise already has had some initial tests.

One example is the ACCESS project,[23] supported by the National Science Foundation. Its purpose was to develop a design for community participation in policymaking at the regional level. Tested in Santa Barbara, California, the design emphasized the importance of graphic techniques in telecommunication to provide information and decision support. The communication tools included a "situation room," computers, television, and remote sensing. One of the tasks of the project was to develop a technique for making computer graphics compatible with two-way coaxial cable television. Computer polling was then used to stimulate dialogue on alternative regional policies. The overall design for ACCESS, however, has never been fully implemented.

The experiments with "new towns" have also included efforts to implement participatory strategies using electronic communications. In Irvine, California, a "Community Cable" connects 15,000 homes. City council meetings are televised every other Tuesday night. At present, the system is largely one-way, but, according to organizers of the cable service, "the ultimate would be to have a system to allow that citizen who is sitting in his home to interact by having the two-way come back, so he can have input to what's going on in the meeting.[24]

In Reading, Pennsylvania, an experimental use of interactive cable television funded by the National Science Foundation has evolved into an ongoing service for the elderly. The program uses video teleconferencing from three neighborhood

[23]William R. Ewald, Jr., *Information, Perception and Regional Policy*, Report to the National Science Foundation, Research Applied to National Needs, 1975.

[24]Ernie Eban, "Blues for Circumstances Beyond our Control: TV Goes Two-Way," *The Village Voice*, November 24, 1976.

centers and one mobile unit. Also, subscribers to the cable system can watch from their homes and interact through their telephones. The service has operated two hours a day, providing a forum for discussions between older citizens and government leaders or social security officials, as well as for meetings among people with common interests. This form of electronic meeting apparently has decreased the sense of isolation felt by many of the elderly in the area and has provided a medium for community expression.[25]

Unlike some other efforts, the Reading project has emphasized the involvement of local citizens in the operation of the system. The technology was only a beginning; far more important were the ways in which the technology was *used*. This emphasis on the *organization* of communication may be a major reason why Reading has been one of the few projects to continue after the initial experimental funding has ended.

The pragmatics of using electronic media to improve citizen-government interaction are only beginning to be understood. Electronic meetings raise basic questions about the nature of the relationship between citizen and government and among citizens. How much direct citizen involvement is manageable? How much is desirable? Will simple procedures for majority rule still work when hundreds of people, all with different viewpoints, can participate in policy formulation? And what about the potential of the media to support propaganda instead of honest exploration of issues? The technology of electronic meetings, by itself, will not provide answers to these questions.

New Ways to Learn

For the education community, teleconferencing media are the newest in a series of electronic temptations. But even as a few people are positing bold transformations of learning through the new media, there is despair over the failures of educational technology to date. Many who have tried electronic media—televised lectures, computer-assisted instruction (CAI), and others—feel that they have been burned. They point to the "dehumanizing" potential of electronic media. They ask if electronic education is not the poor person's education—an inadequate substitute for a "real teacher."

But teleconferencing media are different. They involve group interaction *through* the technology. And this interactive capability means that they do not have to be impersonal, authoritarian, or boring. Learning via teleconference does not require prepackaged instruction programs as does television or programmed learning. The electronic seminar is as possible as the electronic lecture. Furthermore, with media like audio or computer-based conferencing, it is possible for students to put together their own learning networks and call upon people who, because of geographic location, might otherwise be inaccessible. Education might become student-centered rather than institution-centered.

---

[25]For an overview of the Reading experiment, see Mitchell Moss, "The Development of Two-Way Cable Television Applications," in M. C. J. Elton, W. A. Lucas, and D. W. Conrath, eds., *Evaluating New Telecommunication Systems*, New York and London: Plenum, 1978.

The trouble with the vision is this: the potential advantages of teleconferencing may never be realized if the applications are forced to fit existing models of education. If the model remains one-teacher-to-many-students, there will be little chance of more equal interaction between teacher and student. In fact, if the media are viewed as a way to increase the number of students per teacher—as cost considerations might suggest—interaction almost certainly will be more restricted and more unidirectional. When students do exercise the technological option of interrupting, the restricted channels of the media may combine with the unequal status of student and teacher to leave the students feeling awkward and ineffective.

Similarly, if education by means of teleconferencing retains the model of experts assembling learning packages for broad distribution, the potential for tailored learning experiences or for individualized learning networks will be wasted. Education will continue to reflect the concepts which the instructor thinks are important rather than the questions which the student might bring to the instructor.

While there are few nontraditional models of learning which could emphasize the unique strengths of teleconferencing, there is at least one example of a teleconferencing system which has been used to implement a vision of educational reform. In 1907, University of Wisconsin president Charles Van Hise challenged educators to extend "the boundaries of the campus to the boundaries of the state."[26] The idea of using electronic media to assist in implementing this vision was suggested in the 1950s; in 1965, the Educational Telephone Network was begun on a limited scale. Currently, over 25,000 students a year use audio teleconferencing for continuing education. Two hundred locations throughout the state provide convenient access to even the most remote regions. At present, the system is used mainly for scheduled courses, but also for emergency purposes such as providing farmers with critical information about a threatening crop disease. As the use of teleconferencing in Wisconsin continues to expand, the 1907 vision moves closer to reality.

Certainly, this vision of reform is more an expansion of established procedures than a radical reorientation. Furthermore, the expansion itself is limited by organizational constraints: there is no technological reason why teleconferencing cannot extend the boundaries of a university *outside* the boundaries of the state. The technology of teleconferencing is only one factor in a mix of variables which must be marshalled to implement any educational reform. Equally important will be considerations of funding, of unions, of job markets and unemployment levels, and ultimately of social control. Thus, if education is to be revamped by electronic media, the transformation will require major social changes which have little to do with the technology itself.

THE PROBLEMS WITH UTOPIA

Unfortunately, for every positive metaphor inspired by the potential for electronic meetings, there is usually a negative metaphor as well. If the "global village" prom-

---

[26]Cited in Lorne A. Parker, "Teleconferencing as an Educational Medium: A Ten Year Perspective from the University of Wisconsin-Extension," in Lorne Parker and Betsy Riccomini, eds., *The Status of the Telephone in Education*, Madison: University of Wisconsin-Extension Press, 1976, p. 2.

ises peace and brotherhood to the world, its twin, the "wired nation," suggests eavesdropping, domestic espionage, and the possibility of oppressive dictatorship. If immediate access to complete, up-to-date information seems to augur greater problem-solving potential, the prospect of direct electronic signals to the brain threatens manipulation and control at the most basic level.

In contrast to the vital vision of humans more in touch with the world and each other, Asimov depicts a society in which electronic media completely isolate people from one another. On the planet of Solaria, three-dimensional electronic "viewing" has replaced all human communication except for procreation. An Earthman visitor to Solaria comments on the quality of life in this society:

> The Solarians have given up something mankind has had for a million years. . . . the tribe. . . . cooperation between individuals, Solaria has given it up entirely. It is a world of isolated individuals, and the planet's only sociologist is delighted that this is so. That sociologist, by the way, never heard of sociomathematics because he is inventing his own science. There is no one to teach him, no one to help him, no one to think of something he might miss. . . . The human touch is gone. The looked-for future is one of ectogenesis and complete isolation from birth.

Who can say if this vision is less possible than some of the utopian promises summarized earlier?

Utopian perspectives, then, provide only limited views of what actually will happen. They suggest a world in which people behave as they are supposed to behave—at least according to some utopian's perspective. These inhabitants of the better society are clear about their goals; they are cognizant of all of their alternatives and the consequences of these alternatives; they make their choices to maximize their goals. All that is required to ensure successful uses of electronic technology is that the projected use make rational sense.

But every choice regarding the future of new electronic media will not be a rational choice. Decisions about the technology will not always be based on a consideration of alternatives or on complete and accurate information about needs. Often, the choices made will not be the best possible; they will be simply "good enough."

In describing the complexities of organizational decisionmaking, Graham Allison points to the weaknesses of populating scenarios of the future with "rational actors."[27] He observes that organizational procedures and bureaucratic politics are at play in any decision-making situation. According to this view, the future uses of electronic meetings may depend more on the sequence in which each organization plays out its repertoire of standard procedures than on a unitary search for an optimal choice. Applications will likely be determined by a patchwork of decision-making procedures which will almost never deal with a whole problem. Rather, they will address the narrow portion of the problem which falls within this or that person's realm of responsibility. In particular, it is unlikely that anybody will have complete power to deal with a communication problem.

To make things more complex, politics enter the picture. Organizational leaders occupy positions which define both what they may do and must do in in-

---

[27]Graham T. Allison, *Essence of Decision*, Boston: Little, Brown and Company, 1971.

teracting with other organizational leaders. This is a competitive game in which the players all have different amounts of power and different personal and organizational objectives. The game is issue-oriented. The rules are a mix of formal statutes and unexamined conventions which apply only to the specific issue at hand. The result of the game is an outcome of the conflict and bargaining among the players and may not represent anyone's *intended* solution. Utopian perspectives enter the mix, but they seldom determine the future.

In exploring the utopian visions of decentralization, substitution, cross-cultural communication, and others, we have identified some of the organizational and political barriers to their realization. The utopian temptation is to expect widespread societal benefits to emerge *because of* the introduction of the new technology. This technological optimism can easily blind people to major pitfalls in the use of teleconferencing media. The result of such an approach is likely to be an inelegant reality, a scrambling of utopian and more pedestrian possibilities.

SIX

The marketing of teleconferencing has already begun. Polished ads are telling potential teleconference users that the "system is the solution." Newsletters and magazines frequently carry success stories by enthusiastic users of electronic media. There are eloquent claims of improved productivity, decreased communication costs, and more effective decision-making.

The media do indeed offer real opportunities to improve communication by reducing the barriers of space and time. However, a central theme of this book has been that benefits are easily transformed into liabilities, promises into disappointments, and utopias into dystopias. For every possible improvement suggested by electronic media, it is necessary to add at least a word of caution.

BENEFITS AND CAUTIONS: A SUMMARY

If Bill Owens were reviewing his experiences with the Camelia conferences, a half dozen opportunities would probably stand out as most important. First, Bill might tell us that *electronic meetings can be arranged more quickly than face-to-face meetings*. People in Toronto, Canada, can meet with people in Atlanta, Georgia, without having to schedule a day for the trip. They can get together when they need to, when a problem first arises, or when an interesting idea first emerges. But Bill would also point out that the quick start-ups may mean some communication failures, too. Planning is as important for electronic meetings as for face-to-face meetings. Often, the barriers of time and space provide an opportunity to think more carefully about the people who should be at the meeting, the resources the group will need, and the tasks that need to be accomplished. With near-instant connections, some of this planning is bound to be neglected. In the extreme, all meetings could develop a crisis atmosphere with crisis approaches to problem-solving.

Another opportunity, vital for the Camelia conferences, is that *more people, with more perspectives, can participate in an electronic meeting*. And more perspectives can provide more alternatives for untangling a knotty problem. Also, more participation may result in fuller support for the collective decision. At the organizational level, *teleconferencing can open new communication channels*, both within an organization and between different organizations. The warning needed here is that more perspectives may mean more conflict, and protocols have not yet evolved for managing conflict in electronic meetings. Increased communication can actually exaggerate differences in viewpoints, in organizational perspectives, in

131

cultures. Furthermore, the opening of communication channels does not necessarily improve the health of an organization: from the perspective of a division head, new patterns of communication might mean a lower commitment to previous goals and leadership. The new patterns may be an improvement for some members of the division but a threat to the manager.

There are other benefits and other cautions. Just as teleconferencing provides access to more people, it also makes possible easy access *to a wide range of information resources.* The caution: the potential for information overload and for misinformation also increases.

The restricted channels of electronic meetings may encourage *more focus and more objectivity in meetings.* But meetings can become too focused; they may not allow divergent thinking and creativity in solving problems.

Electronic meetings are often more orderly, and the organizer has more control over the interaction. But control may suppress differences of opinion and actually reduce communication.

Finally, the *costs associated with meetings may be reduced by teleconferencing.* However, over the long term, communication costs, as well as travel costs, could actually rise as communication opportunities increase. Direct substitution for travel will be rare.

NEW COMMUNICATION CHOICES

This summary of benefits and cautions suggests an important message for potential organizers of teleconferences: electronic media do not automatically improve communication. In Chapter Two, we noted that the media increase the possibilities for both good and bad outcomes. Similarly, from the practical perspective of someone like Bill Owens, the media increase the choices which a meeting organizer must make. And since these are new choices about communicating—choices which have not been important or even possible before—meeting organizers need to develop new criteria for making basic decisions.

The first decision will probably be the choice among media: Which medium should be used when? Ideally, this choice should be made for each meeting situation. But in reality, the choice may already be made by the time someone begins to plan a meeting. The choice among media will often be made by an entire organization. After all, a video conferencing system is a major investment. So are dedicated audio lines, and the costs of computer terminals can add up. An organization may thus decide to use only one form of teleconferencing. As a result, the choice among media is often a choice between one electronic medium and face-to-face.

Nevertheless, at some point, a group or organization will confront the question of which medium to choose. And several criteria will be important in making this decision. Cost will certainly be one of them, but probably not the most important. Increased cost does not necessarily mean better communication. Video, the most expensive of the three media, has both strengths and weaknesses, as illustrated by the Camelia scenarios; it should never be assumed to be the ideal medium "if only it were affordable."

Portability, Flexibility, and Ease of Use

In fact, other criteria probably will make the real difference in any decision to use one medium or another. Portability is important, particularly if the system is going to be used by many people in different places for different purposes. Flexibility goes hand-in-hand with portability. How quickly can meetings be arranged? How easy is it to vary the number of participants and the number of locations connected? What about flexibility in the use of time? Does everyone have to be present at the same time?

The ability to handle special types of information is another consideration. Computer conferencing, for example, seems uniquely suited to the transfer of technical information. What other types of information might be important for potential electronic meetings? Are there elaborate demonstrations or graphic needs? Do these needs make one medium more attractive than the others?

Each medium also has an inherent "style," which should influence an organizer's choice. As Chapter Two suggests, video conferencing can be very glamorous. Audio, on the other hand, is low-key. Computer conferencing may project a kind of accuracy, authority, and scientific quality that will appeal to certain users. While these styles can interfere with communication if they are overemphasized during a meeting, they may be the source of unfortunate mismatches if their importance is underemphasized in the initial choice of which medium to use.

Finally, all of the new media require new skills for effective use. And different people will be willing to learn different skills. Executives who have never typed—and perhaps associate typing with inferior status—may not be the best candidates for a computer conference. Ease of learning the new skills will also differ among users, and these will be important considerations if the system is not to become a white elephant.

Tasks, Groups, and Personal Styles

Once an electronic medium is chosen, either because it seems most appropriate or because it is the *only* option, more important choices must be made. These are decisions about how the medium is to be used. As the Camelia scenarios demonstrate, such decisions can make the difference between genuine communication and a breakdown in communication. The analyses of the scenarios suggest some of the considerations which will be most important in each meeting. They include choices about the identification of tasks and the organization of the group, about personal styles of communicating and technical arrangements.

Many of the evaluations of teleconferencing media have tried to determine which tasks work best in which medium. Generally, these studies have found that all three media work well for tasks such as exchanging information, giving orders or generating ideas. But tasks involving complex interpersonal communication, such as bargaining and negotiation or even getting to know someone, seem to be more difficult for all three media. However, these tasks are also more difficult in face-to-face meetings. Organizers of electronic meetings need not rule out these difficult tasks; instead, they need to look for effective ways of accomplishing them using the various media.

Critical in these decisions will be considerations of order and timing. Which tasks should be addressed first, and how much time should be allotted for them? Also, can some of the complex tasks be accomplished in a series of simpler stages? When is it appropriate to switch to another medium—for example, to use one-to-one telephone calls? Is the meeting organized in such a way that participants can question and redefine the tasks as necessary?

Users will need to make choices about the organization of the group, too. How many people should participate and what roles should be assigned? What will be the protocols for participation? The previous history of the group will influence these choices. Do the participants know each other? If not, what special arrangements might facilitate entry into the first stages of the meeting? The need to communicate will be another criterion in organizing the group. All of the participants may not have the same perception of the need to communicate. How can roles be defined to encourage participation by those who do not seem to need the group as much as the group needs them? In addition, choices about leadership and facilitation will probably be more critical in electronic conferences than in face-to-face meetings. A visible but flexible leader seems to be the most successful model to date.

While decisions about the group may be made by a single organizer of a meeting, each participant will have choices about his or her participation. Most important will be style of self-presentation. The Camelia scenarios demonstrated that some participants may be more comfortable giving speeches while others will favor intense interactions. These choices will be based on personal skills and qualities as well as intuitive responses to the medium itself. The skilled writer may capitalize on her strength in a computer conference by presenting her views in refined mini-essays. A not-too-self-conscious colleague may respond in messages littered with typing and grammatical errors. These differences in styles may be perfectly acceptable, but they will have to be negotiated in every meeting. If the group cannot agree on a style of self-presentation, there may be no communication.

Even after a medium has been chosen, there will be choices about its technical use. This is the final set of decisions to be made in planning an electronic meeting. How many sites should be connected, and how many people will be at each site? When should the meeting be scheduled, and how long should it last? What additional technical aids, such as tape recorders, slide projectors, or computer data bases, are needed? Perhaps the most important criterion in answering these questions is equality of access. Uneven distribution of participants, inferior equipment, time slots which are easier for some participants than others—all these differences could leave some participants feeling resentful or even prevent their participation altogether.

DEVELOPING A CRITICAL PERSPECTIVE

The Camelia scenarios illustrate a few approaches to decisions about tasks, group organization, personal styles, and technical arrangements. These approaches are suggested by the evaluations of the media to date. The usefulness of the evaluations is limited, however. As in other fields, there is an unfortunate tendency in evaluations of new media to measure only those things which are easily measured. The traditional approach, of course, is to control the use of the independent variable— the teleconferencing medium—while studying the effects on relevant dependent variables, such as measures of the quality of communication. All of this might be done in a laboratory, with student subjects performing artificial tasks through a medium they have never used before. However, it is often difficult to generalize from the laboratory to the real world. Even in field tests with real users, it is extremely difficult to isolate the effects of the medium from effects related to tasks, group dynamics, or individual characteristics of the participants. Thus, while the evaluations may be a source of insight about these components of the meeting, they cannot provide specific guidelines for using the media most effectively.

With the complexity of communication in small groups, there can be no list of "Ten Rules for Successful Teleconferencing." The people who actually hold meetings on a day-to-day basis must develop effective and creative strategies for electronic meetings, and there will be no substitute for experience here. However, it will be helpful to develop a critical perspective for making strategic choices about electronic meetings. We can offer four propositions as the foundation for this perspective.

Proposition 1: The System is *Not* the Solution

Contrary to Bell System ads, the system is definitely not the solution. Teleconferencing is the child of engineering, so it is perhaps not surprising that an undue emphasis has been placed on the technology of teleconferencing—often at the expense of social and organizational structures to support communication. Media designers often perceive electronic communication as inherently more rational or efficient than face-to-face communication. Yet such a "technological fix" orientation, however well-intentioned, seems destined to create teleconferencing failures.

A typical "technological fix" problem arises when users of the media rely on technological features to take the place of social procedures in a meeting. For example, a highly structured computer conference may impose organization on a vast and unruly topic, but it may also be perceived as a manipulative maze through which participants must run like laboratory rats. Technologies usually don't know how to bend rules for people who don't behave quite according to expectations. They also don't know when to depart from the prearranged agenda to explore latent conflicts or perceptual differences. These are subtle choices which have to be made again and again by a group, as it experiences its own communication.

When electronics are expected to solve the problems of cross-cultural communications, the problems may be even more dramatic. The Camelia scenarios have explored some of these possible problems, but more illustrations might easily be drawn from real-world experiences. For example, one demonstration teleconference involved participants in two distant countries; a professor in one country lectured to students in the other. The conference rooms, however, were quite unequal in quality—with the students at the low-quality end. Also, there was little consideration of how the meeting might be conducted most effectively. As it happened, participants in the two countries had very different perceptions about professor-student relationships and about the purpose of the teleconference itself. Ignited by the quality imbalance between the two teleconferencing rooms, this cross-cultural "demonstration" became a shouting match with each side making degrading comments about the other.

An emphasis on the technology as the solution to social problems increases the potential for users to feel that they are being directed by the system rather than using it to their advantage. A large investment in specially tailored equipment could fuel this feeling. Over the long run, those who feel constrained by the gadgetry may simply find excuses for not using it rather than use it "ineffectively." While it is easy to focus on "system effectiveness" in making choices about electronic meetings, it is important to remember that the medium of communication is only the *means* which are used to carry information; one must also consider the *ends* to which the medium is being used.

Proposition 2: Face-to-Face is Not Always Best

It is tempting to think of face-to-face communication as a standard to which media designers should aspire. The goal of teleconferencing, then, would be to produce an environment which is as close as possible to the "real thing"—that is, as close as possible to face-to-face. Such a horseless carriage approach, however, invites fundamental mistakes. In fact, as anyone forced to sit through boring meetings can attest, face-to-face communication is often very inefficient and very undesirable. Does anyone *really* want to create electronic versions of all those boring meetings? Why not explore the ways in which electronic media can improve human communication, regardless of whether the new environment is reminiscent of the old?

Recent experience with the Picturephone® provides a classic illustration of this pitfall. The technologists who developed the equipment simply assumed that if a "live" picture could be added to the telephone, people would like it all the more (presumably because it would be the *next* best thing to being there). Yet in the test marketing of the new technology, it became clear that the situation was not so simple. There are times when people don't *want* to be seen as they talk on the telephone. It may be that one of the "limits" of the telephone—its reliance on voice communication only—is actually a strength of the medium in certain situations.[1]

One limit of face-to-face communication is that everyone must be present simultaneously for communication to occur. Computer-based teleconferencing permits a different sort of communication, in which people "meet" asynchronously. They "attend" meetings at their own convenience. Because of this flexibility, computer conferencing may be more efficient than face-to-face in some situations. To make a computer-based conference more like a face-to-face meeting in this regard would clearly limit its potential as a communications medium.

Candid appraisals of electronic meetings should include candid appraisals of face-to-face meetings. There will be situations in which electronic media are more productive and maybe even more human than face-to-face. These situations need to be acknowledged, along with those in which face-to-face is best.

Proposition 3: First Uses Are Not Likely to Be Future Uses

Old communication habits from face-to-face may also distort initial uses of electronic media, obscuring more likely future uses. First-time teleconferencers tend to follow their familiar and comfortable patterns in electronic meetings; over a period

---

[1]The actual strengths and weaknesses of the Picturephone® are still open to some question, since comprehensive tests are impossible without an adequate number of units in operation. There may still be a role for a video telephone, but it probably won't be as general a role as was originally conceived in the "Tomorrowland"-type science fiction stories. Some of the psychological and sociological aspects of this medium are explored in Edward M. Dickson and Raymond Bowers, *The Video Telephone, Impact of a New Era in Telecommunications*, New York: Praeger, 1973.

of time, though, they gradually acquire usage patterns more authentically related to the new medium. If initial sessions are used as guides for organizing future meetings, organizers of teleconferences may overreact to mistakes which would ordinarily be corrected as users become more experienced.

Martin Elton has commented on his own work with the very successful Communications Studies Group by saying: "The work has been based so far upon meetings that now take place; as important in some instances will be those that do not take place (but, in some sense, should). It is worth considering how well someone 15 years ago might have predicted present use of photocopies from statistics on the use of carbon paper."[2] Rather than simply assessing some remake of current communication activities via electronic media, then, we must also examine new possibilities which promise to improve on the current situation.

If first uses are not likely to be future uses, it is also true that first *users* may not be future users. Often, those who initially try out the media are people already familiar with the technology. For example, initial users of computer conferencing have included a large proportion of people who work with computers anyway— either as programmers or as professionals in building, maintaining, and using computerized data bases. Or first users may be top management personnel, whose pressing communication needs justify the cost of an elaborate video teleconferencing room.

As the media become more widely available, however, new groups of users may become more prominent. The needs of these new users will likely suggest modifications to the technology as well as new rules for their use. A range of "intermediate" technologies may replace plush conference rooms as the electronic meeting becomes a useful tool for people in a variety of organizations and positions. The use of portable audio conferencing units in post-secondary education may be part of a trend in this direction.

One factor which can rarely be captured in initial laboratory tests of the new media is creativity. The long-range impacts of teleconferencing will become apparent only as people with real communication problems and previous experience with the media begin to develop creative applications for them. And these applications may not be at all like those promoted by marketing people or media designers.

Proposition 4: More Communication is Not Always Better

Consideration of teleconferencing media is often accompanied by an unexamined assumption that more communication would most certainly be better. While such a belief could be well founded, it merits serious examination in each situation. In many cases, people already have more information than they are able to absorb effectively. The introduction of yet another source of information could make many situations worse rather than better. Communication pollution and information overload are real problems.

The Advanced Research Projects Agency (ARPA) of the U.S. Department of Defense has had a computer network in operation for about 10 years now. The experience with this network provides a valuable insight into this potential problem

---

[2]Martin Elton, *Evaluation of Telecommunications: A Discussion Paper*, Communications Studies Group, London, England, P/74244/ST, 1974.

area. While only limited amounts of teleconferencing occur over the ARPA network, it is possible to send messages freely to any other participant in any of the distant locations served by the network. In some cases, a copy of a message can be sent to everyone with virtually the same effort as sending it to a single person. While the positive potentials of such a technology are obvious, it has also introduced the concept of electronic "junk mail." In fact, some participants have become so annoyed with unwanted messages that they have written "filtering" programs which sort all incoming messages and only accept those on topics of concern to them. All other messages are then returned "unopened."

Experience with the telephone is another source of guidance about the proposition that more communication is not always better. Many organizational managers are beseiged by telephone calls, even when they have secretaries to "protect" them. The telephone, of course, is an interrupting medium: it rings without regard to one's current activity and even imposes feelings of guilt on those who choose to ignore it. But there is a limit to the number of telephone calls a person can return and still perform other functions; many people are already close to this limit. Must new media be *even more* interruptive than the telephone if they are to find a place in the busy manager's communications system?

THE IMPROVEMENT OF COMMUNICATION

Electronic meetings are alternatives to face-to-face meetings—alternatives designed to improve communication by replacing, enhancing, or extending that which currently occurs. They are responses to two problems of face-to-face meetings. The first is the barrier of geographical distance; the second is the barrier of time. The way in which the technologies of electronic media respond to these problems also produces some secondary benefits, such as increased control over interaction. All of these benefits offer a promise of improved communication. Yet improvements in communication cannot be defined in the abstract. There is no such thing as improved communication *per se;* improvements can be defined only by referring to the specific objectives and values of the participants in the communication situation.

Furthermore, as more people get together without regard for the barriers of time and space, new communication concerns will emerge, and new technologies will attempt to respond to these concerns. These new technologies will further change the definition of "improvement." At the same time, they will likely blur the distinctions we have made in this book among audio, video, and computer-based teleconferencing. Even the distinction between electronic and nonelectronic meetings could become less precise as new combinations of face-to-face and electronic communication are explored. Thus, choices of media for a given communication need will not be simple choices: they will require a careful blending of communication resources and needs.

Communication—electronic or otherwise—is a craft. And as with other crafts, it cannot be taught mechanistically. It must be developed through personal experience. The craft cannot be entirely rational, either. While a systematic evaluation of current and alternative communication patterns will increase the chances of successful meetings, some aspects of communication will resist classification. Differing personal communication styles and unique-to-the-moment group dynamics cannot be calculated in advance. The craft of organizing electronic meetings will depend on intuition in concert with analysis.

POSTSCRIPT

MEMO FROM: Bill Owens, The Foundation
TO: Foundation Staff
REGARDING: Some Conclusions about Electronic Meetings

    Now that the Camelia meetings are over, I wanted to
jot down a few ideas about what I think I have learned from
the experience.

    For one thing, I think we all have been a bit too
starry-eyed about these electronic meetings. The technology,
after all, is only part of the communications puzzle, and
it's usually not even the most important part! Electronic
meetings can be used and misused. They haven't <u>solved</u> anything for us.

    Teleconferencing has, though, provided a really dif-
ferent perspective from which to view our own activities.
I realize now that there is a much broader range of communications possibilities than I ever seriously considered.
I was just making too many assumptions about communications
and the way things are done. Now, even when I decide <u>not</u>
to use teleconferencing, a consideration of the alternatives
is really useful to put things in perspective.

    I also think that the Camelia meetings put too much
stress on the meetings themselves, rather than the potential
for more continuous communication. One lesson I have
learned from the Camelia experience is this: single meetings rarely work. What is important is the building of

ongoing communications. And electronic meetings certainly provide some new alternatives for continuous communication. Now we have to find ways to make good use of these possibilities.

What it finally comes down to is that we should all be thinking more about skills in communicating--by whatever medium. Especially important are leadership skills. It's nice to know that we have more communications options open to us, but there won't be any substitute for good leadership. And the skills for leadership are as elusive as ever--maybe more so now that our ways of communicating are broadening.

APPENDIX A

A review of the literature on social evaluation requires detective skills in addition to conventional library research. The studies are scattered, and many have not been formally published. Some were done as proprietary reports and never distributed broadly. Accordingly, we felt a need for a comprehensive summary of evaluation results; we hope that this summary will spare others the frustrations of reviewing this important—but sometimes inaccessible—body of literature.

The findings from the literature are paraphrased in "strengths" and "weaknesses" which are grouped under a series of summary statements.* A classification of studies then provides basic information about the characteristics of each study in chart form. We have attempted to build a bridge between the summary of strengths and weaknesses and the analyses of the scenarios by using codes. For example, in the analysis of the computer teleconferencing scenario, readers will find a code "C25." This code refers to the 25th finding under computer teleconferencing, that "participants can learn to use computer conferencing quickly." Four studies are cited for this finding: Turoff, 1972b and 1975b; Vallee et al., 1975; and Irving, 1976. If readers wish to know more about these studies, they can consult the chart at the end of this appendix for information about the type of study, the medium used, the number and type of participants, the length of media usage, and the conferencing arrangements and tasks. Full references appear in the bibliography.

We have made no attempt to critique the findings presented here; we have merely summarized them. Also, the studies cited are limited to social evaluations of audio, video, or computer-based teleconferencing. Studies from related fields are cited only when the results bear directly on teleconferencing (i.e., small group communication through an electronic medium). Studies of face-to-face communication are cited only where comparisons with mediated communication were involved.

---

*We owe a special debt to James Craig of the Communications Research Centre in Ottawa, Canada, who first suggested a pro's and con's reporting format in an unpublished paper summarizing results from evaluations of audio teleconferencing.

EVALUATIONS OF VIDEO
TELECONFERENCING: STRENGTHS

Video meetings are satisfactory for a wide range of typical business communication tasks, but are particularly valuable—compared to nonvisual media—for complex communication situations.

1. Picturephone® is perceived as more effective than telephone and less effective than face-to-face for all common business situations.	Wish, 1975
2. Video is perceived as satisfactory for giving or receiving information, asking questions, exchanging opinions, solving problems, and generating ideas.	Champness, 1973 Williams and Holloway, 1974 Jull and Mendenhall, 1976
3. The exchange of information is as effective via video as via face-to-face.	Champness and Reid, 1970 Davies, 1971a,b Williams and Holloway, 1974
4. Video is perceived as more satisfactory than face-to-face for handling regularly scheduled communications and for giving or receiving information.	Noll, 1976
5. Video is more useful than audio for complex group discussions, private conversations, and nonprivate dyadic conversations.	Christie, 1974a
6. The more complicated the task, the more the visual channel is likely to make a contribution (and be perceived as necessary).	Westrum, 1972, in Connors, Lindsey, and Miller, 1976
7. The Bell Laboratories' video system has been used for talking to several people at once, communicating with people of the same rank, and communicating within the company.	Noll, 1976
8. Video is perceived to be satisfactory for committee-like coordination and information exchange.	Noll, 1976

Video is more effective than nonvisual media for tasks which stress interpersonal communication.

9. Video is perceived as better than audio for interpersonal relations.†	Champness, 1972a

---

†Indicates existence of contrary findings.

10. Video is perceived as more effective than audio for forming an impression of others.	La Plante, 1971, in Short, Williams, and Christie, 1976 Williams, 1972a,b; 1974c Not shown in Young, 1974
11. Video provides a greater feeling of social contact than audio.	Communications Studies Group, 1975 Short, Williams, and Christie, 1976
12. Video is perceived as better than audio if participants do not know each other.	Christie, 1974b
13. Video is better than audio when reactions must be carefully noted.	Hammond and Elton, 1975
14. Video is more effective than audio for maintaining friendly relations (tentative conclusion).	Williams, 1974c
15. Eye contact is an important part of communication for feedback, synchronization of speech, and affiliative balance.	Argyle, Lalljee, and Cook, 1968
16. There is less group uncertainty when participants can be seen.	Westrum, 1972
17. The sense of presence of the other people via video may be more important than the specific visual information which is communicated.	Communications Studies Group, 1975 Short, Williams, and Christie, 1976
18. Seeing the other person is of real, but limited, value for conversational tasks.	Klemmer, 1973

The visual capabilities inherent in video systems are important advantages for some types of group communication.

19. Video is better than audio when language barriers exist.	Hammond and Elton, 1975
20. For both Italian and English subjects, higher accuracy scores for communicating information about two-dimensional shapes were obtained when gestures were allowed.	Graham, Ricci Bitti, and Argyle, 1975
21. For both English and Italian subjects, emotional messages can be conveyed through facial expressions alone as effectively as by gestures and other bodily clues combined.	Graham, Ricci Bitti, and Argyle, 1975
22. A person's detection, information processing, and retention are greater when both the audio and video senses are used.	Mowbray and Gebhard, 1961

23. Video communication seems essential for situations involving remote supervision of an anesthetic, speech therapy, and psychiatric diagnosis.	Mark, 1975
24. Video teleconferencing can be used to manage successfully more than 90 percent of the medical problems typically encountered in a general ambulatory clinic.	Murphy and Bird, 1974
25. Teleconferencing can serve as a medium for collegial interaction among distantly located health professionals.	Bashshur, 1975
26. When telediagnosis is used, the physician's time with patients can be optimized.	Park, 1975
27. Telemedicine is an integrative mechanism which counters the proliferation of medical specialization.	Bashshur, 1975

Video meetings are orderly, but not necessarily hierarchical.

28. Time spent for maintaining group organization is lower for video than for audio (but greater for video than face-to-face).	Weston, Kristen, and O'Connor, 1975
29. Meetings seem to be conducted more quickly via video than via face-to-face.	Williams and Holloway, 1974
30. Video meetings are perceived to be more orderly than face-to-face meetings.	Champness, 1973 Williams and Holloway, 1974 Ellis, McKay, and Robinson, 1976
31. Internal group structure and hierarchy do not emerge as clearly in video as in face-to-face.	Strickland, Guild, Barefoot, and Patterson, 1975
32. Video has an implicit "unorganized formality"; people are more polite and solicit participation from quiet members in a way that doesn't happen in face-to-face. Leaders do not emerge spontaneously and indeed seem not to be needed.†	George, Coll, Strickland, Patterson, Guild, and McEown, 1975

New users tend to respond positively to video.

33. Video is more aestheic than audio.	Champness, 1972b
34. People tend to react more positively to video (and face-to-face as well) than to audio.	Weston and Kristen, 1973 Ryan and Craig, 1975

35. New users typically have positive feelings toward the use of video teleconferencing.

Duncanson and Williams, 1973
Williams and Holloway, 1974
British Columbia Telephone, 1974
Champness, 1973
Ellis, McKay, and Robinson, 1976

36. People are generally more confident in their perceptions of others via video than via audio, but not necessarily more accurate.

Reid, 1970

37. Video is perceived to be faster and more convenient than the telephone but this perception is not supported by objective measures.

Woodside, Cavers, and Buck, 1971

38. Doctors appear to be more confident in their diagnoses of patients by video or face-to-face than audio.

Moore, Willemain, Bonanno, Clark, Martin, and Mogielnicki, 1975
Not supported in Conrath, Dunn, Bloor, and Tranquada, 1976

39. In a survey of Bell Laboratories' personnel, only 3 percent of travelers would be willing to substitute a system which did not provide moving picture video.

Snyder, 1973

Video meetings may be more "persuasive" than meetings via other media.

40. More opinion change occurs via video than via face-to-face (but less than or the same as via audio).

Short, 1972a,b; 1973a,b

EVALUATIONS OF VIDEO
TELECONFERENCING: WEAKNESSES

Video meetings are not perceived as satisfactory for communicating with strangers or people of different ranks; furthermore, they may not be *necessary* for many tasks for which they are satisfactory.

41. Bell Laboratories' video system is not used for communicating with strangers, talking to only one or two people, or communiating with subordinates or superiors.	Noll, 1976
42. High-status persons may use video telephones to call subordinates, while subordinates would be more likely to use the telephone when communicating with someone of higher rank.	Dickson and Bowers, 1973
43. Participants are more likely to prefer a face-to-face meeting (rather than video) if they have not known each other previously.	Christie and Holloway, 1975 Jull and Mendenhall, 1976
44. Video is perceived as questionable for getting to know someone, bargaining, and persuasion.	Champness, 1973 Short, 1973 Williams and Holloway, 1974 Jull and Mendenhall, 1976
45. Video systems are only marginally superior to audio systems which include telegraphics.	Casey-Stahmer and Havron, 1973
46. Managers are no more likely to choose to telecommunicate rather than travel when video is an option than when audio is an option.	Christie and Kingan, 1976
47. The addition of a visual channel to audio does not appreciably decrease times to solution of simple problems.	Weeks and Chapanis, 1976
48. Less than 20 percent of existing business meetings need to be conducted by video.	Christie and Elton, 1975

While better than audio for some interpersonal tasks, video meetings may not match the quality of face-to-face meetings.

49. Video is sometimes perceived as lacking a sense of personal contact with other participants.	Champness, 1973 Williams, 1973 Short, Williams, and Christie, 1976
50. The feeling of "presence" is low for normal TV screens. A projection display increases feeling of "presence," but is difficult to use and maintain at the present time.	Midorikawa, Yamagishi, Yada, and Miwa, 1975

51. Some very important aspects of social interaction are visual.†

Argyle, 1969

52. In a seminar taught by video, students at locations remote from the professor felt inhibited, had more negative attitudes toward the course, and earned lower grades than those in the same room with him.

Larimer and Sinclair, 1969

53. While remote patient diagnosis was accurate in primary diagnosis, it was not as effective as face-to-face in detecting secondary illnesses.

Conrath, Dunn, Swanson, and Buckingham, 1975
Wempner, 1975
Not supported in Conrath, Dunn, Bloor, and Tranquada, 1976

Some of the Characteristics of video may be perceived as disadvantages by the users.

54. Video systems are less "private" than audio or face-to-face.

Champness, 1972a,b
Ryan, 1975
British Columbia Telephone, 1974

55. Personal communication style (e.g., referring to personal notes while talking) is sometimes more limited by video.

Short, Williams, and Christie, 1976

56. Features of video (e.g., color necessary for map display, as well as wide-angle shots) may be difficult to match to the specific needs of a group.

Christie, 1974b

57. Video is susceptible to a "Hollywood syndrome" where participants—often unconsciously—use film or television as models for how they are to behave.

Bretz, 1974

58. In group-to-group teleconferencing, "we"-to-"they" tendencies can develop, influencing within-terminal and between-terminal communication patterns.

Casey-Stahmer and and Havron, 1973
Weston, Kristen, and O'Connor, 1975
Williams, 1975a
British Columbia Telephone, 1974

59. Even a small distance to a video studio can be a disincentive to participation in a video conference.

Jull and Mendenhall, 1976
Not supported in Christie and Kingan, 1976

*EVALUATIONS OF COMPUTER
TELECONFERENCING: STRENGTHS*

The print mode provides some advantages over the spoken word of other media.

1. The written record basic to the computer conferencing medium is crucial for some tasks.

Sinaiko, 1963
Vallee, Johansen, Lipinski, Spangler, and Wilson, 1975
Ferguson and Johansen, 1975
Vallee and Wilson, 1976
Vallee, Johansen, Lipinski, Spangler, and Wilson, 1978
Spelt, 1977

2. Handwritten messages are more persuasive than video or face-to-face communications.†

Wall and Boyd, 1971

3. Computer conferencing allows time for reflection on the topic of conversation.

Turoff, 1974a
Vallee, Johansen, Lipinski, Spangler, and Wilson, 1978
Ferguson and Johansen, 1975
Zinn, Parnes, and Hench, 1976
Spelt, 1977

4. Typewritten communications are much less verbose than voice channels for solving the same simple problems.

Weeks and Chapanis, 1976

5. Computer conferencing is well suited for communication involving the deaf, the handicapped, and homebound persons.

Turoff, 1975b

---

†Indicates existence of contrary findings.

Computer conferencing increases continuity of communication by making it less dependent on time and space.

6. Access to computer conferencing can make working hours more flexible.	Turoff, 1974a Vallee, Johansen, Lipinski, Spangler, and Wilson, 1975 Ferguson and Johansen, 1975 Hiltz, 1976b Irving, 1976 Vallee, Johansen, Lipinski, Spangler, and Wilson, 1978
7. Computer conferencing can be used well as a preface and/or follow-up to a face-to-face conference.	Vallee and Wilson, 1976
8. Computer conferencing can provide a continuous link among disseminated researchers.	Vallee, Johansen, Lipinski, Spangler, and Wilson, 1975 Zinn, 1977 Vallee, Johansen, Lipinski, Spangler, and Wilson, 1978
9. Computer conferencing can promote communication among disseminated groups who may not otherwise communicate *if* the need to communicate is high enough.	Ferguson and Johansen, 1975 Hiltz, 1976b Irving, 1976 Spelt, 1977
10. With computer conferencing, as many as 50 people can work together on a project.	Turoff, 1975 Irving, 1976

It is possible to get a sense of interpersonal interaction with computer conferencing.

11. Computer conferencing can support self-presentation and emotional subtleties.	Vallee and Johansen, 1974
12. There can be a strong sense of personal interaction.†	Spelt, 1977 Vallee, Johansen, Lipinski, Spangler, and Wilson, 1978

13. Synchronous sessions are seen as more personal than asynchronous sessions and are desired by users.

Vallee, Johansen, Lipinski, Spangler, and Wilson, 1975
Ferguson and Johansen, 1975

Computer conferencing is particularly well suited to tasks involving the management of technical information.

14. Computer conferencing introduces human judgment at a new level in an information system.

Vallee and Askevold, 1975

15. Users have reported an ability to deal with larger amounts of information more efficiently (though beyond a certain point, information overload can occur).

Vallee and Askevold, 1975
Bennett, 1975

16. Computer conferencing appears particularly useful in coordinating technical projects.

Vallee and Askevold, 1975
Vallee and Wilson, 1976

17. Participants can obtain more deliberate answers to technical questions, backed up by written facts and with less delay.

Vallee and Askevold, 1975

18. Computer conferencing can be used to enhance crisis resolution.

Kupperman, Wilcox, and Smith, 1975

19. Computer conferencing can be used to aggregate group judgment.

Turoff, 1972b; 1974a
Lipinski, Lipinski, and Randolph, 1972
Jillson, 1975

20. Computer conferencing is perceived as satisfactory for exchanging information, asking questions, exchanging opinions or orders, staying in touch, and generating ideas.

Vallee, Johansen, Lipinski, Spangler, and Wilson, 1978

Computer conferencing promotes equality and flexibility of roles in the communication situation.

21. Participants vary their roles from conference to conference.

Vallee and Johansen, 1974
Vallee, Johansen, Lipinski, Spangler, and Wilson, 1975

22. Computer conferencing can enhance candor of opinions.

Turoff, 1972a; 1975b
Day, 1975
Vallee and Askevold, 1975
Irving, 1976

23. The amount of communication per partici-   Krueger, 1976, in
pant is more nearly equal in the real-time   Williams, 1976b
typewritten mode than in audio or face-to-face.
(This equality can sometimes be a negative
factor.)

24. Greater equality in group participation can   Vallee, Johansen,
be facilitated by the use of computer conferenc-   Lipinski, Spangler, and
ing, especially in synchronous sessions.   Wilson, 1975
    Ferguson and Johansen,
       1975

Computer conferencing can be used by people without highly specialized skills.

25. Participants an learn to use computer   Turoff, 1972b; 1975b
conferencing quickly.   Vallee, Johansen,
       Lipinski, Spangler, and
       Wilson, 1975
    Irving, 1976

26. Computer expertise is not a prerequisite to   Vallee, Johansen,
effective use of computer conferencing.   Lipinski, Spangler, and
       Wilson, 1975

27. Lack of typing ability is not a barrier to   Vallee, Johansen,
participation in computer conferencing.   Lipinski, Spangler, and
       Wilson, 1975

EVALUATIONS OF COMPUTER
TELECONFERENCING: WEAKNESSES

The written communications inherent in computer conferencing are less efficient than other media.

28. Both audio and face-to-face allow many more messages to be exchanged in a given time period than does typing.	Sinaiki, 1963 Chapanis, Ochsman, Parrish, and Weeks, 1972; Chapanis, 1973 Chapanis and Overby, 1974 Ochsman and Chapanis, 1974 Weeks and Chapanis, 1976 Krueger, 1976, in Williams, 1976b Not supported in Turoff, 1972b
29. Written negotiations take more time, are more rigid, and are more susceptible to developing intransigent positions.	Kite and Vitz, 1966
30. It is sometimes difficult to focus the discussion in computer conferencing.	Ferguson and Johansen, 1975
31. Problems take longer to solve in written modes.	Chapanis, Ochsman, Parrish, and Weeks, 1972 Krueger, 1976, in Williams, 1976b Ochsman and Chapanis, 1974
32. Participants are sometimes reluctant to make certain statements in writing.	Kite and Vitz, 1966 Vallee, Johansen, Lipinski, Spangler, and Wilson, 1975
33. Computer conferencing is perceived as unsatisfactory for bargaining, resolving disagreements, persuasion,[†] and getting to know someone.	Vallee, Johansen, Lipinski, Spangler, and Wilson, 1978

The self-activated nature of the medium may inhibit its use.

34. Regularity of individual participation is sometimes difficult to enforce in computer conferencing.	Vallee, Johansen, Lipinski, Spangler, and Wilson, 1975 Ferguson and Johansen, 1975 Spelt, 1977
35. A perceived need to communicate is necessary to encourage regular participation in computer conferencing.	Vallee and Johansen, 1974 Vallee, Johansen, Lipinski, Spangler, and Wilson, 1975
36. In written or typewritten communication, the amount of time spent in noncommunicative activities is much greater than in the oral mode.	Ochsman and Chapanis, 1974
37. Managers have a strong preference for verbal and immediate (often unscheduled) communication.	Mintzberg, 1971

The communication process in computer conferencing is very demanding.

38. Training of new users is very important.	Vallee, Johansen, Lipinski, Spangler, and Wilson, 1975 Irving, 1976
39. Participants must learn new skills to use computer conferencing (e.g., how to send a message).	Vallee, Johansen, Lipinski, Spangler, and Wilson, 1975
40. Computer conferencing is vulnerable to poor human/machine interface with both computer networks and computer terminals.	Vallee, Johansen, Lipinski, Spangler, and Wilson, 1975
41. Computer conferencing could easily be used to confuse other participants.	Vallee, Lipinski, Johansen, and Wilson, 1975
42. The volume of information in a computer conference can sometimes become overwhelming.	Ferguson and Johansen, 1975 Vallee, Johansen, Lipinski, Spangler, and Wilson, 1978
43. In synchronous computer conferencing, messages are not sequential and multiple topic threads can appear; information overload can thus result.	Vallee and Wilson, 1976 Vallee, 1976
44. Computer conferencing demands strong leadership.	Johansen, Vallee, and Palmer, 1976

The sense of interpersonal interaction is sometimes weak in computer conferencing.

45. There is often a lack of interpersonal feedback; those who perceive the need for immediate feedback might thus be frustrated.	Ferguson and Johansen, 1975
46. Participants sometimes feel a lack of group interaction.	Ferguson and Johansen, 1975
47. Questions asked within computer conferences often go unanswered.	Hiltz, 1976b
48. The use of surrogates in a computer conference can inhibit levels of trust and security.	Vallee, Johansen, Lipinski, Spangler, and Wilson, 1978
49. French Canadians react more negatively to computers and their potential than do English Canadians.	Ryan and Cummings, 1973

EVALUATIONS OF AUDIO
TELECONFERENCING: STRENGTHS

Audio meetings are adequate for a number of typical business and research situations; they are particularly satisfactory for communications tasks which stress information exchange and problem-solving.

1. The telephone is not in any simple sense inferior to face-to-face contact.	Reid, 1976
2. Audio is perceived as only slightly less satisfactory than face-to-face meetings.	Craig and Jull, 1974 Weston and Kristen, 1973
3. Managers are no more likely to choose to telecommunicate rather than travel when video is an option than when audio is an option.	Christie and Kingan, 1976
4. About 40 percent of existing business meetings *could be* conducted by audio or audio-plus-graphics.	Christie and Elton, 1975 (3 CSG surveys)
5. Simple problem-solving can be effectively conducted via audio.	Davies, 1971a,b Champness, 1971; 1972a,b Short, 1971a,b; 1972a,b Woodside, Cavers, and Buck, 1971 Chapanis, Ochsman, Parrish, and Weeks, 1972 Connors, Lindsey, and Miller, 1976 Thomas and Williams, 1975 Christie, 1975b
6. Meetings which emphasize "information-seeking" and "discussion of ideas" can be effectively conducted via audio.	Williams, 1974c Connors, Lindsey, and Miller, 1976 Thomas and Williams, 1975
7. Audio is satisfactory for giving orders, decision-making, settling a difference of opinion,† and holding briefings.	Stapley, 1973
8. Audio is good for continuing contacts with those with whom one is already acquainted.	Connors, Lindsey, and Miller, 1976
9. There is no difference in output or quality of ideas in audio brainstorming sessions compared to video and face-to-face.†	Williams, 1975a

---

†Indicates existence of contrary findings.

10. The visual channel is not necessary for gaining initial perceptions of others and in understanding how others perceive you.†   Young, 1974b

11. Audio meetings are generally perceived as at least as "rewarding," "friendly," and "enjoyable" as face-to-face committee meetings.   Christie, 1975a

12. Audio can be used as effectively as face-to-face or video for interviewing.   Reid, 1970
Janofsky, 1971
Young, 1974a

13. Audio is perceived to be effective for crisis decision-making when a face-to-face meeting would not be possible.   Thomas and Williams, 1975
Short, 1973c

14. For conducting psychiatric interviews, the telephone can be used as effectively as face-to-face.   Simon, Fleiss, Fisher, and Gurland, 1974

15. Teleconferencing can serve as a medium for collegial interaction among distantly located health professionals.   Bashshur, 1975

16. Audio teleconferencing, used by sophisticated health professionals, is suitable for most neighborhood health clinics, chronic disease follow-up programs, etc.   Mark, 1975

In intense communication situations, such as bargaining or negotiation, audio meetings may offer subtle advantages to some participants.

17. In negotiation, the side with the strongest case is more successful in audio than in face-to-face.   Morley and Stephenson, 1969; 1970
Short, 1971a, b
Weeks and Chapanis, 1976

18. In bargaining and negotiation via audio, effective communication is less dependent on interpersonal than on substantive considerations; a visual image can actually be distracting to the substantive proceedings.   Sinaiko, 1963
Morley and Stephenson, 1969; 1970
Short, 1971a; 1974

19. More opinion change occurs as one effect in conflict situations via audio than face-to-face (implying that audio is better for persuading or adopting another point of view).   Short, 1972a,b; 1973b
Young, 1974b (but not statistically significant)

20. Participants feel it is easier to get a point across without a lengthy debate in audio than in face-to-face.   Christie, 1975a

21. Individuals are perceived as more persuasive and trustworthy via audio than face-to-face or video.

Short, 1972c

22. Lying is easier to detect in audio than in face-to-face.

Krauss, in Williams, 1976
Maier and Thurber, 1968
Reid, 1970 (found no significant difference between audio and face-to-face)

23. Audio is percieved as more revealing than video or face-to-face during interviews.

Young, 1974a

Audio permits rapid communication, with less travel.

24. Audio meetings are shorter than face-to-face meetings.

Craig and Jull, 1974
Short, 1973
Casey-Stahmer and Havron, 1973
Christie, 1975a
Mendenhall and Ryan, 1975
Thomas and Williams, 1975

25. Media which involve voice communication are much faster than writing or typing.

Ochsman and Chapanis, 1974

26. Audio tends to be faster than face-to-face for simple problem-solving experiments when unlimited time is available.

Davies, 1971a
Not supported in Chapanis, Ochsman, Parrish, and Weeks, 1972

27. Audio is most useful when meetings are *short* and *regular*.

Short, Williams, and Christie, 1976

28. Audio can be most useful when people are more than one-half hour apart.

Williams, 1975c
Short, Williams, and Christie, 1976

29. Audio has been highly successful in reducing the total amount of traveling done by a bank's management staff.

Christie, 1975a

Audio permits accurate communication.

30. Accuracy in the transmission and reception of information is not affected by the absence of vision.

Champness and Reid, 1970
Davies, 1971a,b
Reid, 1976
Stapley, 1973
Simon, Fleiss, Fisher, and Gurland, 1974

31. Participants feel they are more attentive to what is being said in an audio system than face-to-face .

Christie, 1975a

32. Audio is at least as effective as face-to-face for assessing other persons.

Giedt, 1955
Maier and Thurber, 1968
Reid, 1970

33. The audio channel can provide all the basic information necessary for preliminary medical diagnosis.

Conrath, Bloor, Dunn, and Tranquada, 1976

Audio promotes controlled participation.

34. Meetings are more orderly ("business-like") in audio than in face-to-face.

Short, 1973c
Jull, McCaughern, Mendenhall, Storey, Tassie, and Zalatan, 1976

35. Audio allows more control over individuals who dominate the conversation and thus more chance for everyone to participate.

Holloway and Hammond, 1976

EVALUATIONS OF AUDIO
TELECONFERENCING: WEAKNESSES

Audio meetings are not satisfactory for tasks which stress interpersonal communication, such as negotiation or getting to know someone.

36. Audio is not satisfactory when emotions run high or nature of the task is "complex."	Connors, Lindsey, and Miller, 1976
37. Participants feel that audio is not satisfactory for such activities as resolving conflicts, persuading others,† resolving disagreements,† or negotiating.	Short, 1973c Craig and Jull, 1974 Thomas and Williams, 1975 Connors, Lindsey, and Miller, 1976 Christie, 1975a
38. There is no more breakdown in negotiation via audio than face-to-face.	Dorris, Gentry, and Kelley, 1970, in Short, 1971a Short, 1971a Champness, 1971
39. Audio meetings are not satisfactory for forming impressions of others.†	Craig and Jull, 1974
40. Audio is not perceived to be satisfactory for getting to know someone.†	Stapley, 1973 Craig and Jull, 1974 Thomas and Williams, 1975 Connors, Lindsey, and Miller, 1976
41. Audio can be poorly received if participants have not known each other previously.	Christie and Holloway, 1975 Connors, Lindsey, and Miller, 1976 Jull and Mendenhall, 1976
42. For "getting to know someone," people who have met face-to-face or via video are judged more favorably than people who have met by telephone.	Williams, 1972a; 1975b

Audio can create an impersonal, uncooperative communications environment.

43. Audio is perceived as less "personal" than face-to-face.	Morley and Stephenson, 1969 Williams, 1972a Short, 1973c Holloway and Hammond, 1976

44. Nonverbal cues are important to indicate the psychological state of each participant (e.g., their reactions) in the progress of the interaction.

Argyle, Lalljee, and Cook, 1969
Duncan, 1969

45. There is often skepticism concerning the content of a message in an audio-only conference, especially when the message is not followed by a written note.

Mendenhall and Ryan, 1975

46. In group-to-group teleconferencing, "we" to "they" tendencies can develop, influencing within-terminal and between-terminal communication patterns.

Casey-Stahmer and Havron, 1973
Weston, Kristen, and O'Connor, 1975
Williams, 1975a

47. Audio environment is considerably more "hostile" than either video or face-to-face.

Weston, Kristen, and O'Connor, 1975

48. In negotiation situations, such as the game called "Prisoners' Dilemma," cooperation is difficult to achieve using audio.

Wichman, 1970
La Plante, 1971, in Short, Williams, and Christie, 1976
Not replicated by Heilbron, 1971, in Wilson, 1974

49. In controlled experiments, individuals will administer more severe shocks to victims they cannot see.

Milgram, 1965
Not supported in Penner and Hawkins, 1971, in Short, Williams, and Christie, 1976

Audio may be less productive than other media.

50. Audio groups spend less time on task-related discussion (about 10 percent less) than either video or face-to-face.†

Weston, Kristen, and O'Connor, 1975

51. An unseen audience inhibits cognitive performance more than a visible audience.

Wapner and Alper, 1952

52. Fewer words were spoken in a given time period via audio than via either video or face-to-face.

Weston, Kristen, and O'Connor, 1975
Not supported in Chapanis, 1973

53. In a conference held to generate recommendations, audio groups made far fewer and less complex recommendations.

Weston, Kristen, and O'Connor, 1975

54. Audio meetings are not satisfactory for generating ideas.†

Craig and Jull, 1974

55. While remote patient diagnosis was accurate in primary diagnosis, it was less effective than face-to-face in detecting secondary illnesses.

Conrath, Dunn, Swanson, and Buckingham, 1975
Not supported in Conrath, Dunn, Bloor, and Tranquada, 1976

Audio meetings are personally demanding.

56. Audio meetings require more chairman control than face-to-face.

Short, 1973c

57. Time spent for maintaining group organization was greater for audio than for face-to-face.

Weston, Kristen, and O'Connor, 1975

58. Audio meetings are more tiring than face-to-face meetings.

Short, 1973c
Jull, McCaughern, Mendenhall, Storey, Tassie, and Zalatan, 1976
Not supported by Mendenhall and Ryan, 1975
Christie, 1975a

59. Varied accents are often difficult to understand over the telephone.

Woodside, Cavers, and Buck, 1971

Users typically have negative expectations about audio.

60. People often react negatively to audio teleconferencing.

Weston and Kristen, 1973
Ryan and Craig, 1975
Christie, 1975a

61. Audio promotes more initial skepticism on the part of users than does video or face-to-face.

Mendenhall and Ryan, 1975

62. In a survey of Bell Laboratories' personnel, only 3 percent of travelers would be willing to substitute a system which did not provide video capability.

Snyder, 1973

63. Patients prefer color video to audio for communicating with a doctor during remote diagnosis.

Conrath, Dunn, Bloor and Tranquada, 1976
Not supported in Moore, Willemain, Bonanno, Clark, Martin, and Mogielnicki, 1975

64. Doctors are more confident in their diagnoses of patients by video or face-to-face than by audio.

Moore, Willemain, Bonanno, Clark, Martin, and Mogielnicki, 1975

EVALUATIONS OF FACE-TO-FACE
CONFERENCING: STRENGTHS

Face-to-face meetings are particularly important for intense, interpersonal communication tasks.

1. Face-to-face is better than audio or video for interpersonal relations and for conflict.	Champness, 1972a

2. Meetings which emphasize "conflict" probably should be conducted via face-to-face rather than via audio or video.	Wichman, 1970
	La Plante, 1971, in
	    Short, Williams,
	    and Christie, 1976
	Dorris, Gentry, and
	    Kelley, 1972, in
	    Williams, 1974c
	Short, 1972a
	Williams, 1974b

3. Meetings which emphasize "negotiation" should be conducted via face-to-face rather than via audio or video.	Morley and Stephenson, 1969; 1970 Champness, 1971 Short, 1971a,b
4. Face-to-face is better than both audio and video for persuasion.	Short, 1973b
5. Meetings for "disciplinary interview" should be conducted via face-to-face rather than via audio or video.	Williams, 1975a
6. Meetings for "presentation of a report" can be conducted more effectively via face-to-face than via audio or video.	Williams, 1975a
7. The most important aspects of social interaction are transmitted in the visual channel.	Argyle, 1969

Face-to-face meetings promote greater information exchange than audio or video.

8. Time spent for maintaining group organization is less for face-to-face than for either video or audio.	Weston, Kristen, and O'Connor, 1975
9. More possible solutions to a problem are discussed in face-to-face than in audio before reaching a decision.	Davies, 1971a,b Champness, 1971

10. More messages are exchanged face-to-face than via other media in a given amount of time.	Chapanis, Ochsman, Parrish, and Weeks, 1972 Chapanis, 1973 Chapanis and Overby, 1974 Ochsman and Chapanis, 1974 Weeks and Chapanis, 1976

Face-to-face is a "friendly" medium.

11. Face-to-face meetings are more friendly than video meetings.	Williams and Holloway, 1974
12. In face-to-face meetings, people are much more likely to address their remarks to the group as a whole; in audio or video meetings, there is more tendency to address individuals or a subgroup.	Weston, Kristen, and O'Connor, 1975
13. There is less tendency to inflict pain when a victim is visible than when he is isolated.	Milgram, 1965

Face-to-face is more "commanding" than other media.

14. There is a greater tendency to obey commands issued via face-to-face than those issued remotely.	Milgram, 1965
15. In controlled experiments in which subjects are ordered to shock another person, subjects are more likely to be obedient when orders are given face-to-face rather than over the telephone.	Milgram, 1965

People generally prefer face-to-face to other media.

16. Face-to-face is generally rated more favorably than audio or video.	Champness, 1972a,b Christie and Elton, 1975 Ryan and Craig, 1975
17. Discussions held by audio or video are generally judged less favorably than discussions held face-to-face.	Christie and Elton, 1975 Champness, 1972a,b Ryan and Craig, 1975

18. Face-to-face is preferred over teleconferencing for meetings which are important or complex.	Connors, Lindsey, and Miller, 1976
19. People are generally more confident in their perceptions of others based on face-to-face meetings than those based on either audio or video, though they are not necessarily more accurate.	Reid, 1970
20. A doctor's confidence in a diagnosis is greater in face-to-face situations than in either audio or video situations.	Moore, Willemain, Bonanno, Clark, Martin, and Mogielnicki, 1975 Not replicated in Conrath, Dunn, Bloor, and Tranquada, 1976
21. Patients prefer face-to-face to remote diagnosis via either audio or video.	Conrath, Dunn, Bloor, and Tranquada, 1976

EVALUATIONS OF FACE-TO-FACE
CONFERENCING: WEAKNESSES

While face-to-face is preferred for many communication tasks, it may not be necessary.

22. Only about 30 percent of all business meetings actually require face-to-face contact.	Christie and Elton, 1975, (3 CSG surveys)

The "personal" nature of face-to-face may inhibit communication in some situations.

23. Face-to-face communication is more dependent on interpersonal or interparty considerations than is audio.	Morley and Stephenson, 1969; 1970 Short, 1971a, 1974
24. In negotiation situations, face-to-face meetings (and video meetings) emphasize the affective content of messages compared to audio or written media.	Wichman, 1970 La Plante, 1971, in Short, Williams and Christie, 1976
25. In conflict situations, face-to-face may create visual distractions which reduce participants' concentration on their arguments and those of others.	Short, Williams, and Christie, 1976
26. For meetings of short duration where long travel time is involved, persons will prefer to telecommunicate rather than attend a face-to-face meeting.	Christie and Kingan, 1976 Duncanson and Williams, 1973
27. Face-to-face meetings tend to be dominated by one person, thus limiting the range of ideas suggested and the quality of the final decisions.	Hiltz, 1975a Hiltz and Turoff, 1976

A CLASSIFICATION OF SOCIAL EVALUATIONS OF TELECONFERENCING

Citation	Organizational affiliation	Type of study	Medium(ia) used
Argyle, 1969	Oxford University	Theoretical analysis; literature review	Primarily face-to-face
Argyle, Lalljee, and Cook, 1968	Oxford University	Laboratory experiments	Face-to-face; simulated audio
Bashshur, 1975	University of Michigan	Literature review; theoretical analysis	Video
Bretz, 1974	Rand Corporation	Field test	Video (the MRC system)
British Columbia Telephone, 1974	British Columbia Telephone	Field test	Video
Casey-Stahmer and Havron, 1973	Human Sciences Research, Inc.	Survey (interviews); theoretical analysis	Bell Canada: video; DINA: audio + facsimile; DOC: audio + graphics; FNCB: video + graphics
Champness, 1971	Communications Studies Group	Laboratory experiment	Face-to-face; television; audio
Champness, 1972a	Communications Studies Group	Laboratory experiment	Audio; close-up television; broader view television

*"Subject" refers to those paid or unpaid subjects who used the media for simulated tasks; all others used the media to perform their normal activities.

**Brief = less than one hour.

Number and type of participants	Length of media usage	Conferencing arrangements	Task(s) or purpose(s) of conferencing usage
Primarily subjects*	——	Varied	Varied
Subjects (28 students at University of Delaware; 32 students at Oxford; 80 middle-aged adult education students)	Brief**	Dyads	Interviews
——	——	Medical professional to patient	Remote diagnosis
Senior and middle level personnel	3 years	Multipoint	Varied
134 British Columbia Telephone employees, businessmen, students (no cost to users)	Varied	Group-to-group	Varied business meetings
7 middle level personnel at Bell Canada; 8 middle level personnel at Department of Indian and Northern Affairs; 6 middle level personnel at Department of Communications, Canada; 4 senior managers at First National City Bank (NY)	Bell Canada, DINA, DOC: several months; FNCB: 12 years	Group-to-group	Bell Canada: demonstration; DINA: coordination with remote sites of DINA; DOC: experimental; FNCB: management meetings
214 male subjects	Brief	Group-to-group (2 acquaintances, 2 strangers)	Bargaining
112 subjects (senior British civil servants)	Brief	Dyads	Varied

Citation	Organizational affiliation	Type of study	Medium(ia) used
Champness, 1972b	Communications Studies Group	Laboratory experiment	Face-to-face; loud-speaking audio; closed-circuit television
Champness, 1973	Communications Studies Group	Survey (question-naires)	Video
Champness and Reid, 1970	Communications Studies Group	Laboratory experiment	Face-to-face; simulated audio; telephone
Chapanis, 1973	Johns Hopkins University	Laboratory experiment	Typewriting; handwriting; simulated audio; face-to-face
Chapanis, Ochsman, Parrish and Weeks, 1972	Johns Hopkins University	Laboratory experiment	Typewriting; handwriting; simulated audio; face-to-face
Chapanis and Overbey, 1974	Johns Hopkins University	Laboratory experiment	Audio; typewriting

Number and type of participants	Length of media usage	Conferencing arrangements	Task(s) or purpose(s) of conferencing usage
72 subjects (managerial British civil servants)	Brief	Dyads	Discussion of personal choices (from Kogan and Wallack's "Choice Dilemmas" questionnaires)
200 subjects (middle level British Post Office personnel)	Brief (almost 75 percent were first-time users)	Group-to-group	Information exchange; trying out Confravision
72 subjects (male students)	Brief (about 5 minutes per medium)	Dyads	Communication of contents of a business letter
Subjects (40 high school boys, 32 Johns Hopkins students)	Brief	Dyads	Finding address of a physician closest to a hypothetical residence; assembling a trash can carrier; similar simple problems
40 subjects (high school boys)	Brief	Dyads	Finding address of a physician closest to a hypothetical residence; assembling a trash can carrier; similar simple problems
32 subjects (college students)	Brief period for each of 4 days	Dyads	Finding address of a physician closest to a hypothetical residence; assembling a trash can carrier; similar simple problems

Citation	Organizational affiliation	Type of study	Medium(ia) used
Christie, 1974a	Communications Studies Group	Laboratory experiment	3 different types of audio; black-and-white television
Christie, 1974b	Communications Studies Group	Survey (interviews)	Video
Christie, 1974d	Communications Studies Group	Laboratory experiment	Face-to-face; television; telephone; letter; audio
Christie, 1975a (Chapter X)	New Rural Society Project	Field test	Stereophonic audio plus facsimile
Christie and Elton, 1975	Communications Studies Group	Literature review of Communications Studies Group studies	Audio; video; face-to-face
Christie and Holloway, 1975	Communications Studies Group	Laboratory experiment	Audio; video
Christie and Kingan, 1976	Communications Studies Group	Laboratory experiment	Audio; video
Communications Studies Group, 1975	Communications Studies Group	Literature review of Communications Studies Group studies	Audio; video; face-to-face
Connors, Lindsey and Miller, 1976	National Aeronautics and Space Administration	Survey (questionnaires)	Audio teleconferencing rooms; portable audio (Bell 50A); conference telephone calls

Number and type of participants	Length of media usage	Conferencing arrangements	Task(s) or purpose(s) of conferencing usage
36 subjects (American business executives)	5 minutes per medium	Group-to-group (3 per group)	General discussion
13 middle level personnel at Department of Environment, London	One group: 6 months; other group: 1 meeting	Group-to-group	Information exchange; general discussion
36 subjects (civil servants)	Three 5-minute discussions per person	Dyads	Attempt agreement on ways of reducing rise of crime, cost of housing, and pollution in British cities
24 upper and middle level management personnel	6 months	Group-to-group	Business meetings between 2 branches of a bank, 45 miles apart
——	——	——	——
104 subjects (management level volunteers from business and government)	Brief	Group-to-group (2 or 3 per group)	Simulated business meetings
50 subjects (volunteer civil servants)	Brief (25–50 minutes)	Group-to-group (2 per group)	Media evaluation
——	——	——	Varied
162 senior and middle level personnel from 5 NASA installations	6 months (less than once per month)	Group-to-group and multipoint	Program review; general planning, management; education

Citation	Organizational affiliation	Type of study	Medium(ia) used
Conrath, Bloor, Dunn, and Tranquada, 1976	University of Waterloo; University of Toronto; Flemingdom Health Center, Toronto	Field experiment	Color television; black-and-white television; still frame black-and-white television; and hands-free telephone
Conrath, Dunn, Swanson, and Buckingham, 1975	University of Waterloo; University of Toronto; Peat, Marwick, and Partners, Toronto	Field experiment	Color television; black-and-white television; hands-free telephone; face-to-face
Craig and Jull, 1974	Communications Research Center, (CRC), Canada	Field experiment	Face-to-face; audio plus graphics
Davies, 1971a	Communications Studies Group	Laboratory experiment	Face-to-face; telephone
Davies, 1971b	Communications Studies Group	Laboratory experiment	Face-to-face; telephone
Day, 1975	Bell Canada	Descriptive analysis; literature review	Computer-based teleconferencing
Dickson and Bowers, 1973	Cornell University	Literature review and analysis (authors call it a "preliminary technology assessment")	Varieties of the video telephone
Duncan, 1969	University of Chicago	Literature review	Primarily face-to-face
Duncanson and Williams, 1973	Bell Laboratories	Field test	Video (Bell Laboratories System)
Ellis, McKay, and Robinson, 1976	Swinburne Institute of Technology; Telecom Australia	Survey (interviews)	Video (Telecom Australia System)

Number and type of participants	Length of media usage	Conferencing arrangements	Task(s) or purpose(s) of conferencing usage
10 doctors (7 male, 3 female); 1 nurse; 1,015 patients visiting a medical clinic (volunteered to be examined via teleconference, as well as normal visit)	Diagnostic session: less than 1 hour per patient; doctors used varied modes	Dyads (physician to patient, with nurse present)	Medical diagnosis
32 patients; 8 physicians; 6 nurses	Brief (average exam less than 15 minutes)	Dyads (physician to patient, with nurse present)	Remote diagnosis
Senior research managers and United Way planning group	Several months	Group-to-group	Normal business meetings
40 subjects (British civil servants; 36 males, 4 females)	Brief	Dyads	Factory-location problem (specially developed)
Subjects (British civil servants)	Brief	Dyads	Factory-location problem (specially developed)
Varied	Varied	Multipoint	Varied
—	—	Primarily dyads	—
Primarily subjects	Varied	Varied	Varied
197 senior and middle level Bell Laboratory employees (no cost to users)	Varied	Group-to-group (3–4 per group)	Normal inter-laboratory meetings between two Bell Labs locations
21 users of the Confravision service who had not continued to use it; paid at rate of $150 per hour	One-half to several hours	Group-to-group	Varied business meetings

Citation	Organizational affiliation	Type of study	Medium(ia) used
Ferguson and Johansen, 1975	Institute for the Future/Lilly Endowment, Inc.	Field test (with postconference questionnaire)	Computer-based teleconferencing
Giedt, 1955	——	Laboratory experiment	Written transcripts; sound recordings; film plus sound
Graham, Ricci Bitti, and Argyle, 1975	Oxford University	Laboratory experiment	Videotape; limited image videotape
Hammond and Elton, 1976	Communications Studies Group	Literature review; descriptive analysis	Audio; video; face-to-face
Hiltz, 1975a	New Jersey Institute of Technology (NJIT)	Literature review of small group research	Face-to-face
Hiltz, 1976a	New Jersey Institute of Technology	Literature review of small group research (face-to-face); descriptive analysis	Computer-based teleconferencing; face-to-face
Hiltz, 1976b	New Jersey Institute of Technology	Literature review of small group research (face-to-face); descriptive analysis	Computer-based teleconferencing; face-to-face
Hiltz Turoff, 1976	New Jersey Institute of technology	Descriptive analysis and projections	Computer-based teleconferencing
Holloway and Hammond, 1976	Communications Studies Group; Open University	Survey (interviews)	Telephone conference calls
Hough, 1976	Stanford Research Institute	Catalogue and descriptive analysis of existing teleconferencing systems	Audio; video; computer-based teleconferencing

Number and type of participants	Length of media usage	Conferencing arrangements	Task(s) or purpose(s) of conferencing usage
19 senior and middle level personnel (no cost to users)	1 week (with brief training period preceding)	Multipoint	Information exchange; discussion of ideas; policy formulation
48 psychiatrists, social workers, and psychologists	Brief	Dyads	Judging patient via recorded interview
Subjects (English and Italian)	Brief	Dyads	Communicating description of a two-dimensional object
—	—	—	Varied
Varied	Varied	Varied	Varied
—	—	—	—
—	—	—	—
—	—	—	—
29 students and faculty using the telephone in teaching at the Open University, London	About 1 year	Multipoint	Faculty/student meetings during academic courses
Varied	Varied	Varied	Varied

Citation	Organizational affiliation	Type of study	Medium(ia) used
Irving, 1976	University of Waterloo	Case study; survey (questionnaires)	Computer-based teleconferencing and message-switching
Janofsky, 1971	University of Oregon	Laboratory experiment	Telephone; face-to-face
Jillson, 1975	Nonmedical Use of Drugs Directorate, Canadian Government	Case study	Computer-based conferencing and response elicitation
Johansen, Vallee, and Palmer, 1976	Institute for the Future	Preliminary analysis of extended field test	Computer conferencing
Jull, McCaughern, Mendenhall, Storey, Tassie, and Zalatan, 1976	Department of Communications (DOC), Canada	Review of research by Department of Communications, Canada; laboratory experiments and surveys, descriptive analysis	Audio; audio plus graphics; video
Jull and Mendenhall, 1976	Department of Communications, Canada	Literature review	Audio; audio plus graphics; video
Kettering Foundation (forthcoming)	Kettering Foundation	Survey	Computer conferencing
Kite and Vitz, 1966	Institute for Defense Analyses	Laboratory experiment	Teletype; audio; face-to-face
Klemmer, 1973	Bell Labs	Theoretical analysis; literature review	Audio; video; face-to-face
Kupperman and Wilcox, 1975	Personal proposal	Theoretical proposal	Computer-based teleconferencing

Number and type of participants	Length of media usage	Conferencing arrangements	Task(s) or purpose(s) of conferencing usage
About 40	10 months	Multipoint	Coordination among regional centers of the Non-medical Use of Drugs Directorate in Canada
160 subjects (paid student volunteers)	10 minutres	Dyads	Interview to get to know strangers
About 20	About 2 months	Multipoint	Information exchange and polling
About 100 energy researchers	12–15 months	Multipoint	Varied; primarily coordination of energy research projects
Varied	——	Primarily group-to-group	Varied
——	——	Primarily group-to-group	Varied
About 50 scientists, teachers, and administrators	1–3 months	Multipoint	Varied
Subjects	Several hours	Multipoint	Crisis simulation ("Summit")
——	——	——	Varied
——	——	Varied	Crisis Management

Citation	Organizational affiliation	Type of study	Medium(ia) used
LaPlante, 1971	University of Windsor	Laboratory experiment (M.A. thesis)	Face-to-face; closed circuit TV; telephone
Larimer and Sinclair, 1969	Pennsylvania State University	Field test	Video
Maier and Thurber, 1968	University of Michigan	Laboratory experiment	Face-to-face; audio; written transcript
Mark, 1975	Varied	Theoretical analysis	Video
Mendenhall and Ryan, 1975	Communications Research Center, Canada	Laboratory experiment	Audio; video; face-to-face
Midorikawa, Yamagishi, Yada, and Miwa, 1975	Electrical Communication Laboratories, Tokyo	Field test	Video plus graphics
Milgram, 1965	——	Laboratory experiment	Face-to-face; audio
Mintzberg, 1971	McGill University	Participant observation	Face-to-face; telephone; mail
Moore, Willemain, Bonanno, Clark, Martin, and Mogielnicki, 1975	Cambridge Hospital	Field experiment	Television; telephone
Morley and Stephenson, 1969	University of Nottingham	Laboratory experiment	Variations of face-to-face and telephone
Morley and Stephenson, 1970	University of Nottingham	Laboratory experiment	Variations of face-to-face and telephone
Mowbray and Gebhard, 1961	Johns Hopkins University	Theoretical analysis	All sensory modes

Number and type of participants	Length of media usage	Conferencing arrangements	Task(s) or purpose(s) of conferencing usage
Subjects	Brief	Dyads	Problem solving ("Prisoners Dilemma" game)
22 teachers taking a graduate course at Pennsylvania State University	1 semester	Group-to-group (11 per group)	Graduate seminar in education
Subjects	Brief	Subject watching, listening, or reading about the role play	Judging accuracy of role-played situation
—	—	Primarily medical professionals to patients	Primarily remote diagnosis
51 subjects (middle level civil servants)	Brief (about 30 minutes per medium)	Group-to-group	Personnel management problem
About 150 senior and middle level personnel	At least 3 hours	Group-to-group	Business meetings
Subjects	Brief	Dyads	Giving orders
Corporate managers	Varied	Varied	Varied
354 patients; 3 practitioner nurses; several physicians	7 months	Dyads (physician to patient, with nurse present)	Remote medical diagnosis
Subjects	40 minutes or less	Dyads	Industrial negotiation problem
Subjects	40 minutes or less	Dyads	Industrial negotiation problem
—	—	Varied	Varied

Citation	Organizational affiliation	Type of study	Medium(ia) used
Murphy and Bird, in Shinn, 1975	——	Field test	Video
Noll, 1976	Bell Laboratories, AT&T	Survey (questionnaires)	Video conferencing
Ochsman and Chapanis, 1974	Johns Hopkins University	Laboratory experiment	Various combinations of teletype, handwriting, typewriting, video, audio, and face-to-face
Panko, Pye and Hough, 1976	Stanford Research Institute and Communications Studies Group	Technology assessment	Video; audio; telephone
Park, 1975	Alternate Media Center	Literature review; theoretical analysis	Video
Penner and Hawkins, 1971	——	Laboratory experiment	Face-to-face audio
Pye, 1976	Communications Studies Group; Stanford Research Institute	Literature review; descriptive analysis	Audio; video; face-to-face
Reid, 1970	Communications Studies Group	Literature review; primarily laboratory experiments	Audio (usually telephone); face-to-face
Reid, 1976	British Post Office	Literature review, primarily laboratory experiments	Telephone; face-to-face
Ryan, 1975	Communications Research Center, Canada	Laboratory experiment	Audio; video; face-to-face
Ryan and Craig, 1975	Communications Research Center, Canada	Laboratory experiment	Video; audio; face-to-face

Number and type of participants	Length of media usage	Conferencing arrangements	Task(s) or purpose(s) of conferencing usage
1,000 subjects (patients)	——	Telediagnosis; patient, physician, and support personnel	Telediagnosis
21 senior and middle level personnel sampled from all users of video system at Bell Labs (represents 7 different user groups)	10 video conferences over last year	Group-to-group	Committee-like coordination; information exchange
120 subjects (male undergraduates at Johns Hopkins University)	Brief	Dyads	Simple problem solving
——	——	Varied	Office decentralization
Varied	Varied	Medical professionals to patient	Remote diagnosis
Subjects	Brief	Dyads	Giving orders
——	——	——	——
Primarily subjects (civil servants)	Typically brief	Primarily dyads	Communicating contents of 9,200-word business letter; interviewing
Primarily subjects	Typically brief	Primarily dyads	Varied
Subjects (51 civil servants)	Brief	Group-to-group	Case study problem ("The Tardy Staff")
51 subjects (Canadian middle and senior level civil servants)	Brief	Group-to-group (3–5 per group)	Solving problem of a tardy employee

Citation	Organizational affiliation	Type of study	Medium(ia) used
Ryan and Cummings, 1973	Communications Research Center, Canada	Survey (questionnaires)	——
Short, 1971a	Communications Studies Group	Laboratory experiment	Face-to-face; telephone
Short, 1971b	Communications Studies Group	Laboratory experiment	Face-to-face; telephone
Short, 1972a	Communications Studies Group	Laboratory experiment	Face-to-face; audio; video
Short, 1972b	Communications Studies Group	Laboratory experiment	Face-to-face; audio; video
Short, 1972c	Communications Studies Group	Laboratory experiment	Face-to-face; audio; video
Short, 1973a	University College, London	Laboratory experiment (Ph.D. thesis)	Face-to-face; audio; video
Short, 1973b	Communications Studies Group	Laboratory experiment	Face-to-face; audio; video
Short, 1973c	Communications Studies Group	Survey (interviews)	Audio (Bell 50A sets)
Short, 1974	Communications Studies Group	Laboratory experiment	Telephone; face-to-face
Simon, Fleis, Fisher, and Burland, 1974	New York State Department of Mental Hygiene	Field experiment	Face-to-face; telephone

Number and type of participants	Length of media usage	Conferencing arrangements	Task(s) or purpose(s) of conferencing usage
120 subjects (French- and English-speaking undergraduates)	——	——	Subjects surveyed about their attitudes toward computer
60 subjects (civil service college volunteers)	Brief	Dyads	Industrial negotiation problem (labor-management)
64 subjects (civil service college volunteers)	Brief	Dyads	Mixed-motive bargaining game
120 subjects (British civil servants)	Brief	Dyads	Arguing opposite points of view on social issues
Subjects	Brief	Dyads	Arguing opposite points of view on social issues
Subjects	Brief	Dyads	Arguing opposite points of view on social issues
Subjects	Brief	Dyads	Arguing opposite points of view on social issues
Subjects	Brief	Dyads	Arguing opposite points of view on social issues
12 administrators and faculty at the University of Quebec	Regularly for at least 1 year	Group-to-group	Administrative meetings
Subjects	Brief	Dyads	Mixed-motive bargaining game
85 incoming psychiatric patients	Brief	Dyads (social scientist to patients)	Admissions interviews for psychiatric care

Citation	Organizational affiliation	Type of study	Medium(ia) used
Short, Williams and Christie, 1976	Communications Studies Group	Literature review and descriptive analysis (based primarily on CSG research)	Audio; video; face-to-face
Sinaiko, 1963	Institute for Defense Analyses	Laboratory experiment	Teletype; telephone; split-screen television
Snyder, 1973	Bell Laboratories	Survey (questionnaires)	Varied
Spelt, 1977	Wabash College	Survey (questionnaires); content analysis	Computer-based teleconferencing
Stapley, 1973	Communications Studies Group	Survey (questionnaires); descriptive cost analysis	Audio (Remote Meeting Table)
Stapley, 1974	Communications Studies Group	Review and descriptive analysis	Audio; video
Strickland, Guild, Barefoot, and Patterson, 1975	Carleton University	Laboratory experiment	Face-to-face; video
Thomas and Williams, 1975	Communications Studies Group	Survey (questionnaires)	Audio (Bell 50A sets)
Turoff, 1972b	Office of Emergency Preparedness (U.S. Government)	Descriptive analysis; cost analysis	Computer-based teleconferencing
Turoff, 1974a	Office of Emergency Preparedness (U.S. Government)	Descriptive analysis	Computer-based teleconferencing

Number and type of participants	Length of media usage	Conferencing arrangements	Task(s) or purpose(s) of conferencing usage
Varied, but primarily subjects	Varied, but typically brief	Varied, but primarily dyads	Varied
Subjects	Several hours	Multipoint for audio and teletype; group-to-group for television	Crisis simulation ("Summit")
3,777 employees at Bell Labs (with travel between Bell Laboratory sites over a 1-month period)	Varied	Varied	——
8 psychology professors at small colleges	20 days	Multipoint	Development of a computer simulation for use in psychology courses
3 separate surveys of RMT users, senior and middle level personnel	Varied	Group-to-group	Varied
Senior and middle level personnel	Varied	Group-to-group	Varied
Subjects (university students)	Brief	Group-to-group	Simulated tasks
186 administrators and faculty at the University of Quebec	Most had used the system at least 5 times	Group-to-group	Administrative meetings
Officials in U.S. Office of Emergency Preparedness	About 1 year	Multipoint	Coordination of responses to emergency situations (e.g., "Price Freeze" in United States)
Officials in U.S. Office of Emergency Preparedness	Several years	Multipoint	Coordination of responses to emergency situations

Citation	Organizational affiliation	Type of study	Medium(ia) used
Turoff, 1975	New Jersey Institute of Technology	Descriptive analysis, based on previous experience	Computer-based teleconferencing
Turoff, 1976	New Jersey Institute of Technology	Descriptive analysis; cost analysis	Computer-based teleconferencing
Vallee and Askevold, 1975	Institute for the Future/U.S. Geological Survey	Field test	Computer-based teleconferencing
Vallee, Johansen, Lipinski, Spangler, and Wilson, 1975	Institute for the Future (IFTF)	Field test	Computer-based teleconferencing
Vallee, et al. (forthcoming)	Institute for the Future	Survey	Computer-based teleconferencing
Vallee and Wilson, 1976	Institute for the Future/National Aeronautics and Space Administration	Field test	Computer-based teleconferencing; audio
Wall and Boyd, 1971	——	Laboratory experiment	Face-to-face; written messages; videotape
Wapner and Alper, 1952	Clark University	Laboratory experiment	Seen and unseen audience
Weeks and Chapanis, 1976	Johns Hopkins University	Laboratory experiment	Audio; video; face-to-face; teletype
Wempner, 1975	U.S. Department of Health, Education, and Welfare	Survey (questionnaires)	Video

Number and type of participants	Length of media usage	Conferencing arrangements	Task(s) or purpose(s) of conferencing usage
Senior and middle level personnel	——	Multipoint	Coordination of responses to emergency situations (e.g., "Price Freeze" in United States)
——	——	Multipoint	——
About 20 senior and middle level personnel	About 6 months	Multipoint	Information exchange; discussion of data base on mineral reserves
About 150 middle level personnel (28 separate conferences; no cost to users)	1 week to 6 months	Multipoint	Primarily information exchange and disucssion of ideas
70 middle and senior level users of the PLANET computer conferencing system	Varied	Multipoint	Varied
13 experts working on a NASA contract and 15 principal investigators on the Communications Technology Satellite	About 8 months	Multipoint (the single audio conference was group-to-group)	Project coordination; information exchange; emergency messages
Subjects	Brief	Dyads	Opinion change exercise
120 subjects (60 male, 60 female undergraduates)	Brief	Person-to-group	Problem solving
96 subjects (male undergraduates at Johns Hopkins University)	Brief	Dyads	2 cooperative problems; 2 conflictual problems
7 physicians who had used telemedicine systems	Varied	Physician-to-patient	Romote diagnosis

Citation	Organizational affiliation	Type of study	Medium(ia) used
Weston and Kristen, 1973	Carleton University; University of Montreal	Field experiment	Audio plus graphics; video; face-to-face
Weston, Kristen and O'Connor, 1975	Carleton University; University of Montreal	Further analysis of data from Weston and Kristen, 1973	Audio plus graphics; video; face-to-face
Westrum, 1972	Purdue University	Survey (questionnaires) (Ph.D. dissertation)	Letter; telephone; face-to-face
Wichman, 1970	Claremont Graduate School	Laboratory experiment	Face-to-face; simulated audio; written notes
Williams, 1972a	Communications Studies Group	Laboratory experiment	Face-to-face; video; audio
Williams, 1973	Communications Studies Group; Bell Canada	Survey (interviews)	Video (Bell Canada's conference television system)
Williams, 1974c	Communications Studies Group	Literature review, primarily of laboratory experiments	Video; audio; face-to-face
Williams, 1975a	Communications Studies Group	Laboratory experiment	Face-to-face; closed-circuit television; audio
Williams, 1972b	Communications Studies Group	Laboratory experiment	Audio; video; face-to-face
Williams, 1975c	Communications Studies Group	Descriptive analysis	Varied types of audio
Williams, 1976a	Communications Studies Group	Literature review of laboratory experiments	Audio; video; face-to-face

Number and type of participants	Length of media usage	Conferencing arrangements	Task(s) or purpose(s) of conferencing usage
About 50 subjects (students, sampled from a population of 650)	3 consecutive weeks, one 45-minute session per week	Group-to-group	Course evaluation
About 50 subjects (students, sampled from a population of 650)	3 consecutive weeks, one 45-minute session per week	Group-to-group	Course evaluation
Sample of U.S. senior and middle level business people	Varied	Varied	——
88 subjects (paid female students at Claremont)	Brief	Dyads	Problem solving ("Prisoners Dilemma")
Subjects	Brief	Dyads	Free discussion; conflicts of opinion
26 senior and middle level Bell Canada employees (no cost to users)	Primarily repeated users	Group-to-group	General business meetings
Primarily subjects	Typically brief	Primarily dyads	Varied
180 subjects (middle level executives and administrators from civil service and nationalized industries)	30 minutes for each group	Group-to-group (2 per group)	Generation of ideas about problems of traveling in Britain
Subjects	Brief	Dyads	Conflictual task
——	——	Group-to-group; multipoint	Varied
Primarily subjects	Typically brief	Primarily dyads	Varied

Citation	Organizational affiliation	Type of study	Medium(ia) used
Williams, 1976b	Communications Studies Group	Literature review of laboratory experiments; analysis of findings	Audio; video; face-to-face
Williams and Holloway, 1974	Communications Studies Group; Bell Canada	Survey (questionnaires)	Video (Bell Canada's conference television system)
Wilson, 1974	Communications Studies Group	Theoretical analysis; comparison with experimental findings	——
Wish, 1975	Bell Laboratories	Survey (questionnaires)	Picturephone®; telephone; face-to-face
Woodside, Cavers, and Buck, 1971	Bell Northern Research	Laboratory experiment	Speakerphone; face-to-face; Project 91 videophone
Young, 1974a	Communications Studies Group	Laboratory experiment	Audio; television; face-to-face
Young, 1974b	Communications Studies Group	Laboratory experiment	Face-to-face; audio
Zinn, 1977	University of Michigan	Case study	Computer-based teleconferencing
Zinn, Parnes, and Hench, 1976	University of Michigan	Case study	Computer-based teleconferencing

Number and type of participants	Length of media usage	Conferencing arrangements	Task(s) or purpose(s) of conferencing usage
Primarily subjects	Typically brief	Primarily dyads	Varied
190 senior and middle level personnel (63 from Bell Canada, others from other Canadian organizations; no cost to users)	Most had used the system only once	Group-to-group	Information exchange; problem solving
——	——	——	——
Middle and senior level personnel	Varied	Varied	Varied
36 engineers from Bell Northern Research	Brief	Dyads	Resource allocation
36 subjects (18 students as interviewees, 18 experienced interviewers)	Brief	Dyads	Simulated interview for civil service employment
48 subjects	Brief	Dyads	Arguing opposite points of view on social issues
Over 100 students and faculty, primarily at University of Michigan	Varied	Multipoint	Professional communication; adjunct to face-to-face convention; courses
About 50 students and faculty at University of Michigan	Several months	Multipoint	Courses; faculty meetings

APPENDIX B

The purpose of this tutorial is to help people discover what teleconferencing is all about. The number of teleconferencing systems is gradually increasing. So is the number of fancy brochures that describe these systems. However, such brochures give few hints about the kinds of *social* issues which may arise once a contract is signed and people get down to the business of communicating via the system. What happens, for example, if fine orators discover they can't dominate a computer conference? How do new users of a video system avoid "Hollywood"-type behavior in front of a camera? What social protocols are necessary for a group to communicate over an audio teleconferencing system? The tutorial encourages users to ask these kinds of questions and then, through their own experience, to find some answers.

HOW TO USE THE TUTORIAL

It may be helpful to think of the tutorial as a stage play. The major difference is that the participants create their own script as they go. They can draw on their own experience; they act the way they would normally act in such a setting.

What is the setting? It's an important meeting of an imaginary consortium. The Consortium has five member organizations who have a long history of cooperation. Recently, however, there have been increasing communication problems. The purpose of the meeting is to choose a teleconferencing system to help solve these problems.

The "Cast" . . .

There are eight basic roles in the tutorial:

- the Leader, whose task is to help the group reach a unanimous decision; the leader has no initial media preference and no vote;
- the representative of the Northcoast Labs, who wants The Consortium to adopt computer conferencing;
- the representative of the Eastridge Center, who wants The Consortium to adopt video conferencing;
- the representative of the Highlands Facility, who wants The Consortium to adopt audio teleconferencing;
- the representative of the Baylands Institute, who must decide for him/herself which system is best suited to the group's needs;

- the representative of the Westridge Academy, who also must make his or her own decision;
- Expert A, who has research findings on the various media and must help the Leader achieve consensus; and
- Expert B, who has a different set of research findings and must make a judgment about which system The Consortium should select and then convince the members to select it.

It is possible to use the tutorial with as few as six people. For this situation, we suggest combining the two Expert roles and having one of The Consortium members also be the Leader. More than eight participants may be involved by assigning small groups to each role. In this way, as many as 25 people can be involved. However, the basic range of the tutorial is 6 to 15 participants.

The Medium . . .

You will first need to decide which medium you will be using during the tutorial. Any teleconferencing medium can be used (even a conference telephone call using standard telephone handsets), or you may choose to meet face-to-face. The tutorial was designed for groups who have already chosen some teleconferencing system— at least tentatively—but want to learn how to use it more effectively. However, groups may also use the tutorial to "try out" a new medium or they may use it in face-to-face mode as a way of considering the options and the issues. Once you decide which medium you will be using, you must make the necessary arrangements to have the system available when you plan to "play" the tutorial. **You should probably allow about two hours for the tutorial itself** and another hour for discussion of the experience.

The Materials . . .

Each participant needs five pieces of information: an instruction sheet for his or her role, three flyers which describe the three different teleconferencing systems, and The Consortium Map. In addition, Expert A receives information about social evaluation results; Expert B receives a "Report on Teleconferencing." We have found that the tutorial is most successful if these materials can be distributed **well before** the "meeting" begins. The "Expert" and "Leader" roles, in particular, require some preparation. At least 15 to 30 minutes should be allowed for such preparation; overnight reading is even better. Of course, if some of your participants are geographically separated, you will have to send their materials well in advance of the scheduled time for the tutorial.

Questions Frequently Asked by Participants and Answers You Should Give . . .

What is "The Consortium"?   The Consortium was organized about 20 years ago as a loosely knit union of free-standing organizations who share a series of needs and objectives. The exact nature of The Consortium is intentionally *not* specified. If this question is asked, you should answer that the exact nature of The Consortium is irrelevant; it is the individual communication needs of each participant which are important. If participants persist in asking the question, tell them they can think of The Consortium in any way they wish—as a group of universities, voluntary organizations, corporations, or whatever.

What are the costs of the various teleconferencing options? While cost would typically be a major factor in which medium to choose, the big problem in the tutorial is COMMUNICATION. The Consortium can afford any **one** of the teleconferencing systems, but the decision should be based on social factors—not economics. What is needed are hard judgments about how the characteristics of each medium will affect the ability of Consortium members to communicate.

Is it possible to combine media (that is, to choose more than one of the teleconferencing media)? NO. While media combinations are certainly possible in the real world, they are *not* possible in the tutorial. Only one system can be selected.

Can both The Consortium and a spinoff survive? NO. If a spinoff is successfully negotiated (that is, if it gathers 10 units of funds), there will not be enough funds remaining for The Consortium to survive. In this sense, the remaining members of The Consortium would be "losers" of the tutorial.

What if someone asks technical questions about the teleconferencing systems which nobody can answer? Such questions are likely to occur no matter how expert your group may be. Rely only on the information in the brochures; the discussion should not become bogged down in these technical issues. If unanswerable questions are raised, suggest that the group write them down so that answers can be sought **after** the tutorial is completed. Please feel free to contact the Institute for the Future for additional information about such questions.

How do we know when the tutorial is over? The tutorial is over when the group reaches a consensus decision **or** when a spinoff is announced.

Discussing the Tutorial Experience . . .

You should allow at least a half-hour after the tutorial for a general discussion of what happened. Typically, the first part of this discussion will focus on who did what to whom. Participants will need an initial period to vent their reactions and frustrations. You might begin such a discussion with a general question such as: "Does anyone have any questions they would like to ask of other participants, now that this experience is over?" You might also ask how the participants perceived each other during the tutorial: were they cooperative? knowledgeable? trustworthy? understanding?

The participants need to shift mental gears during the post-tutorial discussion. They may continue to "play their roles." You need to help them focus on what they learned. As the discussion moves along, you might find it useful to raise questions such as these:

- Do you think you learned anything about the medium you were using during the tutorial (e.g., its strengths and weaknesses)? What special strategies or "tricks" did you use in order to communicate effectively over this medium? What other strategies would you like to try out if you used this medium again?

- Do you feel you could now make an intelligent choice about which medium—face-to-face, audio, video, or computer-based teleconferencing—might be most appropriate for a given situation? What questions do you still have about the strengths and weaknesses of teleconferencing?
- Can you think of instances in which teleconferencing would be **more** desirable than face-to-face? Are there instances in which teleconferencing might be more "human" than face-to-face communication? Are there situations in which you would **never** want to use teleconferencing?
- Are there particular types of people who would be particularly well suited to teleconferencing? Poorly suited?
- How could teleconferencing media be misused?
- What societal changes might be encouraged by the widespread use of teleconferencing media?

A Final Reminder

Make sure each of the participants has a copy of

- the instructions for his or her own role
- the Soundwave Plan flyer
- the Commonet flyer
- the Video Travel flyer
- The Consortium Map

INSTRUCTIONS FOR: THE LEADER

You are about to take part in a critical meeting of The Consortium. At this meeting, the five members of The Consortium will select one of three teleconferencing systems: audio, video, or computer-based conferencing. The members will almost certainly disagree about this choice. You have a difficult leadership job ahead of you.

Your objective is: To ensure a unanimous decision AND prevent a spinoff.

First, select a leadership style . . .

Decide in advance how you want to conduct the meeting. You may want to use this as a chance to "try out" leadership styles. You can have a very formal meeting, an unstructured meeting, or any other format you prefer. *You may even want to call for a decision within a certain time limit which you set.*

Getting started . . .

It is your responsibility to get the meeting off to a good start. As with most meetings, getting underway could prove difficult. Consider ways to get the participants involved quickly. IT'S UP TO YOU.

You don't have a vote!

While you are the leader, you have no vote or no strong preference among the media. Your goal is a unanimous decision by the group.

Using the Experts . . .

Two experts are available for the group. Be sure to introduce them and ask them what kinds of information they have. Also, you should realize that, like most experts, they may have subtle biases or even well-defined preferences. Try to surface these preferences so that the group can judge their information accurately.

BEWARE!

Some of the participants may become frustrated with trying to reach a unanimous decision. They can try to form a spinoff group of like-minded participants. *You should resist any attempts to form a spinoff!*

INSTRUCTIONS FOR: EXPERT A

You are about to take part in a critical meeting of The Consortium. At this meeting, the five members of The Consortium will select one of three teleconferencing systems: audio, video, or computer-based conferencing. They will review the *immediate* benefits and drawbacks of each of these systems as a complement to face-to-face meetings; furthermore, they will be assessing the *future* value of these alternatives. You have expert information on social evaluations of these media; you can help The Consortium reach a decision.

Your objective is: To assist the leader and help the group to reach a unanimous decision.

Ways you can help . . .

- *Provide expert information about research studies of each of these media.* You may want to give a short presentation or show the participants copies of your research results.
- *Suggest ways the group might reach a decision.* For instance, you could suggest that they select only one task which is important to all the groups (e.g., coordination) and decide on a medium based on that task. Or you could show them the comparison charts from your reference materials. Think about alternative ways they might reach a unanimous decision.
- *Remember*, you want to be perceived by the group as a competent expert.

CAUTION!

If the groups can't agree, there is a chance that some participants may try to form a spinoff and destroy The Consortium. You should resist any attempts to form a spinoff and help the leader achieve unanimity.

How to be an instant expert . . .

Experts are confident, even if they don't know what they are talking about. You probably haven't had much time to study your resource materials, but YOU ARE AN EXPERT. The other participants don't know as much as you do about social evaluations of the media. You can be either aggressive or quiet, but the others should see you as competent.

Here are some hints on how to become an Instant Expert:

- Study your resource materials. Look for the major strengths and weaknesses of each medium. Make a list of strengths and weaknesses, if you want.
- Avoid reading to the group whenever you can. Paraphrase the findings.
- If you don't have an answer at your fingertips, tell the group that you would like a few minutes to check your resources. Encourage them to continue talking until you are ready.
- Some questions will be bad questions. They may be too broad or unclear or they may require a value judgment. These questions are probably designed to get you to make a decision for the group. Don't fall into the trap of trying to answer them. Ask the questioner to be more specific, or point out that you can't make their decisions for them.
- You should correct statements which are wrong or misleading even if no one asks you.
- You can always say that you don't have any information on a question. In fact, you should know that the research on teleconferencing is *very limited*. Even the findings that you have are uncertain. Answer when you can, but don't be embarrassed when you can't.

ADDITIONAL INFORMATION FOR EXPERT A

SOME WAYS TO THINK ABOUT
THE CHOICE AMONG MEDIA

Each teleconferencing medium has its own strengths and weaknesses. But it is possible to compare the media for several important features, as the following chart indicates. As an expert, you may want to encourage the group to extend this chart, comparing the media for other features which they feel are important.

MEDIA COMPARISON CHART

	Audio	Video	Computer Conferencing
Does everyone have to be online at the same time?	YES	YES	NO
Can graphics be exchanged?	SLOWLY	YES	SIMPLE CHARTS
Can we exchange facial expressions and other nonverbal clues?	NO	YES	NO
Is a written record immediately available?	NO	NO	YES
Are participant locations flexible?	YES	NO	YES

Another way to help the group reach its decision is to match its communication needs with the capabilities of the medium. For example, you might suggest that the group construct a chart like the following:

Group	Communication Need	Most Appropriate Medium
Highlands Facility	1. 2. 3.	1. 2. 3.
Baylands Institute	1. 2. 3.	1. 2. 3.
Eastridge Center	1. 2. 3.	1. 2. 3.
Westridge Academy	1. 2. 3.	1. 2. 3.
North Coast Labs.	1. 2. 3.	1. 2. 3.

ADDITIONAL INFORMATION FOR EXPERT A

STRENGTHS AND WEAKNESSES
OF THE MEDIA

AUDIO

Participants may be more attentive   BUT   **Meetings are often more tiring**

Audio demands real concentration, and this concentration can be useful for creating an efficient meeting environment.

In a field test with bank personnel, Christie (1975) found that audio was perceived as encouraging participants to be more attentive.

More than an hour in an audio meeting can become very dreary (and perhaps drowsy).

In interviews, actual users of audio teleconferencing have frequently mentioned tiring meetings, especially if they are too long. See Short (1973) and Jull, McCaughern, Mendenhall, Storey, Tassie, and Zalatan (1976).

Efficient for simple problem solving   BUT   **Can create other problems**

Audio has been shown to be faster than (or at least as fast as) face-to-face for simple problem solving.

A series of laboratory experiments has examined simple problem solving over different media. For example, see Davies (1971a, 1971b), Woodside, *et al.* (1971), and Chapanis, *et al:* (1972).

Audio sometimes requires more time to keep the group focused on the tasks at hand. Also, some people may become self-conscious if they have never met people at the other end of the system.

In a field experiment in Canada, Weston *et al.* (1975) found that audio groups spent about 10 percent less time on task-related topics than either video or face-to-face groups. Wapner and Alpen (1952) found in a laboratory experiment that an unseen audience often hindered performance of assigned tasks.

Personalities don't get in the way   BUT   **It can be TOO impersonal**

A "just-give-me-the-facts" approach seems possible in audio and may lead to greater efficiency.

Laboratory tests involving simulated negotiations found that audio encouraged a more substantive (rather than interpersonal) orientation. See Morley and Stephenson (1969, 1970). See also Short (1971, 1974).

A few hours of listening to disembodied voices can be perceived as impersonal and lacking in important social contact.

Morley and Stephenson also concluded that audio is perceived as less "personal." Others had similar findings. See, for example, Williams (1972) and Short (1973).

COMPUTER CONFERENCING

Allows equality of participation

It is possible for each person to "say" more in a computer conference than in other media. In a face-to-face meeting, for instance, only one person can speak at a time. The result is usually very unequal participation. In a computer conference, such a result is not as likely.

Ferguson and Johansen (1975) sent questionnaires to about 20 educational researchers who had used computer conferencing intensively for one week. Vallee, *et al.* (1975) collected usage statistics on participation rates in 28 field test conferences.

BUT Requires strong leadership

Without strong leadership, it is easy for a computer conference to get sidetracked.

Johansen, Vallee, and Palmer (1976) tracked the activities of energy researchers using computer conferencing.

Written record is crucial for some tasks

The written record is built into computer conferencing; there is no need for taping or transcribing. Such a constant record is invaluable for some meetings where misunderstandings could occur.

Sinaiko (1963) has shown in laboratory experiments that the written record is better than a voice or visual medium for some tasks. Vallee, *et al.* (1975), Ferguson and Johansen (1975), and Spelt (1977) all confirm this with questionnaire followups to field tests.

BUT Some may be reluctant to "put it in writing"

It is obvious that some people will not want to be "on the record" for everything they say. Of course, private messages (which are not stored by the computer) help to relieve such reservations.

Laboratory experiments have shown this to be true (Kite and Vitz, 1966) as have field tests (Vallee, *et al.*, 1975). Actually, the finding is more "common sense" than anything.

Allows time to reflect on topic of conversation

Users of computer conferencing have liked the fact that it allows them time to think during a "meeting." Also, they can refer to reference materials without interrupting the discussion.

Turoff (1974) has pointed out this characteristic of computer conferencing, as have later field tests such as Ferguson and Johansen (1975), Zinn, *et al.* (1976), and Spelt (1977).

BUT It is difficult to enforce regular participation

There is no ringing telephone or banging gavel in a computer conference; participants must discipline themselves to participate regularly. Those who don't may be left out of important discussions.

Vallee, *et al.* (1975), Johansen, *et al.* (1976), and Spelt (1977) have all noted this problem in evaluations of field tests.

COMPUTER CONFERENCING

Provides new communication opportunities

Geographically separated groups who do not usually communicate with each other are given the opportunity to communicate with computer conferencing. They can even work together regularly.

The potential for new communications links among geographically separated persons has been both noted and demonstrated. See, for example, Hiltz (1976), Irving (1976), and Spelt (1977).

BUT The need to communicate must be high

Without a perceived need to communicate, it is unlikely that participants will exert the effort required to regularly use computer conferencing.

Field tests of computer conferencing have repeatedly shown that the need to communicate is very important for this new medium. See Vallee and Johansen (1974) and Vallee, et al. (1975).

Good for technical information exchange

Computer conferencing provides a constant written record which can be reviewed. This record is especially valuable for technical discussions since written documents can be an accurate source of reference.

Turoff (1972, 1974) and Kupperman, et al. (1975) have both pointed out this potential utility of computer conferencing. Vallee and Askevold (1975) also support the statement in field tests with geologists.

BUT Information overload can occur

An overreliance on the written record provided by computer conferencing can leave one buried in a sea of computer terminal printouts. Care needs to be taken to ensure that an information overload is not allowed to develop.

Field tests of computer conferencing with researchers in various disciplines have shown that information overload can occur. See Ferguson and Johansen (1975) and Vallee, et al. (forthcoming).

VIDEO

There is a sense of order to the meetings

Video meetings seem to be more orderly than face-to-face.

Williams and Holloway (1974) found that video meetings were perceived as more orderly than face-to-face; these findings come from Canadian field tests. George, et al. (1975), found a similar inherent structure to video meetings in their laboratory tests.

BUT Some people are tempted by the "Hollywood Syndrome"

The "Hollywood Syndrome" occurs when film or TV stereotypes become models for behavior in a video teleconference. ("Okay, everyone got your places? Roll 'em . . . .")

Bretz (1974) found this tendency in an analysis of the use of the Metropolitan Regional Council video system. This is also a "common sense" finding.

Regular usage seems to work best   BUT   **Studio must be nearby**

Video may prove most useful for regularly scheduled meetings. It is important to create ways for the use of teleconferencing to become part of one's normal work activities.

Even a small distance to a teleconferencing facility can discourage usage. Sometimes a trip to the airport doesn't look that much worse than a trip to the studio.

Noll (1976) used a questionnaire to survey 21 senior and middle level personnel at Bell Laboratories. These people had participated in about 10 teleconferences over a period of one year.

Jull and Mendenhall (1976) reached this conclusion in an overview of Canadian evaluations of teleconferencing.

Okay for most business tasks   BUT   **May not always be NECESSARY**

Video is usually perceived as better than the telephone for all common business situations, but usually worse than face-to-face.

Perhaps less than 20 percent of existing meetings *need* to be conducted over video.

Wish (1975) surveyed Bell Laboratory employees who had been using the Picturephone® .

Christie and Elton (1975) reviewed a series of projects by Communications Studies Group in London. Pye and Williams' title is explanatory: "Is Video Valuable or Is Audio Adequate?" (*Telecommunications Policy*, June 1977). They conclude that, in most cases, audio is adequate.

It helps to SEE the person at the other end   BUT   **Video is still not like "being there"**

The sense of "social presence" in video can really add to a meeting, especially if a high degree of interpersonal interaction is involved.

The television screen is not a direct substitute for face-to-face contact.

This finding has come largely from laboratory experiments in Great Britain; subjects performed experimental tasks over different media. See Short, Williams, and Christie (1976) and Champness (1972a).

Midorikawa, *et al.* (1975) did field tests in Japan and found that TV screens lack a feeling of social presence. Champness (1973) and Williams (1973) also note this problem.

INSTRUCTIONS FOR: EXPERT B

You are about to take part in a critical meeting of The Consortium. At this meeting, the five members of The Consortium will select one of three tele-conferencing systems: audio, video, or computer-based conferencing. They will review the *immediate* benefits and drawbacks of each of these systems as a complement to face-to-face meetings; furthermore, they will be assessing the *future* value of these alternatives. You have expert information on social evaluations of these media; you can help The Consortium reach a decision.

Your objective is: To chose the medium which you think best suits The Consortium's needs and to convince the group to invest in that medium

Before you begin . . .

Before the meeting starts, select *which* medium you will advocate. Your choice should be based on the communications needs of each participant, as well as the reference materials you have as an expert.

All the media have been oversold . . .

You must choose the medium which has the fewest limitations for The Consortium. You feel that *all* of the media have been oversold and it is your responsibility to make sure the participants understand their limitations.

AN OPTION . . .

If The Consortium can't agree, some of the participants may try to form a spinoff group of like-minded participants. If the spinoff group is supporting the medium you prefer, you may want to encourage them to break away from The Consortium. You want to ensure that the medium you prefer is adopted, whether by The Consortium as a whole or by a spinoff group.

How to be an instant expert . . .

Experts are confident, even if they don't know what they are talking about. You probably haven't had much time to study your resource materials, but YOU ARE AN EXPERT. The other participants don't know as much as you do about social evaluations of the media. You can be either aggressive or quiet, but the others should see you as competent.

Here are some hints on how to become an Instant Expert:

- Study your resource materials. Look for the major strengths and weaknesses of each medium. Make a list of strengths and weaknesses, if you want.
- Avoid reading to the group whenever you can. Paraphrase the findings.
- If you don't have an answer at your fingertips, tell the group that you would like a few minutes to check your resources. Encourage them to continue talking until you are ready.
- Some questions will be bad questions. They may be too broad or unclear or they may require a value judgment. These questions are probably designed to get you to make a decision for the group. Don't fall into the trap of trying to answer them. Ask the questioner to be more specific, or point out that you can't make their decisions for them.
- You should correct statements which are wrong or misleading even if no one asks you.
- You can always say that you don't have any information on a question. In fact, you should know that the research on teleconferencing is *very limited*. Even the findings that you have are uncertain. Answer when you can, but don't be embarrassed when you can't.

ADDITIONAL INFORMATION FOR EXPERT B

REPORT ON TELECONFERENCING

So far, evaluations of teleconferencing media have included four major types of studies:

- *laboratory experiments,* in which subjects (often students) are given assigned tasks to accomplish using one medium or a combination of media;
- *field tests or experiments,* in which groups are encouraged to use a medium in their normal activities while evaluators observe the impacts of the medium;
- *surveys,* in which the evaluator uses either questionnaires or interviews to determine the attitudes of people toward a medium;
- *theoretical analyses,* in which evaluators consider the characteristics of a medium and speculate about its likely effects.

From these types of studies, evaluators have uncovered several problem areas for each of the media.

ADDITIONAL INFORMATION FOR EXPERT B

Problems of Video Conferencing

Video may be satisfactory for people of HIGH rank who wish to communicate with those of LOW RANK; but subordinates do not feel it is satisfactory for communicating with their superiors.

Dickson and Bowers, 1973; technology assessment of the video telephone.

It has questionable utility for tasks involving PERSUASION and BARGAINING.

Short, 1973; laboratory experiment.

While it provides a visual image, it does not always provide the sense of PERSONAL CONTACT and presence found in face-to-face meetings.

Champness, 1973; questionnaire survey of 200 personnel at British Post Office. Williams, 1973; interview survey of 26 Bell Canada employees.

People who use video feel that the system is LESS PRIVATE than face-to-face.

Champness, 1972a&b; two laboratory experiments with 112 subjects for one and 72 subjects for the other. Ryan, 1975; laboratory experiment with 51 subjects.

Video is susceptible to the "HOLLYWOOD SYNDROME"—people assume a kind of "studio" behavior, using film or television as models for how they behave.

Bretz, 1974; 3-year field test.

Problems of Computer Conferencing

Written communications may be LESS EFFICIENT than other media; fewer messages can be exchanged in a given time period than by face-to-face.

Chapanis and Overby, 1974; laboratory experiments with 32 subjects. Williams, 1976; laboratory experiments.

People may be RELUCTANT TO MAKE CERTAIN STATEMENTS IN WRITING.

Kite and Vitz, 1966; laboratory experiment.

REGULARITY OF PARTICIPATION is difficult to enforce: nobody "calls" you to tell you to come to a computer conference.

Vallee, et al., 1975; field tests.

Participants must learn NEW SKILLS, such as how to use a computer terminal or how to send various types of messages.

Vallee, et al., 1975; field tests.

INFORMATION OVERLOAD can occur because it's so easy to put in a lot of data.

Ferguson and Johansen, 1975; field test.

Participant's sense of INTERPERSONAL INTERACTION is sometimes weak.

Ferguson and Johansen, 1975; field test.

The use of surrogates (a participant can, for instance, give his password to a subordinate to retrieve and enter messages) can INHIBIT TRUST and security.

Vallee, et al., 1977; field tests.

Problems of Audio Teleconferencing

Audio is not satisfactory for tasks which stress INTERPERSONAL COMMUNICATION, such as negotiation, resolving disagreements.

Short, 1973; interview survey of 12 University of Quebec personnel. Thomas and Williams, 1975; questionnaire survey of 186 University of Quebec personnel. Christie, 1975; field test.

Audio is not satisfactory for GETTING TO KNOW SOMEONE.

Stapley, 1973; questionnaire survey of users of Remote Meeting Table. Thomas and Williams, 1975; questionnaire survey of 186 University of Quebec personnel.

Audio is not satisfactory for COMPLEX TASKS.

Connors, Lindsey, and Miller, 1976; questionnaire survey of 162 NASA personnel.

Audio can create an IMPERSONAL, UNCOOPERATIVE, and even HOSTILE communications environment.

Weston, Kristen, and O'Connor, 1975; field experiment. Williams, 1972; laboratory experiment.

Audio may be LESS PRODUCTIVE THAN OTHER MEDIA.

Weston, Kristen, and O'Connor, 1975; field experiment. Wapner and Alper, 1952; laboratory experiment.

Audio meetings are DEMANDING AND TIRING; it's hard to maintain group organization.

Weston, Kristen, and O'Connor, 1975; field experiment.

INSTRUCTIONS FOR: THE HIGHLANDS FACILITY

You are about to take part in a critical meeting of The Consortium. At this meeting, the five members of The Consortium will select one of three tele-conferencing systems: audio, video, or computer-based conferencing. Audio conferencing is best for you. So . . .

Your objective is: To get The Consortium to choose Soundwave OR form a spinoff.

Why you need Soundwave . . .

- *Emergency conferences with outside groups.* There are a half dozen agencies with whom you must meet to discuss your stand on controversial issues. These agencies are not part of The Consortium, and they are scattered across two countries. Sometimes, you talk with them individually over the phone; however, the discussions often require that three or more of you get together very quickly to develop a joint statement. These meetings occur about twice each week and usually last approximately one hour. It is important that the decisions made at these meetings be kept confidential until all members of the participating organizations can be informed of them. *Audio seems best suited to this activity for two reasons:* (1) it is *flexible* enough to allow quickly arranged meetings at varied locations and (2) most people agree that audio is more "private" than video or computer-based conferencing.
- *Joint seminar preparation with the Baylands Institute.* You work closely with the Baylands Institute in the development of public seminars. These seminars are held every other month at both locations. To prepare for each of them, four to seven staff members from each group must meet several times. These meetings involve the preparation of announcements and instructional materials, the selection of speakers, the scheduling of sessions, and the assignment of participants to the various sessions. Since you exchange only simple graphic materials and schedules, an audio system plus a high-speed facsimile should be adequate for this need.

Note: The group may want to know more about your needs. Use your own experience and imagination to answer their questions. You're on your own!

What you should tell others about Soundwave . . .

- No special skills are needed—audio conferencing is a natural extension of the telephone which everyone knows how to use
- The telephone is an intimate medium
- Audio is the least expensive system, so it leaves valuable resources available for other needs
- The telephone is more immediate; meetings are easy to arrange on short notice, and conferences can be direct dialed
- Audio encourages more focus in meetings because participants have to concentrate harder; hence, it is more efficient
- Audio is more "private" than video
- Both video and computer conferencing are more expensive than audio
- Video is not as flexible as audio; the users will be limited to a few permanently installed conference rooms
- Computer conferencing requires typing skills; busy executives won't type
- There is no immediate feedback with computer conferencing because people are not "online"—they join and leave whenever they want, which is confusing and "unnatural"
- Computers are cold and impersonal

What to do if the group does not agree . . .

1. You should negotiate with other representatives to convince them that your needs require serious attention.
2. You should call upon expert information that supports your views.
3. **You cannot combine two systems.** If you cannot convince the whole group to choose Soundwave, you should move decisively to organize a successful spinoff group which favors Soundwave. You may want to request some private meetings for this purpose.
4. **You need at least 10 units of funding to form a spinoff. You have 2 units.**
5. If others form a spinoff favoring another system, you lose.

Your funds: 2 units

INSTRUCTIONS FOR: THE BAYLANDS INSTITUTE

You are about to take part in a critical meeting of The Consortium. At this meeting, the five members of The Consortium will select one of three teleconferencing systems: audio, video, or computer-based conferencing.

Your objective is: To get The Consortium to choose the system which is best for you OR form a spinoff.

Your communication needs are . . .

- *Remote instruction.* You provide instructional programs for people in remote areas. They are designed for professionals and paraprofessionals who are involved in community services. In the past, you have trained local citizens to administer these "prepackaged" courses. But you want to provide higher quality and more interaction with instructors. Your blueprint calls for 2–6 students at up to 10 locations; they would "meet" once a week for 6 weeks. Classes would last 1–2 hours. Class materials, including a few simple graphics, would be mailed in advance. Three Baylands staff members would serve as team teachers for each program. The same programs would be repeated in other locations.
- *Joint seminar preparation with the Highlands Facility.* You work closely with the Highlands Facility in the development of public seminars. These seminars are held every other month at both locations. To prepare for each of them, 4–7 staff members from each group must meet several times. These meetings involve the preparation of announcements and instructional materials, the selection of speakers, the scheduling of sessions, and the assignment of participants to the various sessions. They also involve the exchange of some simple graphic materials and schedules.

Note: The group may want to know more about your needs. Use your own experience and imagination to answer their questions. You're on your own!

What to do if the group does not agree . . .

1. You should negotiate with other representatives to convince them that your needs require serious attention.
2. You should call upon the experts to help you identify which medium is best for your needs.
3. **You cannot combine two systems.** If you cannot convince the whole group to choose the system you want, you should move decisively to organize a successful spinoff group which favors that system. You may want to request some private conferences for this purpose.
4. **You need at least 10 units of funding to form a spinoff. You have 6 units.**
5. If others form a spinoff favoring another system, you lose.

Your funds: 6 units

INSTRUCTIONS FOR: THE WESTRIDGE ACADEMY

You are about to take part in a critical meeting of The Consortium. At this meeting, the five members of The Consortium will select one of three teleconferencing systems: audio, video, or computer-based conferencing.

Your objective is: To get The Consortium to choose the system which is best for you OR form a spinoff.

Your communication needs are . . .

- *Technical Bulletins.* You publish a well-regarded technical *Bulletin* once a month. The editorial board is disseminated: the editor-in-chief is on your staff, but there are editorial representatives from each member of The Consortium as well as five special editors at other locations. The preparation of the *Bulletin* thus involves two important kinds of communication: meetings of the entire editorial board to make policy decisions regarding the content of the *Bulletin* and exchanges between the editor-in-chief and one or more editors regarding the writing and editing of specific articles.
- *Instructional workbooks.* You also prepare instructional workbooks with the Eastridge Center. Your people write the text; the Eastridge staff provides the illustrations and is also responsible for getting the books printed. Producing a book in this fashion requires close cooperation and consultation between artist and writer. The writer must be able to critique the artist's presentation of his or her ideas. Each book requires at least a dozen of these critiquing sessions over three or four months; typically, The Consortium publishes five workbooks each year.
- *Scientific exchange.* You exchange research data—mostly instrument readings—with the Northcoast Labs. This exchange occurs daily.

Note: The group may want to know more about your needs. Use your own experience and imagination to answer their questions. You're on your own!

What to do if the group does not agree . . .

1.   You should negotiate with other representatives to convince them that your needs require serious attention.
2.   You should call upon the experts to help you identify which medium is best for your needs.
3.   **You cannot combine two systems.** If you cannot convince the whole group to choose the system you want, you should move decisively to organize a successful spinoff group which favors that system. You may want to request some private conferences for this purpose.
4.   **You need at least 10 units of funding to form a spinoff. You have 2 units.**
5.   If others form a spinoff favoring another system, you lose.

Your funds: 2 units

INSTRUCTIONS FOR: THE EASTRIDGE CENTER

You are about to take part in a critical meeting of The Consortium. At this meeting, the five members of The Consortium will select one of three tele-conferencing systems: audio, video, or computer-based conferencing. Video conferencing is best for you. So . . .

Your objective is: To get the members of The Consortium to choose Video Travel OR form a spinoff.

Why you need Video Travel . . .

- *Promotional presentations.* You prepare promotional presentations for all members of The Consortium. Each group then uses the promotional material as they see fit. Several years ago, each group was so delighted to have any promotional material that they accepted everything you produced. Not so any more. Each television film clip, press release, magazine ad, and poster must be approved by all five groups, and trying to reach an agreement on even the smallest item is now a difficult task. It means many meetings at which the member groups consider each picture and each word very carefully. Video thus seems vital in order to present and critique films, videotaped sequences, and ad layouts.
- *Instructional workbooks.* You also prepare instructional workbooks with the Westridge Academy. Westridge writes the text, while your staff provides the illustrations and is also responsible for getting the books printed. Producing a book in this fashion requires close cooperation and consultation between artist and writer. The writer must be able to critique the artist's presentation of his or her ideas. Each book requires at least a dozen of these critiquing sessions over three or four months; typically, The Consortium publishes five workbooks each year. A system with a high-quality visual channel could thus save the two groups more than one trip each week.

Note: The group may want to know more about your needs. Use your own experience and imagination to answer their questions. You're on your own!

What you should tell the others about Video Travel . . .

- Video comes closer than any other medium to matching the quality of face-to-face. Participants can see how the others are reacting: smiling, frowning, bored, or interested
- Video lets the group present creative graphic materials much more effectively than a facsimile system
- It encourages more rapid decision-making because participants can see how everyone is reacting; they understand the problem better
- A video conference can be recorded on video tapes if desired
- Computer conferencing is cold and impersonal
- Computer conferencing requires typing skills
- It is difficult to communicate graphic information via computer conferencing
- Audio is tiring and difficult to follow
- Audio is unsatisfactory for complex graphic needs
- It is often difficult to tell who is speaking via audio
- It is difficult to know how others are reacting via audio or computer conferencing

What to do if the group does not agree . . .

1. You should negotiate with other representatives to convince them that your needs require serious attention.
2. You should call upon expert information that supports your views.
3. **You cannot combine two systems.** If you cannot convince the whole group to choose Video Travel, you should move decisively to organize a successful spinoff group which favors Video Travel. You may want to request some private meetings for this purpose.
4. **You need at least 10 units of funding to form a spinoff. You have 2 units.**
5. If others form a spinoff favoring another system, you lose.

Your funds: 2 units

INSTRUCTIONS FOR: THE NORTHCOAST LABS

You are about to take part in a critical meeting of The Consortium. At this meeting, the five members of The Consortium will select one of three teleconferencing systems: audio, video, or computer-based teleconferencing. Computer conferencing is best for you. So . . .

Your objective is: To get The Consortium to choose Commonet
OR form a spinoff.

Why you need Commonet . . .

- *Scientific exchange.* You cooperate with the Westridge Academy and five other centers worldwide in scientific research. This activity involves daily exchange of information in the form of tables and instrument readings. You have been frustrated in these exchanges by slow, unreliable mail; unreadable carbon copies; and costly telephone calls which all too often lead to errors in the information exchanged. Also, joint report writing has been disastrous. Often, after several months in which manuscripts are lost in the mail and telephone changes are not incorporated to anyone's satisfaction, the authors must fly to a central location to finish the paper together. If The Consortium had access to Commonet, the outside organizations would secure their own terminals and pay a fee proportionate to their use of the service.
- *Field work.* Approximately half of your staff is in the field for extended periods collecting and recording technical data. Periodically, these data are mailed to the central office where other staff members analyze them. There has been considerable dissent between the field staff and the central staff for some time. The central staff complains that the data are received in too many different formats. The field staff feels that the central staff is insensitive to the constraints on their collection activities. The group is hoping that Commonet will allow staff to view all of the data which are being collected and to jointly discuss procedures for reporting and updating data from the field.

Note: The group may want to know more about your needs. Use your own experience and imagination to answer their questions. You're on your own!

What you should tell others about Commonet . . .

- It is faster, more reliable than mail
- A permanent accurate record is always available
- You can participate when you want, where you want. No need to leave your office; no need for everyone to be present at the same time
- It costs much less than video or a face-to-face meeting
- It provides online access to data bases and mathematical models to support technical work
- It provides continuous communication rather than a one-time meeting
- It is difficult to handle a lot of technical information using either audio or video
- It is awkward to record and review proceedings of audio and video conferences
- Both audio and video require all members of the group to be available at the same time, which is particularly difficult across time zones
- Both audio and video require participants to go to a central location; with computer conferencing, you can join a meeting anywhere as long as you have a portable terminal and access to a telephone

What to do if the group does not agree . . .

1. You should negotiate with other representatives to convince them that your needs require serious attention.
2. You should call upon expert information that supports your views.
3. **You cannot combine two systems.** If you cannot convince the whole group to choose Commonet, you should move decisively to organize a successful spinoff group which favors Commonet. You may want to request some private meetings for this purpose.
4. **You need at least 10 units of funding to form a spinoff. You have 4 units.**
5. If others form a spinoff favoring another system, you lose.

Your funds: 4 units

The Soundwave Plan features permanent conference rooms for highest quality sound. Our conference room team . . . which includes sound engineers, electricians, communications analysts and interior decorators . . . will wire and furnish a room of your choice for acoustically perfect audio conferencing. Our audio equipment is built into the conference table, so you never have to worry about complicated setups. Just flip the "on" switch, dial another conference room, and you are ready to hold your conference.

The Soundwave Plan is an audio conferencing service with a difference.

What makes Soundwave unique is its versatile dedicated network. This network reaches all over the world. It means that you can have a permanent conference room installed at your site. Or if flexibility is a must, you can simply plug in our lightweight, portable conferencing unit and place it on any table. Individual telephones can even be used with the conference rooms simply by dialing your private account number.

You need no operator. No special training. And it costs surprisingly little money to use the Soundwave Plan. Doesn't Soundwave make sense for you?

The Soundwave Plan

Some common questions about Soundwave

How do we know who is speaking at the other locations?

Each conference table has a built-in speaker with a lighted panel which indicates who is speaking. Also, most people begin to recognize voices after only 5 or 10 minutes.

Can we exchange graphics with distant locations?

Yes. Each conference room will be fitted with a facsimile system for transmitting flat art. An average page takes 20 seconds to transmit. Black-and-white photographs and simple color artwork are reproduced with great accuracy. Full-color photographs are reproduced in black-and-white.

How many people can participate in a Soundwave conference?

We have found that five people at each location is the ideal size for an audio conference. So our conference tables are set up with five microphones. Technically speaking, up to 20 locations can be "online" at the same time; however, from an organizational standpoint, 15 participants seems to be a maximum. Our communications analyst will help you analyze your conferencing needs and schedule meetings which make the best use of Soundwave equipment . . . and your valuable time.

Can we record our meetings?

Yes. All of our conference rooms include recording equipment. (A lighted panel at each site indicates that the recorder is in operation.) In addition, the Soundwave Plan includes dial-up secretarial and transcription services: if you call us one half hour before your conference begins, one of our highly skilled secretaries will be on line to record your conference. Typed transcripts are mailed to you the following day.

Do we have to "fight" for the microphone?

The Soundwave system uses an open microphone so anyone can speak at any time ... just like a face-to-face conference. Of course, you may have interruptions just as you do in a face-to-face conference.

Our portable

Because it's not always convenient to get everyone together at one of your permanent conference room sites, the Soundwave Plan includes a portable conferencing unit. This inexpensive, lightweight unit allows up to four people to join a conference with any of your permanent sites. They simply plug the unit into an ordinary telephone jack, dial the local Soundwave number, and ask for your account and extension number. Since they are inexpensive and easy to maintain, many Soundwave users supply these units to their most important clients or contacts in the field. Then, when an emergency arises, it's easy to hold a quick, efficient conference.

commonet

wherever you are . . .

Computer conferencing is conferencing where and when you want it. It's timely information. It's accurate information.

Computer conferencing is print-based communication. When you want to exchange information with colleagues in any country, you turn on your computer terminal, call the local Commonet office on your phone, and plug the phone into the terminal. Instantly, you're in touch with the world.

The computers used by Commonet are fast and reliable. However, the computer itself is not the most important part of computer conferencing. The most important part is the sharing of facts and ideas. So with the Commonet system, you will not need to learn any complicated procedures or computer languages. All you will need to do is enter your thoughts into the network.

just some simple equipment . . .

a portable terminal . . .The most important piece of equipment in computer conferencing is the terminal. It looks and works like a typewriter. But—a pleasant surprise—it's lighter than a typewriter. You can carry it anywhere.

. . . **and a telephone** To join a conference, you just call Commonet and plug the telephone receiver into your terminal. It's a local telephone number, so there's never a long-distance charge.

and a lot of service . . .

like information storage . . . In computer conferencing, the computer retains everything that you and your colleagues say. So if you just want to review what your friend Mitchell had to say about the building codes in Gahanna, Ohio, you can.

a transcript . . . But you don't have to rely on the computer's memory. You can have the whole conference down in black and white. The transcript is available immediately, with names, dates, and time of day matched to each comment. Accurately.

training for your staff . . . Computer conferencing is easy to use. But it may be unfamiliar to your staff. Commonet will help them get to know the system.

translation service . . . In a worldwide network, language barriers are bound to be a problem. Commonet's translators are available online whenever you want them.

round-the-clock communication . . . Commonet provides continuous, round-the-clock communication. Schedules seem to disappear. While your associate is drifting off to sleep in Beirut, you can be responding to his questions in Chicago. The Commonet computer never sleeps, so you can.

commonet

VIDEO TRAVEL

Why travel when you can be there electronically?

Video Travel is the fast, comfortable way to meet with your associates.

How many times have you arrived at an important meeting feeling cramped, wrinkled, and tired from a three-hour flight in a seat designed for a toddler rather than a busy executive?

How many times have you missed your important meeting because you couldn't land in Tokyo, London, Rome, Chcago, or Atlanta?

How many times have you just skipped an important meeting because you couldn't afford the extra day it takes to get there and back?

No more.

Video Travel lets you be there in luxurious, electronic comfort. Refreshed. On time. In familiar surroundings.

VIDEO TRAVEL

- permanent, attractively designed, conference rooms wherever you want them
- full-color television screens
- voice-switched cameras with manual override
- pushbutton controls for split-screen arrangements or close-up zoom of speaker
- training for your staff in the effective use of the video medium
- a special graphics camera for sharing slides, photographs, charts, and even 3-dimensional objects with your colleagues at other locations
- film projection facilities
- video recording facilities
- hard-copy print-out of graphics if needed
- up to five sites connected simultaneously

The Westridge Academy
Technical bulletins
Instructional workbooks
Scientific exchange
Funds: 2 units

The Northcoast Labs
Scientific exchange
Field work
Funds: 4 units

The Eastridge Center
Promotional presentations
Instructional workbooks
Funds: 2 units

The Baylands Institute
Remote instruction
Seminar preparation
Funds: 6 units

The Highlands Facility
Emergency conferences with
outside groups
Seminar preparation
Funds: 2 units

The Consortium

BIBLIOGRAPHY

Anonymous, 1963. *An Experimental Task*, Aircraft Armaments, Inc. and Institute for Defense Analyses, Arlington, Virginia, Research Paper P-111, NTIS*: AD-601 929.

——, 1973. *The 1972/73 New Rural Society Project*, Report to the U.S. Department of Housing and Urban Development.

——, 1973. *Technical and Economic Analysis of Interactive Television*, The Mitre Corporation.

——, 1976. *Telecommunications and Regional Development in Sweden*, Expert Board for Regional Development and National Swedish Board for Technical Development.

Argyle, M., 1969. *Social Interaction*, London, England: Methuen.

——, 1975. *Final Report to the Social Science Research Council for the Period September 1970–August 1975*, Programme on Social Interaction, Department of Experimental Psychology, Oxford University.

——, M. Lalljee, and M. Cook, 1968. "The Effects of Visibility on Interaction in the Dyad," *Human Relations*, Vol. 21, pp. 3–17.

Aronson, Sidney, 1971. "The Sociology of the Telephone," *International Journal of Comparative Sociology*, Vol. 11, September 1971, pp. 153–67.

Bailey, Gerald C., Peter G. Nordlie, and Frank Sistrunk, 1963, revised 1966. *Literature Review, Field Studies, and Working Papers*, Institute for Defense Analyses, Arlington, Virginia, Research Paper P-113, NTIS*: AD-480 695.

†Barker, Glenn and Terry McCoy, *Tele-Training for Personnel Development: Course Directors'/Designers' Report*, Public Service Commission of Canada [no date given].

Bashshur, Rashid L., 1975. "Telemedicine and Medical Care," in Rashid L. Bashshur, Patricia A. Armstrong, and Zakhour I. Youssef, eds., *Telemedicine*, Springfield, Illinois: Charles C. Thomas.

---

†This document was received after our survey of social evaluations was completed; as a result, any findings reported here are not included in the text of this book or in Appendix A.

*National Technical Information Service, U.S. Department of Commerce, 5285 Part Royal Road, Springfield, Virginia 22151.

Bavelas, Alex, 1963a. *Teleconferencing: Background Information*, Institute for Defense Analyses, Arlington, Virginia, Research Paper P-106, NTIS*: AD-601 924.

————, 1963b. *Teleconferencing: Guidelines for Research*, Institute for Defense Analyses, Arlington, Virginia, Research Paper P-107, NTIS*: AD-601 925.

Belden, Thomas G., 1963. *Teleconferencing: Procedures*, Institute for Defense Analyses, Arlington, Virginia, Research Paper P-111, NTIS*: AD-601 928.

†Bell, Daniel, 1977. "Teletext & Technology," *Encounter*, June 1970, pp. 9–29.

Bennett, J. L., 1975. *User Acceptance of Decision Support Systems: The Role of the Integrating Agent*, IBM Corporation, Yorktown Heights, New York, Research Report RJ 1502.

Bentz, Carol A. and Thomas M. Potrykus, 1976. "Visual Communications in the Phoenix Criminal Justice System," *International Communications Conference Proceedings*, Philadelphia, Pennsylvania; available through American Telephone and Telegraph Company, Morristown, New Jersey 07960.

Billowes, C. A., G. W. Jull, H. C. Frayn, W. S. Tigges, and M. A. Maclellan, 1974. *An Audio-Graphics System for Teleconferencing*, Communications Research Centre, Department of Communications, Ottawa, Canada, CRC Technical Note No. 670.

†Botros, Radamis, 1977. "Audio Teleconferencing—The Telephone and the Environment," *Telesis*, Vol. 5, No. 1, pp. 16–21.

Bretz, Rudy, 1971a. *Taxonomy of Communication Media*, The Rand Corporation, Report R-697-NLM/PR.

————, 1971b. *Selection of Appropriate Communication Media for Instruction: A Guide for Designers of Air Force Technical Programs*, The Rand Corporation, Report R-60-PR.

————, 1972. *Omaha Veterans Hospital Closed-Circuit TV System: A Case Study*, The Rand Corporation, Working Note WN-8901-MRC.

————, 1974. *Two-Way TV Teleconferencing for Government: The MRC-TV System*, The Rand Corporation, Report R-1489-MRC.

————, James H. Carlaisle, Jim Carlstedt, David H. Crocker, James A. Levin, and Laurence Press, 1976. *A Teleconference on Teleconferencing*, Information Sciences Institute, University of Southern California, Marina Del Rey, California 90291.

British Columbia Telephone, 1974. *An Experiment in Conference TV*, British Columbia Telephone, 768 Seymour Street, Vancouver, British Columbia V6B 3K9, Canada.

Brown, David, "Teleconferencing and Electronic Mail," *EDUCOM Bulletin*, forthcoming.

Carlisle, James H., 1975. *A Selected Bibliography on Computer-Based Teleconferencing*, Information Sciences Institute and Annenberg School of Communications, University of Southern California, Marina Del Rey, California 90291.

————, 1976. *Evaluating the Impact of Office Automation on Top Management Communication*, University of Southern California, Los Angeles, California

Carter, George, 1974. *Confer—A Preliminary Design Concept*, Department of Electrical Engineering, University of Illinois, Urbana, Illinois.

†Casey-Stahmer, Anna, 1978. "Telehealth Care in Canada," in M. C. J. Elton, W. A. Lucas, and D. W. Conrath, eds., *Evaluating New Telecommunication Systems*, New York and London: Plenum.

—— and M. Dean Havron, 1973. *Planning Research in Teleconference Systems*, Human Sciences Research, Inc., McLean, Virginia.

Cavert, C. Edward, 1972. *Procedures for the Design of Mediated Instruction*, State University of Nebraska Project.

Champness, Brian, 1971. *Bargaining at Bell Laboratories*, Communications Studies Group, London, England, Paper, E/71270/CH.

——, 1972a. *The Perceived Adequacy of Four Communications Systems for a Variety of Tasks*, Communications Studies Group, London, England, Paper E/72245/CH.

——, 1972b. *Attitudes towards Person-Person Communications Media*, Communications Studies Group, London, England, Paper E/72011/CH.

——, 1972d. *The Effectiveness and Impact of New Telecommunications Systems*, Symposium on Human Factors and Telecommunications, Stockholm, Sweden.

——, 1972e. *Experimental Research Team: October 1971 to January 1972*, Communications Studies Group, London, England, Paper W/72310/CH.

——, 1973. *The Assessment of Users' Reactions to Confravision*, Communications Studies Group, London, England, Paper E/73250/CH.

—— and M. F. Davies, 1971. *The Maier Pilot Experiment*, Communications Studies Group, London, England, Paper E/71030/CH.

—— and Alex Reid, 1970. *The Efficiency of Information Transmission: A Preliminary Comparison between Face-to-Face Meetings and the Telephone*, Communications Studies Group, London, England, Paper P/70240/CH.

†Chan, Paulina Y. B., 1976. "A Model of Some Psychological Factors in Teleconferencing, Including Social Relationships, Participant-Satisfactions and Group Performance," in Lorne A. Parker and Betsy Riccomini, eds., *The Status of the Telephone in Education*, Madison: University of Wisconsin-Extension Press.

——, 1977. "Some Prerequisites on Designing Training-Needs to Applying Teleconferencing in Oriental Societies," *Proceedings of European Conference on Electrotechnics '77*, AEI and IEEE, Venezia.

—— and Colin Cherry, "Some Social Criteria for the Technological Assessment of Teleconferencing," Imperial College, London, England [no date given].

—— and E. C. Cherry, 1977. "The Implications of Teleconferencing as a People-Images Communication System," *Proceedings of the 20th Midwest Symposium on Circuits & Systems*, Lubbock, Texas.

Chapanis, Alphonse, 1971. "Prelude to 2001: Explorations in Human Communications," *American Psychologist*, Vol. 26, No. 11, pp. 949–61.

——, 1973. "The Communication of Factual Information through Various Channels," *Information Storage and Retrieval*, Vol. 9, pp. 215–31.

————, R. Ochsman, R. Parrish, and G. Weeks, 1972. "Studies in Interactive Communication: The Effects of Four Communications Modes on the Behavior of Teams during Cooperative Problem-Solving," *Human Factors,* Vol. 4, No. 6, pp. 487–509.

———— and Charles M. Overbey, 1974. "Studies in Interactive Communication: III. Effects of Similar and Dissimilar Communication Channels and Two Interchange Options on Team Problem-Solving," *Perceptual and Motor Skills,* Monograph Supplement 2-Vol. 38, pp. 343–74.

†Chapuis, R. J., 1978. "Technology and Structures—Man and Machine," in M. C. J. Elton, W. A. Lucas, and D. W. Conrath, eds., *Evaluating New Telecommunication Systems,* New York and London: Plenum.

Christie, Bruce, 1974a. "Perceived Usefulness of Person-to-Person Telecommunications Media as a Function of the Intended Application," *European Journal of Social Psychology,* Vol. 4, No. 3, pp. 366–68.

————, 1974b. *A Summary of the D.O.E. Teleconferencing Experience,* Communications Studies Group, London, England, Paper P/74280/CR.

————, 1974c. *Semantic Differential Judgements of Communications Media and Other Concepts: 1. Differences between the Media,* Communications Studies Group, London, England, Paper E/74120/CR.

————, 1975a. "The Role of the Electronic Meeting in the Decentralization of Business," Chapter 10 in unpublished Ph.D. thesis, University of London.

————, 1975b. *Travel or Telecommunicate? Some Factors Affecting the Choice,* Communications Studies Group, London, England, Paper E/75030/CR.

————, and Martin Elton, 1975. *Research on the Differences between Telecommunication and Face-to-Face Communication in Business and Government,* Communications Studies Group, London, England, Paper P/75180/CR.

———— and S. Holloway, 1975. "Factors Affecting the Use of Telecommunications by Management," *Journal of Occupational Psychology,* Vol. 48, pp. 3–9.

———— and Stephen Kingan, 1976. *Electronic Alternatives to the Business Meeting: Managers' Choices,* Communications Studies Group, London, England, prepublication copy.

†Cinar, Unver, 1978. "A Methodology for Design of Advanced Technology-Based Health Care Systems in Developing Countries," in M. C. J. Elton, W. A. Lucas, and D. W. Conrath, eds., *Evaluating New Telecommunication Systems,* New York and London: Plenum.

†Cohen, Jean-Claude, David W. Conrath, Philippe Dumas, and Gabriel du Roure, 1978. "Information and Communication: Is There A System?," in M. C. J. Elton, W. A. Lucas, and D. W. Conrath, eds., *Evaluating New Telecommunication Systems,* New York and London: Plenum.

Cohen, William C. and Stuart L. Meyer, 1975. "Development of the Educational Uses of Slow-Scan Televideo," *Bioscience Communications,* Switzerland, Vol. 1, pp. 169–83.

Collins, Hugh, 1972. *The Telecommunications Impact Model, Stages I and II,* Communications Studies Group, London, England, Reference No. P/72031/CL.

†Commission for the Development of the Telecommunication System, 1976. *Telecommunications Report*, Bonn, Germany: Federal Ministry of Posts and Telecommunications.

Communications Research Centre [1975?]. *The Communications Behaviour Laboratory*, Communications Research Centre, Department of Communications, Ottawa, Ontario, Canada.

Communications Studies Group, 1969. *Annotated References*, Communications Studies Group, Wates House, 22 Gordon Street, London WC1H 0QB, England.

———, 1973a. *Final Report*, Communications Studies Group, London, England, Paper P/73273/EL.

———, 1973b. *The Scope of Person-to-Person Telecommunications in Government and Business*, Communications Studies Group, London, England, Reference No. P/73272/EL.

———, 1975. "The Effectiveness of Person-to-Person Telecommunications Systems: Research at the Communications Studies Group, University College, London," *Long Range Research Report 3*, Post Office Telecommunications, England, Reference No. LRRR 003/ITF.

Connors, Mary M., 1973. *Teleconferencing Systems: Current Status and Effects on the User Population*, Stanford University Area Exams, Stanford, California.

———, George Lindsey, and Richard H. Miller, 1976. *The NASA Teleconferencing System: An Evaluation*, Ames Research Center, National Aeronautics and Space Administration.

†Conrath, David W., 1973. "Communication Patterns, Organizational Structure, and Man: Some Relationships," *Human Factors*, Vol. 15, No. 5, pp. 459–70.

†———, *Organizational Communication Behavior: Description and Prediction*, Department of Management Sciences, University of Waterloo, Waterloo, Ontario, Canada, and Institut d'Administration des Entreprises, University d'Aix-Marseille, Aix-en-Provence, France [no date given].

———, E. V. Dunn, W. G. Bloor, and B. Tranquada, 1976. *A Clinical Evaluation of Four Alternative Communication Systems as Used for the Delivery of Primary Health Care*, Department of Management Sciences, University of Waterloo, Waterloo, Ontario, Canada.

———, J. N. Dunn, J. N. Swanson, and P. Buckingham, 1975. "A Preliminary Evaluation of Alternative Telecommunication Systems for Delivery of Primary Health Care to Remote Areas," *IEEE Transactions on Communications*, COM-23, pp. 1119–26.

Craig, James G. and George W. Jull, 1974. *Teleconferencing Studies: Behavioural Research and Technological Implications*, Communications Research Centre, Department of Communications, Ottawa, Ontario, Canada.

†Daniel, J. S., Michele L. Côté, and Murray Richmond, 1977. *Evaluation Education, Bulletin 5*, Department of Communications, Canada.

†———, M. L. Côté, and M. Richmond, 1978. "Educational Experiments with the Communications Technology Satellite: A Memo from Evaluators to Planners,"

in M. C. J. Elton, W. A. Lucas, and D. W. Conrath, eds., *Evaluating New Telecommunication Systems*, New York and London: Plenum.

Davies, Martin, 1971a. *Cooperative Problem-Solving, An Exploratory Study*, Communications Studies Group, London, England, Paper E/71159/DV.

————, 1971b. *Cooperative Problem-Solving: A Follow-Up Study*, Communications Studies Group, London, England, Paper E/71252/DV.

†Davis, Peter and Edward Freeman, 1978. "Technology Assessment and Idealized Design, An Application to Telecommunications," in M. C. J. Elton, W. A. Lucas, and D. W. Conrath, eds., *Evaluating New Telecommunication Systems*, New York and London: Plenum.

Day, Lawrence H., 1973. *The Future of Computer and Communications Services*, National Computer Conference and Exposition, New York City.

————, 1975. *Computer Conferencing: An Overview*, Airlie House 1975 Conference on Telecommunications Policy; available from Bell Canada, Business Planning Group, 620 Belmont, Montreal, Quebec, Canada.

†————, 1978. "The Role of Telecommunications Policy Analysis in Service Planning," in M. C. J. Elton, W. A. Lucas, and D. W. Conrath, eds., *Evaluating New Telecommunication Systems*, New York and London: Plenum.

Dickson, Edward M. and Raymond Bowers, 1974. *The Video Telephone, Impact of a New Era in Telecommunications*, New York: Praeger Publishers, Inc.

†Dormois, M., F. Fioux, and M. Gensollen, 1978. "Evaluation of Potential Market for Various Future Communication Modes via Analysis of Communication Flow Characteristics," in M. C. J. Elton, W. A. Lucas, and D. W. Conrath, eds., *Evaluating New Telecommunication Systems*, New York and London: Plenum.

Dorris, J. W., G. C. Gentry, and H. H. Kelley, 1972. *The Effects on Bargaining of Problem Difficulty, Mode of Interaction, and Initial Orientations*, prepublication draft.

†Douglas, Paul M., 1977. *A Conference on International Economic Cooperation via Communication Satellite*, Proposal for an International Telecommunication Experiment, The Aspen Institute for Humanistic Studies, Program in International Affairs, Princeton, New Jersey.

†Drioli, B., L. A. Ciavoli Cortelli, and J. L. Jankovich, 1978. "A Possible European System for Teleconferencing via Satellite," in M. C. J. Elton, W. A. Lucas, and D. W. Conrath, eds., *Evaluating New Telecommunication Systems*, New York and London: Plenum.

Duncan, Starkey, 1969. "Nonverbal Communication," *Psychological Bulletin*, Vol. 72, No. 2, pp. 118–37.

Duncanson, James P. and Arthur D. Williams, 1973. "Video Conferencing: Reactions of Users," *Human Factors*, Vol. 15, No. 5, pp. 471–85.

Ellis, Susan, Vince McKay, and Michael Robinson, 1976. *A Preliminary Report of the Follow-Up Study of Users of the Melbourne-Sydney Confravision Facility*, Swinburne Institute of Technology, Australia.

Elton, Martin, 1975. "The Use of Field Trials in Evaluating Telemedicine Applications," in Rashid L. Bashshur, Patricia A. Armstrong, and Zakhour I. Youssef, eds., *Telemedicine*, Springfield, Illinois: Charles C. Thomas.

Ernst & Ernst, 1975. *A Market Study on the "Conference T.V." Services Offered by Bell Canada*, Ernst & Ernst, Canada.

Ferguson, John and Robert Johansen, eds., 1975. *Teleconference on Integrated Data Bases in Postsecondary Education*, Lilly Endowment, Inc., Indianapolis, Indiana, and Institute for the Future.

†Fields, Craig, 1978. "Exploiting the Tele- in Teleconferencing," in M. C. J. Elton, W. A. Lucas, and D. W. Conrath, eds., *Evaluating New Telecommunication Systems*, New York and London: Plenum.

†Fjaestad, Björn and P. G. Holmlöv, 1978. "The Swedish Market for a Public Switched Multi-Purpose Broadband Network," *Evaluating New Telecommunication Systems*, New York and London: Plenum.

†Flowerdew, A. D. J., J. J. Thomas, and C. M. E. Whitehead, 1978. "Problems in Forecasting the Price and Demand for On-Line Information Services," in M. C. J. Elton, W. A. Lucas, and D. W. Conrath, eds., *Evaluating New Telecommunication Systems*, New York and London: Plenum.

Fordyce, Samuel W., 1974. *NASA Experience in Telecommunications as a Substitute for Travel*, NASA Headquarters, Washington, DC.

†Ganz, C. and J. D. Goldhar, 1978. "The Impact of Telecommunications Technologies on Informal Communication in Science and Engineering—Research Needs and Opportunities," in M. C. J. Elton, W. A. Lucas, and D. W. Conrath, eds., *Evaluating New Telecommunication Systems*, New York and London: Plenum.

George, Donald A., D. C. Coll, S. A. Patterson, and P. D. Guild, 1976. "Video via the Telephone," in Lorne A. Parker and Betsy Riccomini, eds., *The Status of the Telephone in Education*, Madison: University of Wisconsin-Extension Press.

————, D. C. Coll, L. H. Strickland, S. A. Patterson, P. D. Guild, and J. M. McEown, 1975. *The Wired City Laboratory and Educational Communication Project, 1974–75*, Carleton University, Ottawa, Ontario, Canada.

Giedt, F. Harold, 1955. "Comparison of Visual, Content, and Auditory Cues in Interviewing," *Journal of Consulting Psychology*, Vol. 19, No. 6, pp. 407–19.

†Gleiss, Norman and Ingemar Klingén, 1977. "Conference Telephony," *Tele*, Swedish Telecommunications Administration, S-123 86 Farsta, Sweden, pp. 56–62.

Glenn, Edmund S., 1973. *Language and Cultural Factors*, Institute for Defense Analyses, Arlington, Virginia, Research Paper P-109, NTIS*: AD-601 926.

Goddard, J. B., 1971. "Communications and Office Location: A Review of Current Research," *Regional Studies*, Vol. 5, pp. 263–80.

———— and D. Morris, 1976. "The Communications Factor in Dispersal," *Progress in Planning Series*, Vol. 6, Part 1, Oxford, England: Pergammon Press.

———— and R. Pye, 1975. *Telecommunications and Office Location*, Communications Studies Group, London, England, Paper P/75175/PY.

Goldmark, Peter C., 1971. *Communications Technology for Urban Improvement*, Committee on Telecommunications, National Academy of Engineering, Washington, D.C.

Graham, J. A., P. Ricci Bitti, and M. Argyle, 1975. "A Cross-Cultural Study of the Communication of Emotion by Facial and Gestural Cues," *Journal of Human Motivation Studies*, Vol. 1, pp. 68–77.

Gray, Paul, 1973. *Prospects and Realities of the Telecommunications/Transportation Tradeoff*, Center for Futures Research, Graduate School of Business Administration, University of Southern California, Los Angeles, California.

†Hall, Edward T., 1976. "How Cultures Collide," *Psychology Today*, July, pp. 68–97.

Hall, Thomas, 1971. "Implementation of an Interactive Conference System," in *Proceedings of the 1971 Spring Joint Computer Conference*.

Hammond, Sandy and Martin Elton, 1976. *Getting the Best Out of Teleconferencing*, Communications Studies Group, London, England, Paper P/76075/HM.

Heilbronn, M. and W. L. Libby, 1973. *Comparative Effects of Technological and Social Immediacy upon Performance and Perceptions during a Two Person Game*, paper read at the 1973 Annual Conference of the American Psychological Association in Montreal, Quebec, Canada.

Hiltz, Starr Roxanne, 1975a. *Communications and Group Decision-Making: Experimental Evidence on the Potential Impact of Computer Conferencing*, Computerized Conferencing and Communications Center, New Jersey Institute of Technology, Newark, New Jersey, Research Report No. 2.

————, 1975b. *The Potential Social Impacts of Some Near Future Developments in Computer Conferencing*, paper presented at the World Future Society Second General Assembly.

————, 1976a. "A Social Scientist Looks at Computer Conferencing," in Pramode K. Verma, ed., *Proceedings of the Third International Conference on Computer Communication*, pp. 203–7.

————, 1976b. *Computer Conferencing: Assessing the Social Impact of a New Communications Medium*, Upsala College and The Center for Technology Assessment, presented at the American Sociological Association Annual Meeting, New York.

†————, 1978. "Social-Psychological Processes in Computerized Conferencing," Chapter 3 in *The Network Nation*, Reading, Massachusetts: Addison-Wesley.

———— and Murray Turoff, 1976. *Potential Impacts of Computer Conferencing upon Managerial and Organizational Styles*, New Jersey Institute of Technology.

Hiratsuka, Ken'ichi and Hideto Kakihara, 1976. "Video Conference System," *Japan Telecommunications Review*, July, pp. 145–51.

Holloway, Susan and Sandy Hammond, 1976. "A Case Study of Users' Reactions of Two Telephone Teaching Systems at the Open University," in Lorne A. Parker and Betsy Riccomini, eds., *The Status of the Telephone in Education*, Madison: University of Wisconsin-Extension Press.

Hough, Roger, 1976. *Teleconference Systems: A State of the Art Review*, Stanford Research Institute.

Imberger, L. A., 1975. *The Substitution of Telecommunications for Travel*, unpublished report from the National Telecommunication Planning of the Australian Post Office.

Irving, R. H., 1976. *Usage of Computer-Assisted Conferencing in an Organizational Environment*, Nonmedical Use of Drugs Directorate, 365 Laurier Street, Ottawa, Ontario K1A 1B6, Canada.

†———, 1978. "Computer Assisted Communication in a Directorate of the Canadian Federal Government—A Pilot Study," in M. C. J. Elton, W. A. Lucas, and D. W. Conrath, eds., *Evaluating New Telecommunication Systems*, New York and London: Plenum.

Janofsky, A. Irene, 1971. "Affective Self-Disclosure in Telephone versus Face-to-Face Interviews," *Journal of Humanistic Psychology*, Vol. 11, No. 1, pp. 93–103.

Jillson, Irene N., 1975. *Final Evaluation Report: Nonmedical Use of Drugs Computer Conferencing System Pilot Phase*, Nonmedical Use of Drugs Directorate, 365 Laurier Street, Ottawa, Ontario K1A 1B6, Canada.

Johansen, Robert, 1976. "Pitfalls in the Social Evaluation of Teleconferencing Media," in Lorne A. Parker and Betsy Riccomini, eds., *The Status of the Telephone in Education*, Madison: University of Wisconsin-Extension Press.

———, R. Miller, and J. Vallee, 1974. "Group Communication through Electronic Media," *Educational Technology*, August, pp. 7–20.

——— and J. Schuyler, 1975. "Computerized Conferencing in an Educational System: A Short-Range Scenario," in M. Turoff and H. Linstone, eds., *Delphi: Methods and Applications*, Reading, Massachusetts: Addison-Wesley.

†———, Jacques Vallee, and Kent Collins, 1978. "Learning the Limits of Teleconferencing: Design of a Teleconference Tutorial," in M. C. J. Elton, W. A. Lucas, and D. W. Conrath, eds., *Evaluating New Telecommunication Systems*, New York and London: Plenum.

———, Jacques Vallee, and Michael Palmer, 1976. *Computer Conferencing: Measurable Effects on Working Patterns*, Institute for the Future, Paper P-44.

†Jull, G. W., 1978. "Use and Traffic Characteristics of Teleconferencing for Business," in M. C. J. Elton, W. A. Lucas, and D. W. Conrath, eds., *Evaluating New Telecommunication Systems*, New York and London: Plenum.

——— and C. A. Billowes, 1974. *Human and Technical Factors in Teleconferencing Services*, Communications Research Centre, Department of Communications, Ottawa, Ontario, Canada.

———, R. W. McCaughern, N. M. Mendenhall, J. R. Storey, A. W. Tassie, and A. Zalatan, 1976. *Research Report on Teleconferencing*, Communications Research Centre, Department of Communications, Ottawa, Ontario, Canada, Report No. 1281-2.

———— and N. M. Mendenhall, 1976. "Prediction of the Acceptance and Use of New Interpersonal Telecommunication Services," in Lorne A. Parker and Betsy Riccomini, eds., *The Status of the Telephone in Education*, Madison: University of Wisconsin-Extension Press.

Kite, W. Richard and Paul C. Vitz, 1966. *Teleconferencing: Effects of Communication Medium, Network, and Distribution of Resources*, Institute for Defense Analyses, Arlington, Virginia, NTIS*: AD-636 143.

Klemmer, E. T., 1973. *Interpersonal Communication Systems: Relevance, Credibility, Impact*, presidential address before the Society of Engineering Psychologists, Montreal, Quebec, Canada.

Kohl, Kay, Thomas G. Newman, and Joseph F. Tomey, 1975. "Facilitating Organizational Decentralization through Teleconferencing," *IEEE Transactions on Communications*, pp. 1098–104.

Kollen, James H. and John Garwood, 1975. *Travel/Communication Tradeoffs: The Potential for Substitution among Business Travelers*, The Business Planning Group, Bell Canada, Montreal, Quebec, Canada.

Krueger, G. P., 1976. *Teleconferencing in the Communication Modes as a Function of the Number of Conferees*, unpublished doctoral dissertation, The Johns Hopkins University.

Kupperman, Robert H., Richard H. Wilcox, and Harvey A. Smith, 1975. "Crisis Management: Some Opportunities," *Science*, Vol. 187, No. 4175, pp. 404–10.

La Plante, D., 1971. *Communication, Friendliness, Trust, and the Prisoners Dilemma Game*, M.A. thesis, University of Windsor, Ontario, Canada.

Larimer, George S. and W. Ward Sinclair, 1969. "Some Effects of Two-Way Television on Social Interaction," *AV Communication Review*, Vol. 17, No. 1, pp. 52–62.

Lathey, Charles E. and Joseph R. Bewick, 1975. *Selected Abstracts of Documents Related to Energy Conservation through Telecommunications*, Office of Telecommunications, U.S. Department of Commerce, Washington, D.C., OT Special Publication 75-5.

†Lloyd, John, 1977. "Workers' Dilemma at the Post Office," *The Financial Times*, London, England, August 24, p. 17.

†Lortie, Rene, *Teleformation pour le perfectionnement du personnel*, Modele Theorique, Public Service Commission of Canada [no date given].

Maier, Norman R. F. and James A. Thurber, 1968. "Accuracy of Judgments of Deception When an Interview is Watched, Heard, and Read," *Personnel Psychology*, Vol. 21, pp. 23–30.

†Mandelbaum, Seymour J., 1978. *The Design of the Designing Community*, in M. C. J. Elton, W. A. Lucas, and D. W. Conrath, eds., *Evaluating New Telecommunication Systems*, New York and London: Plenum.

Mark, Roger G., 1975. "Communication Requirements in Telemedicine Systems," in Rashid L. Bashshur, Patricia A. Armstrong, and Zakhour I. Youssef, eds., *Telemedicine*, Springfield, Illinois: Charles C. Thomas.

†Mason, Robert M., 1978. "The Economics and Cost Benefit of Analysis Services—The Case of Information Anaysis Centers," in M. C. J. Elton, W. A.

Lucas, and D. W. Conrath, eds., *Evaluating New Telecommunication Systems*, New York and London: Plenum.

†McKendree, John D., 1977. "Decision Process in Crisis Management: Computers in a New Role," in Belzer, Holzman, and Kent, eds., *Encyclopedia of Computer Science & Technology*, Vol. 7, Marcel Dekker, pp. 115–56.

†Mendenhall, Nicole, Pat Grygier, and Jerzy Jarmasz, *Tele-Training for Personnel Development: Evaluators' Report*, Public Service Commission of Canada [no date given].

†——— and George Jull, "L'Evaluation de deux systemes audio interactifs: Comportement et technologie," *Tele-Training for Personnel Development: Telecommunication Research*, Public Service Commission of Canada [no date given], pp. 55–73.

†——— and Rene Lortie, "Evaluations of Interactive Tele-Education in the Public Service Commission," *Tele-Training for Personnel Development: Telecommunication Research*, Public Service Commission of Canada [no date given], pp. 40–54.

——— and Michael Ryan, 1975. *L'Effet des communications mediatisees: L'affectivite sociale, la melancolie, la fatigue et le scepticisme de l'utilisateur*, Communications Research Centre, Department of Communications, Ottawa, Ontario, Canada, Rapport 1286 Du CRC.

Meyer, Stuart L., 1975a. *Extending the Reach of the University with Narrow-Band Telecommunications: The Present and Potential Uses of Slow-Scan Tele-video for Continuing, Off-Campus Education*, The Transportation Center, Northwestern University, Evanston, Illinois.

———, 1975b. *Research and Development on Narrow-Band Telecommunications*, Northwestern University, Evanston, Illinois.

——— and David Brown, 1976. "A Review of Available Technology for Narrow-Band Transmission of Visual Material," *Bioscience Communications*, Vol. 2, pp. 38–48.

Midorikawa, Masahiro, Kingo Yamagishi, Ken'ichi Yada, and Kiyoski Miwa, 1975. "TV Conference System," *Review of the Electrical Communication Laboratories*, Vol. 23, Nos. 5–6.

Milgram, S., 1965. "Some Conditions of Obedience to Authority," *Human Relations*, Vol. 18, pp. 57–75.

Millard, Gord C., 1975. *Computer Mediated Interaction (CMI) User Guide*, The Computer Communications Group, Bell Canada, Ottawa, Ontario, Canada.

——— and Hilary Williamson, 1976. "How People React to Computer Conferencing," *Telesis*, Vol. 4, No. 7, pp. 214–219.

Mintzberg, Henry, 1971. "Managerial Work: Analysis from Observation," *Management Science*, Vol. 18, No. 2, pp. B97–B110.

Moore, G. T., T. R. Willemain, R. Bonanno, W. D. Clark, A. R. Martin, and R. P. Mogielnicki, 1975. "Comparison of Television and Telephone for Remote Medical Consultation," *The New England Journal of Medicine*, Vol. 292, pp. 729–32.

Morley, Ian E. and Geoffrey M. Stephenson, 1969. "Interpersonal and Inter-Party Exchange: A Laboratory Simulation of an Industrial Negotiation at the Plant Level," *British Journal of Psychology*, Vol. 60, No. 4, pp. 543–45.

————, 1970. "Formality in Experimental Negotiations: A Validation Study," *British Journal of Psychology*, Vol. 61, No. 3, pp. 383–84.

Mowbray, G. H. and J. W. Gebhard, 1961. "Man's Senses as Information Channels," in H. Wallace Sinaiko, ed., *Human Factors in the Design and Use of Control Systems*, New York: Dover Publications, Inc.

Murphy, Raymond and Kenneth T. Bird, 1974. "Telediagnosis: A New Community Health Resource," *American Journal of Public Health*, Vol. 64, No. 2, pp. 113–9.

Noll, A. Michael, 1976a. "Teleportation through Communications," *IEEE Transactions on Systems, Man, and Cybernetics*, pp. 753–56.

————, 1976b. "Teleconferencing Communications Activities," *Communications Society*, Vol. 14, No. 6, pp. 8–14.

Ochsman, R. B. and A. Chapanis, 1974. "The Effects of Ten Communication Modes on the Behavior of Teams during Cooperative Problem-Solving," *International Journal of Man-Machine Studies*, Vol. 6, pp. 579–619.

O'Neil, J. J., J. T. Norcerino, and P. Wolcoff, 1975. *Benefits and Problems of Seven Exploratory Telemedicine Projects*, The Mitre Corporation, Washington, D.C., Report No. MTR-6787.

Orlansky, Jesse, 1963. *Feasibility of a Research and Development Program*, Institute for Defense Analyses, Arlington, Virginia, Research Paper P-105, NTIS*: AD-601 923.

†Palmer, A. W. and R. J. Beishon, 1970. "How the Day Goes," *Personnel Management*, April, pp. 36–40.

Panko, Raymond R., Roger Pye, and Roger Hough, 1976. "Telecommunications for Office Decentralization: Apparent Needs and Investment Requirements." in Pramode K. Verma, ed., *Proceedings of the Third International Conference on Computer Communication*.

Park, Ben, 1975. "Communication Aspects of Telemedicine," in Rashid L. Bashshur, Patricia A. Armstrong, and Zakhour I. Youssef, eds., *Telemedicine*, Springfield, Illinois: Charles C. Thomas.

†Parker, Lorne A., Marcia A. Baird, and Dennis A. Gilbertson, *Introduction to Teleconferencing*, Instructional Communications Systems, University of Wisconsin-Extension, Madison, Wisconsin [no date given].

———— and Betsy Riccomini, eds., 1976. *The Status of the Telephone in Education*, Madison: University of Wisconsin-Extension Press.

Penner, L. A. and H. L. Hawkins, 1971. "The Effects of Visual Contact and Agressor Identification on Interpersonal Aggression," *Psychonomic Science*, Vol. 24, pp. 261–63.

†Phillimore, Lynda, 1977. *Audioconferencing in ICI*, Communications Studies and Planning Ltd., London WIN 5LH, England, Report No. ICI/77069/PH.

Polishuk, Paul, 1975. "Review of the Impact of Telecommunications Substitutes for Travel," *IEEE Transactions on Communications*, Vol. COM-23, No. 10, pp. 1089–98.

————, 1976. *Draft Bibliography: Telecommunications, Travel, and Energy Conservation*, Dedham, Massachusetts: Horizon House International.

Price, Charlton R., 1974. *Conferencing via Computer-Cost/Effective Communication for the Era of Forced Change*, George Washington University.

Pye, Roger, 1972a. *The Telecommunications Impact Model, Stages III and IV*, Communications Studies Group, London, England, Paper P/72031/PY.

————, 1972b. *Projections of Office Location in Great Britain at Year 2001*, Communications Studies Group, London, England, Paper P/72048/PY.

————,1976a. "Communications Effectiveness and Efficiency," *Technology Assessment of Travel/Communications Relationships*, Stanford Research Institute, Impact Paper 14.

————, 1976b. "Effect of Telecommunications on the Location of Office Employment," *Omega, The International Journal of Management Science*, Vol. 4, No. 3, pp. 289–300.

————, Brian Champness, Hugh Collins, and Stephen Connell, 1973. *The Description and Classification of Meetings*, Communications Studies Group, London, England, Paper P/73160/PY.

————, Michael Tyler, and Brian Cartwright, 1974. "Telecommunicate or Travel?," *New Scientist*, pp. 642–44.

Reid, Alex A. L., 1970a. *Electronic Person-to-Person Communications*, Communications Studies Group, London, England, Paper B/70244/CSG.

————,1970b. *The Costs of Travel and Telecommunication*, Communications Studies Group, London, England, Paper P/70220/RD.

————, 1971a. *Needs Technology, Effectiveness, and Impact*, Communications Studies Group, London, England, Paper P/71128/RD.

————, 1971b. *New Directions in Teleconferencing Research*, a report prepared for the Sloan Commission on Cable Communications.

————, 1971c. *Face-to-Face Contacts in Government Departments*, Communications Studies Group, London, England, Paper P/71270/RD.

————, 1971d. "What Telecommunication Implies," *New Society*, pp. 1284–86.

————, 1973. *Telecommunications/Transportation Substitution*, Communications Studies Group, London, England, draft.

————, 1976. *Comparing Telephone with Face-to-Face Contact*, Post Office Telecommunications Headquarters, London, England.

†Rivers, William L., Wallace Thompson, and Michael J. Nyhan, 1977. *Aspen Handbook on the Media, 1977–79 Edition, A Selective Guide to Research, Organizations and Publications in Communications*, New York: Praeger Publishers and Aspen Institute for Humanistic Studies.

†Rockoff, Maxine L. and Arthur M. Bennett, 1978. "The 'Patient Trajectory': A Modeling Tool for Planning and Evaluating Rural Telemedicine Systems," in M. C. J. Elton, W. A. Lucas, and D. W. Conrath, eds., *Evaluating New Telecommunication Systems*, New York and London: Plenum.

†Ryan, Michael G., *Tele-Training for Personnel Development: Staff Training by Satellite*, Public Service Commission of Canada [no date given].

†————, 1973. *Interrogative Behavior in Business Telephone-Communication*, Staff Development Branch, Public Service Commission, Ottawa, Ontario, Canada.

————, 1975. *The Influence of Teleconferencing Medium and Status on Participants Perception of the Aestheticism, Evaluation, Privacy, Potency, and Activity of the Medium*, Communications Research Centre, Department of Communications, Ottawa, Ontario, Canada.

————, 1976. "Interrogative Behavior in Business Telephone-Communication," in Lorne A. Parker and Betsy Riccomini, eds., *The Status of the Telephone in Education*, Madison: University of Wisconsin-Extension Press.

———— and James G. Craig, 1975. *Intergroup Telecommunication: The Influence of Communications Medium and Role Induced Status Level on Mood, and Attitudes towards the Medium and Discussion*, Communications Research Centre, Department of Communications, Ottawa, Ontario, Canada.

———— and H. Wayland Cummings, 1973. *Man-Machine Communication: Computer Credibility for French and English Canadians*, International Communication Association, Montreal, Quebec, Canada.

†———— and Guy Jean, "The Impact of the Communications Technology Satellite on a Government Organization," *Tele-Training for Personnel Development: Telecommunication Research*, Public Service Commission of Canada [no date given], pp. 24–39.

†———— and Nicole Mendenhall, "Canadian Satellite Experiments: Implications for Human Communication," *Tele-Training for Personnel Development: Telecommunication Research*, Public Service Commission of Canada [no date given], pp. 14–23.

†———— and Nicole Mendenhall, "Interaction: A Canadian Theme in Education by Satellite," *Tele-Training for Personnel Development: Telecommunication Research*, Public Service Commission of Canada [no date given], pp. 1–13.

Schuyler, J. and R. Johansen, 1972. "ORACLE: Computerized Conferencing in a Computer-Assisted Instruction System," *Proceedings of International Conference on Computer Communications*, Washington, D.C.

Seyler, Jim, 1976. *Electronic Blackboard Permit Graduate Engineering Course Offerings to Engineers in Industry*, Continuing Education and Engineering, University of Illinois, Champaign, Illinois.

†Sheridan, Thomas B., 1975. "Community Dialog Technology," *Proceedings of the IEEE*, Vol. 63, No. 3, pp. 463–75.

Shinn, Alan M., Jr., 1975. "The State of the Art in Telemedicine and the Need for Research," in Rashid L. Bashshur, Patricia A. Armstrong, and Zakhour I. Youssef, eds., *Telemedicine*, Springfield, Illinois: Charles C. Thomas.

†————, 1978. "The Utility of Social Experimentation in Policy Research," in M. C. J. Elton, W. A. Lucas, and D. W. Conrath, eds., *Evaluating New Telecommunication Systems*, New York and London: Plenum.

Short, John A., 1971a. *Bargaining and Negotiation—An Exploratory Study*, Communications Studies Group, London, England, Paper E/71065/SH.

————, 1971b. *Cooperation and Competition in an Experimental Bargaining Game Conducted over Two Media*, Communications Studies Group, London, England, Paper E/71160/SH.

————, 1972a. *Conflicts of Opinion and Medium of Communication*, Communications Studies Group, London, England, Paper E/72001/SH.

————, 1972b. *Medium of Communication, Opinion Change, and Solution of Problem of Priorities*, Communications Studies Group, London, England, Paper E/72245/SH.

————, 1972c. *Medium of Communication and Consensus*, Communications Studies Group, London, England, Paper E/72210/SH.

————, 1972d. *Telecommunications Systems and Negotiating Behavior*, Symposium on Human Factors and Telecomnunications, Stockholm, Sweden.

————, 1973a. *The Effects of Medium of Communication on Two Person Conflicts*, Ph.D. thesis, University College, London, England.

————, 1973b. *The Effects of Medium of Communication on Persuasion, Bargaining, and Perception of the Other*, Communications Studies Group, London, England, Paper E/73100/SH.

————, 1973c. *A Report on the Use of the Audio Conferencing Facility in the University of Quebec*, Communications Studies Group, London, England, Paper P/73161/SH.

————, 1974. "Effects of Medium of Communication on Experimental Negotiation," *Human Relations*, Vol. 27, pp. 225–34.

————, Ederyn Williams, and Bruce Christie, 1976. *The Social Psychology of Telecommunications*, London, England: John Wiley & Sons, Ltd.

†Shulman, Arthur D. and Jerome I. Steinman, 1978. "Interpersonal Teleconferencing in an Organizational Context," in M. C. J. Elton, W. A. Lucas, and D. W. Conrath, eds., *Evaluating New Telecommunication Systems*, New York and London: Plenum.

Simon, Robert J., Joseph L. Fleiss, Bernice Fisher, and Barry J. Gurland, 1974. "Two Methods of Psychiatric Interviewing: Telephone and Face-to-Face," *The Journal of Psychology*, Vol. 88, pp. 141–46.

Sinaiko, H. Wallace, 1963. *Teleconferencing: Preliminary Experiments*, Institute for Defense Analyses, Arlington, Virginia, Research Paper P-108, NTIS*: AD-601 932.

Snyder, Frank, 1973. *Travel Patterns: Implications for New Communications Facilities*, Bell Laboratories, Holmdel, New Jersey, working draft.

Spelt, Philip F., 1977. "Evaluation of a Continuing Computer Conference on Simulation," *Behavior Research Methods and Instrumentation*, forthcoming in the Spring 1977 issue.

Stapley, Barry, 1973. *Collected Papers on the Remote Meeting Table*, Communications Studies Group, London, England, Paper W/73298/ST.

————, 1974. *A Comparison of Field Trials of Teleconferencing Equipment*, Communications Studies Group, London, England, Paper P/74244/ST.

†Stockbridge, C. D., *Planning Exploratory Trials of New Interpersonal Telecommunications*, Bell Telephone Laboratories, Holmdel, New Jersey 07733 [no date given].

Strickland, L. H., P. D. Guild, J. R. Barefoot, and S. A. Patterson, 1975. *Teleconferencing and Leadership Emergence*, Carleton University.

†Takasaki, Nozomu, 1977. *Our Study of "Quality of Life" and Contribution of Telecommunications*, Research Institute of Telecommunications and Economics, Japan.

†——— and Takahiro Ozawa, 1977. *The Scheme of the Study of Information Flow*, Research Institute of Telecommunications and Economics, Japan.

†———, Teruo Tuneki, and Yoshiko Saito, 1977. *Psychological Experiment, Video Conference Communication*, Research Institute of Telecommunications and Economics, Japan.

Thomas, Hilary B. and Ederyn Williams, 1975. *The University of Quebec Audio Conferencing System: An Analysis of Users' Attitudes*, Communications Studies Group, London, England, Paper P/75190/TH.

Thompson, Gordon B., 1971. *The Greening of the Wired City*, Bell Northern Research, P.O. Box 3511, Station "C", Ottawa, Ontario, Canada.

———, 1972. "Three Characterizations of Communications Revolutions," *Proceedings of the International Conference on Computer Communications*, Washington, D.C.

†———, *Information Technology and Society*, Bell Northern Research, Ottawa, Ontario, Canada [no date given].

Thorngren, Bertil, 1972. *KOMM 71: A Communication Study of Government Relocation in Sweden*, preliminary summary in English, Economic Research Institute, Stockholm School of Economics, Sveagen 65, Stockholm, Sweden.

†———, 1977. "Silent Actors—Communication Networks for Development," in Ithiel de Sola Pool, ed., *Social Impact of the Telephone*, Cambridge, Massachusetts: MIT Press.

Turoff, Murray, 1971. "Delphi and Its Potential Impact on Information Systems," *AFIPS Conference Proceedings*, Vol. 39.

———, 1972a. "Delphi Conferencing: Computer-Based Conferencing with Anonymity," *Technological Forecasting and Social Change*, No. 2, pp. 159–95.

———, 1972b. "'Partyline' and 'Discussion' Computerized Conference Systems," *Proceedings of the International Conference on Computer Communications*, Washington, D.C.

———, 1973a. "Human Communication via Data Networks," *Computer Decisions*; also in Blanc and Cotton, eds., *Computer Networking*, IEEE Press, 1976.

———, 1973b. "Communication Procedures in Technological Forecasting," *Intercom Papers*, Vol. 7, IEEE Press.

———, 1974a. "Computerized Conferencing and Real Time Delphis," *Proceedings of the International Conference on Computer Communications*, Stockholm, Sweden.

————, 1974c. "The State of the Art: Computerized Conferencing," in N. Macon, ed., *Views from ICCC 1974*, International Council for Computer Communication, P.O. Box 9745, Washington, D.C. 20016.

————, 1975a. *Initial Specifications, Electronic Information Exchange System (EIE)*, Computerized Conferencing and Communications Center, New Jersey Institute of Technology, Newark, New Jersey, Research Report No. 1.

————, 1975b. "The Future of Computer Conferencing," *The Futurist*, Vol. 9, No. 4, pp. 182–95.

————, 1975d. "Computerized Conferencing for the Deaf and Disabled," *Urban Telecommunications Forum*, IV/33; also, *SIGGAPH (Association for Computing Machinery) Newsletter*, No. 16; and 141st Meeting of the American Association for the Advancement of Science.

————, 1976. "The Costs and Revenues of Computerized Conferencing," *Proceedings of the Third International Conference on Computer Communication*, pp. 214–21.

————, 1977. "An On-Line Intellectual Community or MEMEX Revisited," *Proceedings of the Annual Meeting of the American Association for the Advancement of Science*.

†———— and Starr Roxanne Hiltz, 1978. "Computerized Conferencing: A Review and Statement of Issues," in M. C. J. Elton, W. A. Lucas, and D. W. Conrath, eds., *Evaluating New Telecommunication Systems*, New York and London: Plenum.

———— and Marion Spector, 1976. "Libraries and the Implications of Computer Technology," *Proceedings of the National Computer Conference*.

†Tyler, Michael, *User Research and Demand Research: What's the Use? An Enquiry into the How and Why of Telecommunications Studies*, Communications Studies and Planning Ltd., 56/60 Hallam Street, London W1N 5LH, England [no date given].

————, Brian Cartwright, and David Bookless, 1974. *Long Range Intelligence Bulletin 1—Long-Range Economic Forecasts: The Economic Consequences of Energy Scarcity*, Long Range Intelligence Division, Long Range Studies Division, Telecommunications System Strategy Department (TSS6), Post Office Telecommunications, England.

————, Brian Cartwright, and Geoffrey Bush, 1974. "Interaction between Telecommunications and Face-to-Face Contact: The Energy Factor," *Long Range Intelligence Bulletin No. 3*, Post Office Telecommunications, England. Reference No. LRIB 003/ITF.

————, Brian Cartwright, and Hugh Collins, 1975. "Interaction between Telecommunications and Face-to-Face Contact: Prospects for Teleconference Systems," *Long Range Intelligence Bulletin No. 9*, British Post Office, England.

————, B. Cartwright, and H. A. Collins, 1977. *Long Range Intelligence Bulletin No. 9, Demand for Teleconference Services*, Long Range Studies Division, Post Office Telecommunications Headquarters, England.

†Valery, Nicholas, 1977. "Foot in the Door for the Home Computer," *New Scientist*, April 14, pp. 63–65.

Vallee, Jacques, 1974. "Network Conferencing," *Datamation*, May, pp. 85–86, 91–92.

———, 1976a. "The FORUM Project: Network Conferencing and Its Future Applications," *Computer Networks*, Vol. 1, pp. 39–52.

———, 1976b. "There Ain't No User Science," in *Proceedings of the 1976 American Society for Information Science Annual Meeting*, San Francisco, California.

———, 1976c. "The Outlook for Computer Conferencing on ARPANET and PLATO," *Proceedings of the Society for General Systems Research*, Denver, Colorado.

——— and Gerald Askevold, 1975. "Geologic Applications of Network Conferencing: Current Experiments with the FORUM System," in Peter Lykos, ed., *Computer Networking and Chemistry*, American Chemical Society.

——— and Bradford Gibbs, 1976. "Distributed Management of Scientific Projects," *Telecommunications Policy*, Vol. 1, No. 1, pp. 75–85.

——— and Robert Johansen (Robert H. Randolph and Arthur C. Hastings, consultants), 1974. *Group Communication through Computers, Volume 2: A Study of Social Effects*, Institute for the Future, Report R-33.

———, Robert Johansen, Hubert Lipinski, Kathleen Spangler, and Thaddeus Wilson (Andrew Hardy, consultant), 1975. *Group Communication through Computers, Volume 3: Pragmatics and Dynamics*, Institute for the Future, Report R-35.

———, 1978. *Group Communication through Computers, Volume 4: Social, Managerial, and Economic Issues*, Institute for the Future, Report R-40.

———, Hubert Lipinski, Robert Johansen, and Thaddeus Wilson, 1976. "Pragmatics and Dynamics of Computer Conferencing," *Proceedings of the Third International Conference on Computer Communication*, Toronto, Ontario, Canada.

——— and Thaddeus Wilson, 1975. "Computer Networks and the Interactive Use of Geologic Data: Recent Experiments in Teleconferencing," *Proceedings of the COGEODATA Symposium*, Paris, France.

——— and Thaddeus Wilson, 1976. *Computer-Based Communication in Support of Scientific and Technical Work*, Institute for the Future, Report NASA CR 137879.

†Vernimb, Carl O. and Garth W. P. Davies, *Communication Aspects of EURONET*, Commission of the European Communities, Luxembourg [no date given].

Wall, V. D. and J. A. Boyd, 1971. "Channel Variation and Attitude Change," *Journal of Communication*, Vol. 21, pp. 363–67.

Wallenstein, Gerd D., 1975. "Sound and Image in Interactive Telecommunication," *Systems Thinking and the Quality of Life, Proceedings of the 1975 Annual North American Meeting of the Society for General Systems Research and American Association for the Advancement of Science*, Washington, D.C., pp. 546–56.

Wapner, Seymour and Thelma G. Alper, 1952. "The Effect of an Audience on Behavior in a Choice Situation," *The Journal of Abnormal and Social Psychology*, Vol. 47, pp. 222–29.

Weeks, G. D. and A. Chapanis, 1976. "Cooperative versus Conflictive Problem-Solving in Three Telecommunication Modes," *Perceptual and Motor Skills*, Vol. 42, pp. 879–917.

Wempner, Jon D., 1975. "The Clinical Applications of Telemedicine: Some Remarks," in Rashid L. Bashshur, Patricia A. Armstrong, and Zakhour I. Youssef, eds., *Telemedicine*, Springfield, inois: Charles C. Thomas, pp. 113–25.

Weston, J. R. and C. Kristen, 1973. *Teleconferencing: A Comparison of Attitudes, Uncertainty and Interpersonal Atmospheres in Mediated and Face-to-Face Group Interaction*, The Social Policy and Programs Branch, Department of Communications, Ottawa, Ontario, Canada.

———, C. Kristen, and S. O'Connor, 1975. *Teleconferencing: A Comparison of Group Performance Profiles in Mediated and Face-to-Face Interaction*, The Social Policy and Programs Branch, Department of Communications, Ottawa, Ontario, Canada, Report No. 3, Contract OSU4-0072.

Westrum, Ronald, 1972. *Communications Systems and Social Change*, unpublished Ph.D. dissertation, Department of Sociology, Purdue University.

Wichman, Harvey, 1970. "Effects of Isolation and Communication on Cooperation in a Two-Person Game," *Journal of Personality and Social Psychology*, Vol. 16, No. 1, pp. 114–20.

Williams, Ederyn, 1972a. *The Effects of Medium of Communication on Evaluation of a Conversation and the Conversation Partner*, Communications Studies Group, London, England, Paper E/72131/WL.

———, 1972b. *Factors Influencing the Effect of Medium of Communication upon Preferences for Media, Conversation, and Persons*, Communications Studies Group, London, England, Paper E/72227/WL.

———, 1973. *The Bell Canada Conference Television System: A Case Study*, Communications Studies Group, London, England, Paper P/73173/WL.

———, 1974. *A Summary of the Present State of Knowledge of the Substitution of Face-to-Face Meetings by Telecommunicated Meetings: Type Allocation Revisited*, Post Office Corporation, London, England.

———, 1975a. "Coalition Formation over Telecommunications Media," *European Journal of Social Psychology*, Vol. 5, No. 4, pp. 503–7.

———, 1975b. "Medium or Message: Communications Medium as a Determinant of Interpersonal Evaluation," *Sociometry*, Vol. 38, pp. 119–30.

———, 1975c. *A Review of Audio-Only Teleconferencing*, Communications Studies Group, London, England, Paper P/75290/WL.

———, 1975d. *Communications Chains: A Method for Tying Down Generation Effects and Other Beasties*, Communications Studies Group, London, England, Paper S/75135/WL.

———, 1976. "Experimental Comparisons of Face-to-Face and Mediated Communication: A Review," *Psychological Bulletin*, forthcoming.

†———, *Research at the Communications Studies Group*, 1970–1977, Long Range Intelligence Division, Post Office Corporation, Cambridge CB2 1PE, England, Long Range Research Report 14 [no date given].

—— and Alphonse Chapanis, 1976. "A Review of Psychological Research Comparing Communications Media," in Lorne A. Parker and Betsy Riccomini, eds., *The Status of the Telephone in Education*, Madison: University of Wisconsin-Extension Press.

—— and S. Holloway, 1974. *The Evaluation of Teleconferencing: Report of a Questionnaire Study of Users' Attitudes to the Bell Canada Conference Television System*, Communications Studies Group, London, England, Paper P/74247/WL.

Wilson, Chris, 1974. *Interpretation of Media Effects*, Communications Studies Group, London, England, Paper P/74157/CW.

Wish, Myron, 1975. "User and Nonuser Conceptions of PICTUREPHONE® Service," *Proceedings of the 19th Annual Convention of the Human Factors Society*.

†——, *Multidimensional Measurement of Interpersonal Communication*, Department of Interpersonal Communications Research, Bell Laboratories, Murray Hill, New Jersey [no date given].

Woodside, C. M., J. K. Cavers, and I. K. Buck, 1971. *Evaluation of a Video Addition to the Telephone for Engineering Conversations*, Bell Northern Research, P.O. Box 3511, Station "C", Ottawa, Ontario, Canada.

Young, I., 1974a. *Telecommunicated Interviews: An Exploratory Study*, Communications Studies Group, London, England, Paper E/74165/YN.

——, 1974b. *Understanding the Other Person in Mediated Interaction*, Communications Studies Group, London, England, Paper E/74266/YN.

Zinn, Karl L., 1977. "Computer Facilitation of Communication within Professional Communities," *Behavioral Research Methods and Instrumentation*, Spring.

——, Robert Parnes, and Helen Hench, 1976. "Computer-Based Educational Communications at the University of Michigan," *Proceedings of the Association for Computing Machinery 1976 National Conference*, Houston, Texas.